AMONG THE MOSQUES

AMONG THE MOSQUES

A Journey Across Muslim Britain

ED HUSAIN

BLOOMSBURY PUBLISHING
LONDON · OXFORD · NEW YORK · NEW DELHI · SYDNEY

BLOOMSBURY PUBLISHING
Bloomsbury Publishing Plc
50 Bedford Square, London, WC1B 3DP, UK
29 Earlsfort Terrace, Dublin 2, Ireland

BLOOMSBURY, BLOOMSBURY PUBLISHING and the Diana logo are trademarks of
Bloomsbury Publishing Plc

First published in Great Britain 2021

A catalogue record for this book is available from the British Library

ISBN: HB: 978-1-5266-1865-8; EBOOK: 978-1-5266-1866-5

2 4 6 8 10 9 7 5 3 1

Typeset by Newgen KnowledgeWorks Pvt. Ltd., Chennai, India
Printed and bound in Great Britain by CPI Group (UK) Ltd, Croydon CRO 4YY

To find out more about our authors and books visit www.bloomsbury.com
and sign up for our newsletters

To all the brave women and men who laid down their lives in two world wars for the liberties that we now cherish. They came from all continents. Travelling across Britain made me more aware of our debt to them; this book is a contribution to that generational conversation.

Contents

Introduction

Muslims are the fastest growing community in Britain. The religious, political and social direction of travel inside this demographic will shape the future of this country.

A hundred years ago, there were two mosques in England. There was a small terraced house in Liverpool founded in 1887 for a handful of eccentric English converts to laud the virtues of the Ottoman Turks.[1] And then in 1889 in Woking, Surrey, a Jewish scholar who also converted to Islam built a magnificent mosque with minarets and domes. Named the Shah Jahan Mosque, after the Mughal emperor who constructed the Taj Mahal, this mosque was an institution of learning and awarded degrees from the University of Punjab. In short, Liverpool and Woking were outposts of the Islamic empires of the Mughals and Ottomans in England.

Along with the British Empire's rise and fall, its Muslim populations ebbed and flowed. Disraeli liked to remind Queen Victoria that she was the queen-empress of more Muslims in her domain than the Turkish sultan in his. British Muslims are the grandchildren of the British Empire.

Today, there are almost 2,000 mosques in Britain's towns and cities. On some roads, we have multiple mosques to cater for sectarian, ethnic and tribal differences. The Turks, Arabs, Pakistanis and Indians all want their own mosques in parts of north London, for example. The differences among Muslims constantly call on our tolerance levels as local councils are being lobbied daily to approve new mosques. Liverpool and Woking were open places of learning and discussion, but what of today's mosques? What is happening inside mosques and how do these institutions influence the lives and localities in which they are established? The skylines of Luton, Slough, Nelson, Birmingham, Leicester, Bradford, Dewsbury, Keighley, Blackburn and the London suburb of Hounslow are changing, with minarets, domes and mosques appearing more frequently. Who is behind this proliferation of mosques? What type of mosques are they?

I visited nine major towns and cities across Great Britain in order to write this book. Always, I turned up unannounced at the central mosque or at the largest weekly gathering: communal Friday prayers, to experience its sermon, its announcements and its conversations. I also visited mosques that are prominent for locals, even if they are not the 'central mosque'. I stopped people in streets. Wherever and whenever I had a question, I mostly asked. Where I failed to do so, I confess that too.

Between 2001 and 2016, the whole population of England grew 10.9 per cent from 49,128,831 to a general population of 54,516,822, according to Britain's largest independent producer of official statistics, the Office for National Statistics (ONS). At the same time, the Muslim population of England grew by 107.3 per cent, going from 1,524,877 in 2001 to 3,161,629 people by 2016. The Muslim population in Britain is estimated to be thirteen million people by 2050.[2]

In 2004, the Home Office predicted the arrival of no more than 13,000 European migrants if the Blair government joined the EU's free movement of workers from ten new EU member states. In reality, Britain attracted over two million EU citizens in the decade that followed, particularly from Poland and Eastern Europe.[3] Britain's exit from the European Union was, in large part, an outcome of European immigration and the free movement of people. What awaits the future of this country and this continent as Muslim numbers increase? If Britain could not tolerate white

Christian Europeans, what is the fate of its Muslims? We must not shy away from these difficult questions: for, if we do, extremist voices will force a future upon us that will be divisive and destructive.

By 2031, based on the ONS census of 2001–11 projections, several areas in Bradford, Blackburn, Birmingham, Leicester, Slough, Luton and some London boroughs will be Muslim-majority. What implications will that have, and how will it change power dynamics for the wider population?

I am a Muslim. For most of my life I have lived in London, but I spent two years studying Arabic and Islam in Damascus, Syria (2003–5). I have lived in Jeddah, Saudi Arabia, for almost a year (2006). I have also worked and lived in New York and Washington DC (2010–15) – and I believe in the world we have inherited: cosmopolitan, multi-ethnic, multi-faith, open, liberal and secular.

Based on my family and faith background, I was able to converse in the various languages, both cultural and linguistic, of the people I met across Britain. My studies and my travels in Turkey, Syria, Israel, Egypt, India and the Arabian Gulf have given me an awareness of the different ways of being Muslim in varied contexts that still remain loyal to the spirit of my religion. My assumptions from the outset while writing this book were that organised religion is a force for good; community is something positive and to be supported; clerics and religious leaders are generally sincere people committed to virtue. I assumed that the concept of a caliphate was something from history, and attempts by the Taliban or ISIS to resurrect the imperial past of Islam in recent years has led to failure. Therefore, most Muslims living in a liberal democracy will have little truck with a caliph, or the yearning for a caliphate, either now or for the future.

During the course of writing this book, my view of my own country, continent, community and city has changed. My starting point was, and remains, honesty in outlook and behaviour. With an open mind, I went out to the towns and cities of England, Scotland, Wales and Northern Ireland. I thought we were Europeans and had a sense of history, present and future direction.

Great Britain is a country that, despite our faults, still provides intellectual leadership around the world. Developments here matter to thinking people in Africa, Europe, Asia and America. We forget that our language, laws and liberties are the bedrock of the modern world. Philosophers from these islands, John Locke, David Hume, Adam Smith, Edmund Burke and John Stuart Mill, shaped the cultures and constitutions of countless countries.

My editor at Bloomsbury, Michael Fishwick, encouraged me to ask questions and be open to their answers. I followed the crumbs; I was led by observations, conversations, by leads, by suggestions. I questioned as much as decently possible. I went everywhere, every mosque, every bookshop, clinic, community centre, shelter, street, town and city that my interviewees recommended.

Nothing less than the future of our country depends on us studying, debating and deciding together where we are headed. If we do not consciously shape our own future, forewarned and forearmed, we will be shaped by it. As Heraclitus of Ephesus warned five centuries before Christ, life is all about change; change is the only constant. We cannot even step into the same river twice, taught Heraclitus. The problem is *not* that the Muslim population is increasing: the question is what *type* of Islam is on the rise in British mosques.

Abraham Lincoln's words about his own country that he helped unite after a civil war apply to us today as we leave the European Union and try to maintain a 'United' Kingdom: 'America will never be destroyed from the outside. If we falter and lose our freedoms, it will be because we destroyed ourselves.'

What is the state of these freedoms in our towns and cities?

I

Dewsbury

It is a damp, grey Friday morning. A taxi pulls up outside Dewsbury railway station and an Asian teenager in Adidas sneakers leaps out. He's wearing a white skullcap and a long, white flowing dress that reaches from his neck down to his ankles. The Arabs would wear such a thing, a *thawb*, out in the desert to help ward off the searing heat and glaring sunlight. As he hurries towards the station, I can see he has a faint, wispy beard of the sort grown by adolescent boys if they don't shave at the first appearance of facial hair.

'*Salam alaikum*,' I call out to him.

'*Alaikum as-salam*,' he replies.

This exchange of Muslim greetings – words of peace in Arabic – stops him in his tracks. Even when in haste, a Muslim is expected to respond and help a traveller. The boy wears spectacles, and raindrops linger on his thick lenses. He looks like he might be a religious student at the place I want to visit, and where I'm planning to perform my weekly Friday devotions.

'Where is the Markazi Mosque, please?' I ask.

'I'd take you, but I have to go to Huddersfield,' he says in a heavy Yorkshire accent, elongating the vowels. 'Go down that road there, and you'll see the mosque.' Then off he goes in a rush.

The Markazi Mosque is the European central office of the largest Muslim organisation in the world, the Tableeghi Jamaat. It was founded in India in 1927 in opposition to the British Raj and to stop the dilution of Muslim identity in the cosmopolitan cities of British India. Its founder's slogan was '*Ai Musolmano, Musolman bano!*', meaning 'O Muslims, become [real] Muslims!'[1] With over 150 million adherents, the Tableeghis are present in virtually every country of the world, and are known for their door-to-door proselytising in groups of three or more. '*Tableegh*', an Arabic word, means 'conveying' or 'delivering', as in delivering a message. '*Jamaat*', again an Arabic term, means 'group'; thus 'Tableeghi Jamaat' means 'Group of Conveyance' of a religious message. Almost every Muslim home, office and shop across the globe has had a Tableeghi knock on the door and invite those inside to prayer, to the mosque, or to travel the world to call Muslims to return to traditional ways of piety. They are essentially the (male-only) Muslim version of Jehovah's Witnesses.

The Tableeghi Jamaat is, in turn, the evangelical arm of the Deobandi movement in India. Named after Deoband, a town on the outskirts of Delhi, the movement arose to emphasise Muslim religious identity after the failed uprising against the British Raj in 1857. It was in Deoband that a group of anti-British clerics created their first madrasa, or Islamic seminary, known as the Darul Uloom (Arabic for 'House of Knowledge'), in 1866. Free from any government ties, the madrasa was and remains dedicated to educating and creating Muslims who are decidedly not modern, but hold firmly to literalist interpretations of religious texts. Its students then took the teachings of the Deoband school across the world through their Tableeghi missionary activities. The two things reinforce each other: acquiring knowledge and spreading ideas.

Each year, Tableeghi international missionaries gather at a conference in Dhaka, Bangladesh, with dignitaries attending from over 140 countries. By way of comparison, the annual Hajj pilgrimage draws two million Muslims, women and men, to Mecca in Saudi Arabia; the Tableeghi convention attracts five million Muslims (and only men). Such is the pulling power today of the Deobandi movement that was born in hostility in British-controlled

India, with its undertaking to be separate from government and secular society.

And now here I am in Dewsbury, in Yorkshire, almost 200 years later, encountering the legacy of that interaction between Empire and Islam. Today, more than half of Britain's mosques belong to the Deobandi movement[2] and, away from media headlines, I want to visit their headquarters in Dewsbury to see and feel how Islam in Britain is shaping up.

The boy from the station was right: I couldn't miss the mosque. As I walk towards Daisy Hill the mosque is clearly visible, with its simple white-and-green minaret atop a dark green dome that dominates the low-rise buildings of the town. Against the deep sandy buff of local York stone brickwork that gives Dewsbury a visual unity, the green-and-white mosque stands out incongruously. Daisy Hill is lined with Victorian streetlamps. As I walk along for a few minutes, I notice that all the shops and businesses lining the road – solicitors, accountants, miscellaneous offices – seem to be closed. A row of white taxis, all with Asian drivers, are parked outside Asda, B&Q and an adjacent retail park. There was no such queue of cabbies outside the railway station.

It is just two hours since I left my home city – London – and already I feel as though I am in a different country and century. At King's Cross station I had to squeeze past Harry Potter fans from all over the world trying to get a glimpse of J. K. Rowling's magical Platform $9^{3/4}$. Here, I am seeing Dickensian streets with grimy, derelict buildings, and neglected churchyards amid signs pointing towards the 'Town Centre'. I promise myself that I will see if Dewsbury gets any better after Friday prayers.

The first Asian workers arrived to work in the famous woollen mills of Dewsbury in the 1960s. Only twenty years earlier Gandhi had advocated the boycott of English factories, yet within a decade of India's independence, Indians started arriving in England. The old connection between Britain's empire and her subjects may have changed in terms of names and locations, but the battered old relationship remains alive beyond the Commonwealth.[3] India and Indians are still fascinated with Britain's universities, politics, law and language, and Britain, in turn, remains infatuated with Indian food, history, tourism, culture and cricket. Few, however, remember that another outcome of Britain's imperial domination of India was the Deobandi movement and its offshoot, the Tableeghi Jamaat.

It looks like a long walk to the Markazi Mosque, and it is drizzling, so I approach the first cab. The driver has a long beard and wears a white skullcap. He is reading the Quran and munching peanuts from a pot on the dashboard. As I get into the warm car from the cold outside, the smell of the nuts makes me feel hungry. He tucks the holy book away above the steering wheel as I close the door.

'I am very sorry to interrupt your *tilawat*, your Quran reading,' I apologise. 'But please will you take me to the Markazi Mosque? Is it far?'

'About five minutes,' he replies.

I feel genuine remorse for disturbing his reading of the Quran on a Friday morning.

'My son went to the Markaz,' he volunteers.

'What did he study?' I ask.

'He memorised the entire Quran. He is a *hafiz*. My younger son will also attend and become an *'alim*, a scholar.'

'Both your sons will be religious scholars, *ma sha Allah*,' I say. ('As God wills', in Muslim culture, is an acknowledgement of God's blessings.) 'I suppose it's like a private school?'

'Yes, we have to pay fees to the Markaz. It's hard, but if you want your children to be good Muslims, you must struggle and spend the money,' he declares.

'Is it a good school?' I ask next. 'If you think it's good, I might consider sending my nephew here to study.'

'Oh, yes, you must. My son has children from all over England studying here with him. Your nephew will be a very successful *da'ee* after studying at the Markaz.'

Through the Quran, the Prophet Mohamed was instructed to carry out '*da'wa*' – which literally means 'calling' or 'inviting' – by calling the pagans of Mecca to worship the One God, Allah, and do good deeds. Today, the Tableeghi Jamaat and others have made it their mission of *da'wa* to invite ordinary Muslims to create Islamic societies and government. Someone who does this work, mostly as a voluntary commitment, is given the honorific title of '*da'ee*'.

'What does your son do?' I ask.

'He works in a post office in the daytime and teaches Quran in the evening.'

'So he works two jobs?'

'Yes.'

'And what will your younger son do after he finishes his *'alim* course?'

'He will be an imam at a mosque.'[4]

As we approach the large mosque structure, he gives me directions. 'The school's there, on your left,' he says. 'Go inside and ask for Mawlana Abdul Samad.'

'Thank you. How much do I owe you?'

'That will be six pounds,' he says.

I give him ten and don't take any change. I ask for his prayers and he seems happy with the tip, saying, '*Jazak Allah khair* [God reward you]'.

It seems to work better in Arabic than English. Not only in Dewsbury but all across Britain, Muslims feel that much holier when saying a kind word in Arabic.

I am conscious that although the door of the mosque is physically open, there is an unseen barrier that stops most people in Britain from entering. I can enter a church if I want to, and in Turkey, Syria or Egypt anybody can enter a mosque, but outsiders cannot just walk into a British mosque.

I don't immediately follow the cab driver's advice. Rather than go straight to the madrasa, I head first to the mosque. I remove my shoes and place them on one of the shoe shelves by the door. As it is a Friday, there will be thousands coming to pray at the mosque, which can hold up to 4,000 worshippers. I want to pray alongside them, but the Quranic requirement to perform *wudhu*, pre-prayer ablutions, means I could also end up sharing the washrooms with hundreds of other people. I know that technically, as a traveller far from home, I'm not required to take my socks off and can instead simply wipe over them. But I'd rather not have to explain that to other Muslims who may not be so familiar with the intricacies of medieval Muslim jurisprudence, so to avoid the crowd I do my own *wudhu* ahead of the expected arrival of the masses.

In the washrooms there are rows upon rows of wooden benches in front of taps set at intervals along a network of bare pipes. There is an elderly gentleman inside already when I enter, who is still there when I leave. He holds a *miswak*, a traditional tooth-cleaning twig made from a particular tree, and rubs the bristles into his teeth with great attention.

Next, I want to say a prayer of thanks to God for my safe journey and the blessings of faith and a healthy life, so I head for the main prayer hall.

At the door there is a sign that reads, in capital letters:

PUBLIC NOTICE
ALL ACTIVITIES AND PROGRAMMES IN DEWSBURY TABLIGHI MARKAZ PREMISES WILL BE CONDUCTED ACCORDING TO THE PROGRAMME APPROVED BY THE MANAGEMENT OF THE MARKAZ. NO INDIVIDUAL OR ORGANISATION HAS THE PERMISSION TO DO ANY ACTIVITIES OR PROGRAMMES HERE WITHOUT PRIOR PERMISSION OF THE MANAGEMENT. NO ONE IS ALLOWED TO COLLECT ANY DONATION OR ADVERTISE HERE AT THE MARKAZ IN ANY WAY.

I suspect this is to keep extremist preachers out of the mosque. It feels a tad ironic, given that the Tableeghi Jamaat is renowned for starting up events and programmes at mosques all around the world without permission. Yet here, in their own headquarters, they impose even stricter rules.

Inside, the main hall of the mosque is very plain. There is no calligraphy on the walls or any impressive architectural features. There is space on the simple brown carpet for ten rows of about a hundred worshippers in each line, all facing the equivalent of a small pulpit, called a *minbar* in Arabic – a seat from which the imam is expected to deliver his sermon – and to the left of it a small semicircular niche, or *mihrab*, with a microphone, facing which he will lead the communal prayers.

For now, I am alone in the hall except for a group of four men listening to an elderly preacher who is talking to them in quiet whispers. They beckon me to join them as I put a white cotton prayer cap on my head. I don't ordinarily wear caps any longer, but I do on this occasion as most mosque attendees in Dewsbury wear traditional attire. It is a decorated, angular cap from one of my father's religious friends, similar to that of India's first prime minister, Nehru.

I pray, giving God thanks in Arabic, and then follow the usual movements that accompany reciting the shorter chapters of the Quran from memory – bowing, praising God, prostrating myself in adoration – and then I raise my hands and pray for my parents, friends and family and humanity at large.

Before visiting the madrasa, I want to see the entirety of the great and famous mosque that is Dewsbury Markaz. I walk over to the other, smaller, hall only to be reminded what it is like to be a member or activist with the Tableeghis: communal living, men in sleeping bags all over the floor, and the room filled with that musky odour of men who have not opened a window overnight. Some are awake, some talking to each other, in a room full of men in a mosque far from their homes and families, committed to preaching, doing *da'wa*, conveying the call to other Muslims. No other organisation, not even the mosques of Saudi Arabia, packs in as many sleeping bags as a Tableeghi mosque – and this is their European headquarters.

One of the men, with a short beard and wearing Pakistani clothes, catches my eye. 'Come in, brother,' he beckons.

I politely say that I am looking for Mawlana Abdul Samad in the madrasa.

'They are in the other building, brother,' he says. I touch my right hand to my chest and lower my head a little, and slowly move away.

Followers of the Tableeghi teachings often prioritise their literalist principles and dedication to worship over family and other duties. As I walk over to the madrasa, I recall something my father told me long ago. When they were living in London's East End in the 1970s, he and my mother were once woken late at night by the agonised shrieks of the Muslim lady living next door. My father rushed out to see what had happened.

'Call me an ambulance, please,' she yelled.

My mother stayed with the lady while my father arranged transport. The neighbour was pregnant and had gone into labour. Her husband, a Tableeghi, was absent: he was busy doing *da'wa* abroad, leaving his wife at home alone. My father would often repeat the story of this shunning of family duty, and the way the Tableeghis would justify this abdication in the name of God.

I collect my shoes and walk out across the small car park.

'Press and wait' says a notice under the buzzer, so I do. Suddenly I hear someone shouting from an open door inside, not through the intercom: 'You can come in!'

The receptionist is a man in his twenties with a bushy beard, without a moustache, dressed in Pakistani-style salwar kameez.

'I've come from London to find out more about the madrasa,' I tell him.

'What do you want to know?'

'I want to meet Mawlana Abdul Samad to discuss the education system here,' I say.

'He's not here,' says the moustache-less youth abruptly. He offers no alternatives.

'How much are the annual fees?' I ask.

His interest piqued, he gets out a form and gives it to me.

'Three thousand pounds per year for food, accommodation and studies, but books and clothes are separate.'

I explain to him that if I am impressed by what I see, I will bring my nephew back to visit the madrasa.

'He doesn't need to visit,' the man interrupts. 'If you just fill in the form and pay, it will be okay.'

At this point, feeling the need for more situational awareness, I turn my head and look around.

'Whoa!' I exclaim, unexpectedly. The man looks at me, surprised. 'Why are there so many pairs of trainers here?!' I ask.

I have never seen so many pairs of colourful branded footwear in one place. Nike, Adidas, Reebok, Puma – there are hundreds upon hundreds of sports shoes piled up on some shelves against a wall.

'Those belong to the students,' he says.

'They are all here?'

'They live here,' he says.

'Can I see, please? If my nephew can't visit, as you say, at least let me meet one of your students, and then I'll take the form to fill in for three thousand pounds.'

The receptionist disappears through the door behind him and returns with a student who looks identical to the teenager from the station.

'Usman will show you the madrasa,' he says. 'But we cannot show you the sleeping area, because ...'

'I understand,' I quickly interrupt. I have no plans to inspect the sleeping quarters of underaged boys, either.

Usman is a very pleasant and polite young boy, again bespectacled and wearing a white *thawb*, and deeply respectful in his manner. He shakes my hand before opening a side door, and we enter a vast, narrow hall where dozens of young boys in white *thawbs* and skullcaps are engaged in all sorts of activities.

'This is our break time before Friday prayers,' Usman informs me.

Some of the boys are playing snooker and pool; others are playing table tennis. There is much laughter and joyful shouting.

Two payphone booths are prominent – for students to call home? Usman himself is from Spain, he explains. 'Two of my brothers are also here,' he volunteers.

'Really? How long will you be here?' I ask.

'Our parents want us to study here. I'm seventeen now, and I have eight more years to complete my *'alim* course.'

'God bless you,' I say. I can't stop myself from expressing my thoughts in English.

Usman, not knowing that I speak Arabic, kindly translates some Arabic posters on the wall. 'This one says: The best of you are those who help others,' he tells me. '*Khair al-nas man yanfa' al-nas*.'

Literally, it translates as: 'The best humans are those who benefit other humans.' The word 'human' is mentioned twice, and some would argue that this is a call to humanism, but I don't want to argue semantics and translation with a teenager.

'Why are you here?' I ask him, as we walk along a narrow corridor. 'So far from home?'

'This is our home. In Spain, there is too much *fitna* and tourism.'

We both understand what he means. '*Fitna*' (literally meaning 'temptation', or 'discord') has come to refer to the sexual freedoms of the nude beaches in Spain. The madrasa is a place of safety and shelter, away from the modern freedoms and *fitna*.

'This is a classroom,' he points out.

'Hold on,' I say. 'Where are the chairs?'

'We don't use chairs and tables unless we are in a science class, or computing.'

'But why?'

'It's *sunnah*, innit?' he says. '*Sunnah*' ('customary practice') refers to the habits and sayings of the Prophet recorded in books of '*hadith*', which Muslims seek to follow, often literally. Sitting on the floor because the Prophet did so reflects the same literalism as using a twig, the *miswak*, to clean one's teeth.

But I am distracted now by something more instinctive. The aroma of delicious Indian curry fills the next corridor as we walk towards the kitchen. Several male chefs in Pakistani attire are stirring the contents of a number of vast cooking vessels. Groups of men are eating on the floor nearby.

'These are some of our teachers,' murmurs Usman.

'Brother, please join us,' one says, calling me over with his hand.

He seems genuinely warm and inviting. I look at the floor-based arrangement and am tempted. I am still hungry from the car that smelled of peanuts. I smile and look at their food. There is a pile of chapati bread and two curry pots. But they are all sitting on the floor, eating from the same plate, and there are no knives or forks.

They are dipping their chapati into a curry dish shared by them all – I can see their fingers dripping with sauce. I want to say, 'what about hygiene?'

But I don't. They are building bonds of brotherhood and sharing. By sitting with one knee raised in order to eat less, as the Prophet taught, they are trying to imitate a great man. I thank them and touch the left side of my chest, bow a little again, and walk away slowly. Many members of the Tableeghi Jamaat live and eat in communities like this to emulate the behaviour, as traditionally imagined, of the community of believers around the Prophet in seventh-century Arabia.

Usman then takes me to the doctor's room. If a student is ill, he doesn't need to go outside the madrasa: there are medical facilities for administering drugs on site, and a doctor who visits regularly.

'All of us know about the medicine room,' grins Usman. The *hadith* literature emphasises the use of olives, honey, black seed oil, dates, and even blood-cupping therapy as traditional ways to heal, and also prevent, illnesses. But here in the madrasa I see boxes of pills and pads for prescriptions and chemists – the medicine is modern, not traditional.

As we walk along another corridor, Usman tells me how they raised £250 for a Muslim charity last week by selling doughnuts to the mosque congregation, and that they play football with the local church. I ask if they would also play with a synagogue or temple, and he replies without hesitation: 'Yes, we are open to all religious schools.'

I ask how my nephew would live if he came here. Usman explains that he would sleep in a room with his whole form, approximately fifteen to twenty boys in the same space together.

As we talk, he leads me into a vast room where they are memorising the Quran. A younger boy is sitting there on the floor, bobbing to and fro, reciting verses:

'Idha al-shamsu kuwwirat, wa idha al nujum inkadarat ...'

(When the sun is wrapped in darkness, and the stars fall, dispersing ...)

These verses on the movement of the sun and stars helped give birth to an active intellectual interest in astronomy and the pursuit of science among medieval Muslims, including the great Ibn Sina or Avicenna (d. 1037). Now Muslim youths memorise the Quran in one class, sitting on the floor, completely detached from 'secular science' in another class with chairs and lab benches. The connection between faith and science has been lost.

'Let me show you the library,' Usman offers, recognising that I am mentally far away from the Quran memorisation room. I am eager to see the madrasa's book collection.

We enter a small room with two sleeping bags on the floor and a messy assortment of poorly bound Arabic books on the shelves. A cursory look through the books is enough for me to understand that these are volumes of *hadith*, collections of sayings attributed to the Prophet, and *tafseer*, Quranic exegesis. There is nothing on ethics, physics, philosophy and logic, history or maths in this 'Islamic' library. The bestsellers in fiction and non-fiction have also been kept out.

Finally, Usman shows me the class in which he most aspires to sit and learn. His excitement is palpable. It is not the classroom for studying the Quran, or one of the labs for science or computing. This venerated class is for lessons on the *hadith* collection of Imam Bukhari (d. 870), and once again the room is furnished with benches.

After the Prophet passed away almost two centuries later, pious Muslims started to collect reports of his supposed sayings. There are six such collections popular among Sunni Muslims, of which Bukhari's is considered to be the most reliable in terms of authenticity, but also, to rational minds, the most controversial in terms of content. For example, the Bukhari collection several times quotes Abu Huraira, one of the Prophet's companions, as reporting that the Prophet said: 'If a house fly falls in the drink of any one of you, he should dip it in the drink and take it out, for one of its wings has a disease and the other has the cure for that disease.'[5] Many still take such *hadiths* literally as the actual words of the Prophet.

As I stand outside the *hadith* classroom, about to get ready to leave, I wonder how much I have accepted the madrasa's terms of debate. I have only asked about sending my nephew here: why not my nieces, or my daughters? Has fear of causing offence, upset and who knows what consequences constrained me to remain silent on male-dominated institutional collectivism?

Usman, ever courteous, asks me to pray for him and shakes my hand with both of his before passing me back to the receptionist. I thank the youngster and say a prayer for him. I genuinely like him. I also thank the receptionist, but there is no shaking of hands with him. I take the application form with me: a single A4 sheet with two sides of questions, asking for student information, contact details, previous schools attended and any criminal convictions.

The Deobandis are creating these madrasas all over the country: in Bury, Bradford, Oldham, Manchester, London and other major towns and cities. There are more than thirty such institutions operating across Britain, turning out the imams who will lead the congregations and communities of the future.

* * *

I walk through the car park back to the mosque. It is now prayer time, and hundreds of men are beginning to arrive in their cars. I re-enter the mosque and sit on the floor waiting for the call to prayer. There are no pews in a mosque. As our movements include bowing and prostrating, much like yoga, sitting on the floor to worship God somehow always feels right. But the mosque hall seems very bleak. Most mosques are well lit, either naturally or by means of chandeliers. Calligraphy of Quranic verses can further illuminate a mosque, for God, in the Quran, is called *al-Noor*, the Light. The Markazi Mosque has very little natural light, though, and as the hall slowly begins to fill with worshippers three observations strike me.

First, the men all, without fail, have beards of various lengths. A beard is a hallmark of religiosity, in emulation of the Prophet Mohamed. *Hadith* literature tells us that Mohamed had a beard, as did Moses and Jesus, and there are *hadiths* that curse men who look like women. So Muslim men often grow beards in order to look like the Prophet of God and not appear effeminate. For myself, because I believe that godliness is internal, I have slowly removed all outward signs that help to breed hypocrisy. But Dewsbury mosque is clearly not the place for such mysticism. Here everybody has a beard.

Second, as I look around I see only about five other men wearing shirts and trousers. All the others are wearing either Pakistani-style salwar kameez or an Arab-style *thawb*. There is no such thing as 'Islamic dress': the Prophet wore the same attire as his pagan enemies. When I lived in Saudi Arabia, I wore a *thawb*, and many of my Saudi and Gulf Arab friends wear English chinos or American jeans away from their own countries. Most worshippers at mosques in Turkey, Syria and Egypt wear Western clothes. Yet here in England, thousands are wearing traditional clothing from Asia and the Middle East.

Third, a surprising number of the men are following an eighth-century Islamic dispensation that allows the wearing of leather socks that they can simply wipe over when making their ablutions before prayers, rather than having to remove their socks to wash their feet. They could also, just as legitimately, wipe over their ordinary socks, but the focus here is on a more rigid interpretation of the rules. Yet leather is slippery when walking on carpet, and the wearer also has to take an extra size in shoes. I know, because I too once wore these leather socks, and I realised within a week just how uncomfortable they were.

And yet, despite these niggling thoughts at the back of my mind, there is a beautiful humming of worshippers reciting prayers from the Quran. I take out my Egyptian prayer beads and join the harmony, whispering prayers of salutation to the Prophet. For almost an hour there is outward bliss as every individual engages in a personal act of worship, meditation, recitation or contemplation.

At this point on a Friday, at mosques in most of the Middle East, the homeland and birthplace of Islam, a *qari* (trained reciter of the Quran) will melodiously recite a portion of the Quran. Then the imam will stand up and address the congregation in the local language – say

Turkish, or Persian, or Urdu. This is usually the most educational and relevant part of Friday prayers. There is no such pre-sermon lecture here today in Dewsbury. Instead, the imam suddenly launches into a sermon in classical Arabic, to a hall full of non-Arabs. The Friday lecture is not in English, or even Hindi or Urdu, the languages that the mosque's elders and younger congregants understand.

I do understand the Arabic, because my parents taught me the Quran as a child and then I studied classical Arabic in the Middle East in my twenties. The focus of the imam's sermon is on the importance of fasting for Ashura, a practice based on the Jewish Yom Kippur fast. If the Jews fasted for a day and a night, the Prophet declared, the Muslims, being more worthy of Moses, would therefore fast for ten days. I record the sermon. It is somewhat functional and feels devoid of soul. And then the collective prayer is offered, in a rapid manner and again with no melody, as we stand, bow and prostrate ourselves. Here in this Indian-dominated mosque in Yorkshire, the recital smacks of the Arabian deserts of Najd: fast-paced and lacking in any of the Ottoman, Egyptian or even Meccan melodies of old. The Ottomans and Mughals had their imams trained in the classical musical notes, but this is not the practice any more.

In Britain's synagogues on Saturday mornings, as in many of its churches on Sundays, a prayer is always said for the good health of the Queen. Historically, Muslims too have always prayed for the head of state's wellbeing, as a symbol of thanksgiving for the security and stability of the lands in which they live. This prayer is more important now than ever to connect young Muslims to their country, monarch and government. But no such supplication is forthcoming from the imam in Dewsbury.

After the prayers led by the imam, I await the Friday *dua*, usually the high point of the week, where Muslims raise their hands to God together. The more literalist mosques these days consider this *bid'ah*, an evil innovation, which under widespread Saudi Salafi influences they are encouraged to avoid. The elders of early Islam used to believe that among any large gathering there might be one particularly pious person present, and that God would answer the prayers of everybody there for the sake of that one special, humble lover of God. Such mysticism now seems to have vanished: I sit there and raise my hands to the heavens alone. I pray a few more *raka'as* and then prepare to leave. On the far side of the hall, readings of the old Tableeghi books are taking place. It is *bid'ah*, it seems, to deliver a pre-sermon speech in English, or to raise hands together in *dua*, but to sit together reading the books of their organisation's twentieth-century founders from India is not *bid'ah* at all.

For the entire day, from the moment I arrived, I have been surrounded by men. As I get up to leave, an elderly gentleman comes up to me.

'How are you, brother?' he asks. 'Where are you from?'

'London,' I reply.

'You have come so far, how can I help you?'

He has a neatly trimmed beard, beautifully dark skin and deep, kind eyes. He holds my hand as he speaks, with a smile on his face. Out of all the people in the mosque, he has spotted me as an outsider of sorts. He now tells me he has been in Dewsbury for fifty-two years and is a retired train driver. Every week he goes to London to see his daughter. Three of his sons are *'alims*. One works as an imam and one at HMRC, and the other is looking for a job. They are all also Tableeghi preachers.

As we stand talking, the friendly gentleman points out that the son of the founder of Dewsbury's Markazi Mosque, Hafez Patel, is sitting nearby with a couple of clerics. 'Would you like to meet them?' he asks.

'Yes, I'd like to ask them a question.'

The gentleman kindly takes me over to the group, and we again sit on the floor together. The son of the founder is a chubby man with a friendly face behind a full beard.

'Why are there no women in the mosque?' I ask. 'Or in the madrasa?' The question sounds abrupt because it is abrupt. 'Even in Saudi Arabia,' I continue, 'there are women in the mosques. They're segregated, but at least they're there. In Turkey, I've seen them walking around freely. You're from India – in the main mosque in Delhi women walk freely everywhere, even Hindu women, right at the very front of the mosque. Why are you stopping women in a free country like Britain being in a mosque?'

The cleric doesn't approve of my questions. His friendly expression is starting to fade, but he waits courteously until I have finished my thoughts.

'My brother,' he says. 'You're an intelligent man, but there can be no discussion of there being women in the mosque. This would be a temptation for many. I suggest you read the following books by our teachers and students.'

I jot down several titles of books in English that he recommends – books with titles that refer to women as wives and sexual creatures, but I resolve to keep an open mind and read them before coming to any conclusions.

'Where can I buy them?' I inquire – needlessly, as it transpires.

'All of the bookshops in Dewsbury,' he says.

There are several bookshops outside the mosque, so I decide to go and buy his recommendations. I thank the elderly uncle, who now offers to give me a lift to the station. His incredible politeness continues despite my questioning of his respected clerics.

* * *

Out on the streets, I see row after row of terraced houses with only Asian Muslims standing by the doors and on the streets. The women shopping at the butchers and fruit stalls are all out with their faces covered with black veils. Again, in Turkey or Syria or Egypt you would rarely find such uniformity in clothing. After Friday prayers in Damascus, for example, the women and men at the local shops in Souq al-Jum‘a come from an array of backgrounds, and many women don't even cover their hair, much less conceal their faces. Not so in this part of Yorkshire.

All around Savile Town there are shops selling books, plane tickets, headscarves, face veils, long women's gloves, *miswaks*, cheap Arabian perfumes, *thawbs*, honey, olives and black seed oil, and within this subculture the cleric's recommended books on women are on prominent display. I buy the ones I'd noted down and decide to read them on the train back to London.

It is a subculture of different food and lifestyle, clothes and books –
a culture of caliphism.* The Tableeghi Jamaat separates itself from
secular society, and preaches from door to door, to create a Muslim
society from which a caliphate is expected eventually to emerge.
While political Islamists in the Muslim Brotherhood target the state
and seek to change its laws through elections and parliaments, as
in Egypt and Syria, and their jihadi cousins in al-Qaeda and ISIS
use violence in seeking to restore a caliphate in several Muslim
countries, the Tableeghi Jamaat believe in bottom-up change, and
work for their caliphate from the masses upwards.

Its caliphism may be slow and populist, in theory at least,
but Tableeghi-dominated Dewsbury has produced impatient
and violent followers, too. The separatism and caliphism of the
Tableeghi literalists gave Britain the ringleader of the 7 July 2005
London Tube bombings. Mohammad Sidique Khan, a worshipper
at the Markazi Mosque, led the operation, killing himself and over
fifty Londoners and injuring 700 more; the attack was planned
from his home in Dewsbury.

The caliphism did not stop there. In June 2015 Britain's youngest
ISIS suicide bomber, Talha Ismail, carried out an attack for the
caliphate in Iraq at only seventeen years of age. His best friend,
Hasan Munshi, also from Dewsbury, had travelled with him to
the ISIS caliphate. In 2006 Hasan's older brother, Hamad Munshi,

---

* Caliphism is not only a political ideology but also a set of cultural and social attitudes,
influenced by a sense of separatism and a desire to be governed more by a rigid
interpretation of sharia as state law. Many Muslim organisations support the ultimate
aim and aspiration of creating a caliphate – an Islamist state headed by a caliph – in a
return to the glory of days of an imperial Islam. Turkey abolished the caliphate with the
break-up of the Ottoman Empire after the First World War.

Tableeghi Jamaat and others believe that if Muslims become closer to the sharia in
their personal and social lives, then God will grant them a caliphate. Islamists such as the
Muslim Brotherhood, meanwhile, take the view that a government of God would help to
make Muslims more sharia-compliant. Both groups, despite their different approaches,
have the same goal of a caliphate or Islamist state.

then fifteen, had become the country's youngest convicted terrorist. He was found on his way home from school with a pocket full of ball bearings, and had instructions on martyrdom and explosives hidden in his bedroom.

The hatred and anger also went beyond caliphist Muslims in Dewsbury. In Birstall, four miles up the road, Jo Cox, the Labour MP for Batley, was shot and stabbed to death in 2016 by a man reportedly shouting 'Britain First', apparently for her support for the local Muslim community and for calling for Syrian refugees to be allowed into Britain. Where will this mutual separatism lead in modern Britain?

* * *

The town centre feels lifeless and barren. It is desolate: not a single major retail outlet is present on the high street. The shopkeepers in the pound stores look bored, as customers are few and far between. I want some lunch, but not a single restaurant seems to be open or welcoming. There is not even a McDonald's to be seen. What do young people do in Dewsbury? There's no cinema that I can see, or any clubs and bars.

I walk back to the railway station. The West Riding pub next door seems tranquil enough, and it's open. I need the lavatory, but I also want something to eat. I've been feeling hungry ever since smelling peanuts in the car and curry in the mosque.

It's strange to think that this pub is a forbidden space for the thousands who were at the mosque today, while, conversely, the few people who are in the pub would not go to the mosque either. Yet the pub has traditionally been a key social space for most Brits, as the mosque is the weekly gathering space for most Muslims. Inside the West Riding an elderly couple sit quietly alone. I smile at them and, as I often enjoy the company of people older than myself, I sit down at the table next to them. Predictably, they invite me to join them. Tom and Jane previously lived in Dewsbury, but have moved to nearby Batley now. Both in their sixties, they are almost an advert for Marks & Spencer with their fleece jackets and neighbourly warmth.

'I'm visiting from London,' I say, in case they are under the misapprehension that I'm a local gone astray who shouldn't be in the pub.

'Yeah, we can tell from your accent and behaviour,' says Tom. 'The locals here don't talk to us. They see us as leftovers from an old Dewsbury, not part of the town they are creating.'

'What do you mean?' I ask.

'Have you seen the number of mosques?' Jane chimes in. 'All the pubs are shut. We had more than thirty pubs in Dewsbury when I was young. Now we have fewer than five.'

'What's wrong with mosques?' I ask, trying to get a better sense of what is on their minds.

'It's not just a few mosques here and there. There are several all on the same road.'

'But, still, if they want more mosques in Dewsbury, why not?'

'You don't understand,' interjects Tom, visibly annoyed by my persistent probing. 'A few years ago our neighbours applied to Kirklees – that's the local council – for permission to build a small flagpole outside their house. This is England, and we want to fly our flag. He served in the war and wanted to remember …'

Jane takes over.

'The council delayed and delayed. So we joined our friend and also asked for a permit. Guess what? We were all denied permission. Do you understand now? We couldn't get a permit for a flag, yet the council keeps giving them permission to build more and more of their mosques.'

If these people feel so separate from the Muslims in Dewsbury that they have left the town, then what future is there for the separate frequenters of pubs and mosques in Britain? Where can they both meet? What do these two tribes have in common?

I suddenly realise that Jane is the first woman I have spoken to all day. I'm tempted to show her the books recommended to me by the mosque-dwellers, but after the insult over their flag I daren't raise any more issues. It is time to head back home to London, and to read the texts on the train.

* * *

The cleric asked me to read three books to get a better understanding of why women cannot enter mosques, and why this cannot even be discussed in Dewsbury. *Intermingling of the Sexes* is a tiny pamphlet produced by Mohamed bin Lutfi al-Sabbagh. It started life as the author's admonitions transmitted on Riyadh Radio in Saudi Arabia two decades ago. From Riyadh, his words were translated in India and now find an audience in Yorkshire, England. Here are a few extracts from the publication:

> The call for the woman to come out of the home and intermingle with men has caused many tragedies and misfortunes. This call started off in a very glittering and attractive way in an effort to make the woman the splendour of society and the focus of honour and reverence. But she ended up in disgrace and humiliation where she is either a street sweeper or a worker in a bar. Quite often, this emergence of hers exposes her to things that threaten her chastity and put an end to her future.[6]

> Being in seclusion with a strange woman, and the reckless intermingling between men and women, is most certainly *haram*, forbidden in the religion of God.[7]

> It has been historically established that one of the biggest causes for the downfall of Greek civilisation was the exposure of the woman, her intermingling with men, and her over-indulgence in self-beautification and free intermingling. And exactly the same thing happened with the Romans. In the beginning of their civilisation the women were virtuous and modest. They were able to conquer places upon places and reinforce the pillars of their mighty empire. But the moment the women began to exhibit themselves and began frequenting clubs and public gatherings in their best attire and most beautiful jewellery, then the morals of the men became corrupt, their military power became weak, and then civilisation collapsed very quickly.[8]

The corruption of political foundations is found in every era and time. But the surprising and astonishing thing is that its causes are the same today as they were in the past: i.e. the woman was the strongest factor in destroying noble characteristics.[9]

Muhammad ibn Adam al-Kawthari is a British Muslim cleric of the Deobandi school who lives in Leicester. According to the bookseller, his *Islamic Guide to Sexual Relations* is a bestseller and has been reprinted every two years since it was first published in 2008. From the very outset al-Kawthari is keen to remind his readers of the caliphism: 'It is a common fallacy that Islam is restricted to particular forms of devotional worship and has nothing to say about social issues, marriage, divorce, politics, economics and so on.'[10] This is a reminder that the private practices of the Tableeghi Jamaat have a caliphist intent, the aspiration towards Muslim rule over society, politics and economics to which the movement's *da'wa* is oriented. But in the meantime, Deobandi-influenced books give young Muslims in Britain guidance on how to prepare for that pure caliphate.

He bans all musical instruments: it is *haram* to play or listen to music:

Musical instruments designed exclusively for entertainment and dancing, and which are capable of captivating the listener, even when unaccompanied by the human voice, such as the drum, violin, guitar, flute, lute, mandolin, harmonium and piano, are all prohibited to use and listen to.[11]

Al-Kawthari justifies his ban by citing a *hadith* from *Sahih al-Bukhari*, the same collection of *hadith* that the teenager Usman was yearning to study in the most prestigious class of the madrasa in Dewsbury. Was that why the Quran recital in the Dewsbury Markazi Mosque was so bland, lest it appear musical?

I have one book left to read before I arrive in London.

Guidance for a Muslim Wife was written by Majaz Azmi and published in India in 2013. Here is a sample of the author's selection of *hadith* material:

When a woman leaves her home without her husband's consent then all the angels of the skies and the entire universe curse her for this act until she returns home.[12]

The woman who applies perfume and passes by men is an adulteress.

When a husband calls his wife at night to have relations with her and she refuses without a valid reason, she is cursed throughout the night by the angels.

The rights of the husband on the wife are so great that if pus flows on the husband's body and the woman cleans it, then too his rights will not be fulfilled.

The book prohibits women from entering the mosque wearing perfume because this would draw lustful male attention. In Dewsbury, the European hub of the Deobandi Islam of the Indian subcontinent, the Muslim men go even further to prevent inappropriate desires: they stop women entering the mosque at all.

I wonder if Muslim women fare any better at mosques in Manchester, a city of radical feminism and home to the first suffragettes? I decide to make my next Friday prayer in Manchester.

2

Manchester

The taxi drivers at Manchester Piccadilly station are all Asian. The driver at the front of the queue is on his phone.

'The Radisson Blu Edwardian, please,' I say. 'OK,' he grunts, and I assume he has ended his call and will help me load my luggage for the two nights I plan to stay in Manchester, along with the gifts I have brought for the Mancunian Muslims who have agreed to meet me. I lift the bags into the taxi myself and hear the driver break into Punjabi.

'*Haan ji*,' he says to the person on the phone. 'Yes, sir.'

I can't fully understand what he is saying, but I know he is talking about numbers and money. When a moment of silence presents itself, I press the button to speak to the driver and ask, 'The Radisson Blu is the old Free Trade Hall, right?'

He looks at me in the rear-view mirror and shows no sign of comprehension.

I try again. Again, a blank look.

He speaks some more Punjabi on the phone, and then I hear him say '*Allah hafiz*' ('God keep you' or 'goodbye'), words of farewell. The original Persian and Urdu version of the phrase is '*Khuda hafiz*', but much has changed with the recent rise of Arab culture in Pakistan, including certain aspects of the language. Arabic words have supplanted their Urdu and English equivalents in religious matters, in keeping with Pakistan's new religious culture. The driver doesn't use the non-Arabic words 'God' or '*Khuda*'; only the Arabic '*Allah*' will do.

The ride to the hotel is relatively short and costs less than £10.

The receptionist, Victorija, is from somewhere in Eastern Europe. She's very pleasant: blonde, smiling and keen to help.

'This is the old Free Trade Hall, right?' I try again.

'I'm sorry?' she says, inquiringly.

'Isn't this where the Suffragettes' "Votes for Women" campaign began?'

She smiles at me, and then trots out what I imagine is her standard answer when a question doesn't resonate:

'We have had refurbishment work done recently. The spa is downstairs and the massage parlour, too. Please enjoy your stay.'

I don't think there'd be any point in asking her about Disraeli, the great British prime minister who made his famous 'One Nation' speech here, on these hallowed grounds, in 1872. Addressing a vast crowd at what was then the Free Trade Hall in Manchester, and building on the themes of his book *Sybil*, Disraeli spoke for four hours to explain his vision of a new, one-nation Britain with more rights for working-class people. The historic hall was itself built on the site of the 1819 Peterloo Massacre, in which cavalry charged into a crowd of demonstrators for parliamentary reform, on the orders of local magistrates, killing several and injuring hundreds. The shocking event was ironically named 'Peterloo' in reference to St Peter's Field, where the demonstrators had gathered peacefully to listen to a well-known radical orator, and Waterloo, the famous British military victory that had taken place four years earlier.

Local people, I suspect, would once have known about the past of such places, and been able to understand their present significance – but that is no longer the case. The now refurbished Free Trade Hall seems to house the hotel's main restaurant for dinner and breakfast, but the exterior façade still stands in all its grandeur. A neoclassical building of tan-coloured stone, the hall is adorned with symmetrical round arches on the ground floor, repeated on the floor above with twinned pillars and carved floral designs. It is a stunning building.

I leave my bags in my sixth-floor room and head out to my dinner meeting. St Peter's Square in the city centre, near the tram station and interchange and shopping malls, is busy. I walk past Chanel and Selfridges, both staffed by white and Asian workers. Gary, my gay waiter at an Indian restaurant, seems comfortable and confident in telling me I've come to the wrong restaurant, while serving me hot water and lemon – my favourite drink for keeping bugs at bay while travelling. Gary doesn't charge me for the drink, and his Asian colleague escorts me to the taxi rank. I am soon heading for another restaurant on Manchester's Oxford Road, near the 'Curry Mile' and university area, where my hosts are patiently waiting.

Faiza is a Muslim woman born and raised in Manchester, and a volunteer at her local mosque. Fifteen years ago she emailed me an invitation to attend an event at a Manchester mosque to celebrate the *mawlid*, the birthday of the Prophet Mohamed, and over the years we have stayed in touch. For the past fifteen years Faiza has emailed me, including while I was living in Damascus, New York, Jeddah, Washington DC and London. She has an inquisitive mind and has always wanted to know more about the Sufi shrines and historical sites I visited during my travels abroad. I always responded courteously and asked, 'Shall we meet when next in London?' Each time I have visited Manchester, often for party political conferences or to speak at their fringe events, I have written to Faiza, inviting her to meet me for a cup of tea. She knows a lot about Muslims in Manchester and understands the various political and social issues they encounter like no one else. For fifteen years she has refused to meet me. When I emailed her three weeks ago, she turned down my invitation yet again. Her reason all these years has been consistent. As a Muslim woman in Manchester, her local Muslim community observed her movements and meetings. Contact with men was limited to family, marriage or religious settings. There was a bond between Faiza and me: we were each trying to find a way of being both

British and observantly Muslim. So why could we two Brits not meet for coffee?

Faiza used to wear a face veil, a niqab, and each time opposition to the face veil was voiced in the British media she would write to me in a fury. First, back in 2006, there was the former MP Jack Straw's uneasy questioning of a woman in his constituency wearing the full veil in a private meeting. Later, in 2017, there was the uproar over former Prime Minister Theresa May's support for women to wear the hijab 'without fear'. Then, finally, there was the backlash faced by Boris Johnson in 2018 over his comments about women in burkas 'looking like letterboxes'. Throughout all this time, Faiza and I discussed this controversy that was so close to her heart and appearance. After debating the correctness of wearing a face veil for more than a decade, she finally decided to remove hers after leaving her job at an Islamic girls' school several years ago.

For years a single mother, whose daughter is now over the age of eighteen, Faiza stands outside the restaurant waiting for me in case I have got lost. Her husband, Taj-Paul, is with her, a convert to Islam, bearded, well-mannered and softly spoken. He maintains steady eye contact. Taj-Paul has no idea who I am or why he is meeting a friend of his wife, but he has agreed to come because Faiza, as a woman, cannot meet me without a *mahram*. Having a *mahram*, or chaperone, present to ensure that a man and a woman do not meet together alone (which would be *haram*, forbidden) is a commonly observed religious practice drawn from an interpretation of scripture accepted across much of the Muslim Middle East, from Saudi Arabia to Iran. Specific *hadiths* are cited in justification of this practice, for example: 'If a woman does speak to a man who is neither her husband nor her *mahram* (a close relative she is permanently barred from marrying) then the two may not be alone, for otherwise the third of them is Satan.'[1]

A year ago I told Faiza I was in Manchester and was free finally to meet in person, but Taj-Paul refused to permit her to meet any male friend alone. Faiza told me via WhatsApp the story of a previous meeting with a male friend: 'I wanted to see an American friend who was visiting, and my husband insisted that we meet him at home together,' Faiza wrote. 'Then when my friend arrived, he was only allowed to sit with my husband, and I met only the wife. So yes, please, let's meet, but you'll be in a separate room from me.'

I accepted her terms.

One week before our meeting, I decided to ask if I could invite them both for dinner at a restaurant, a public place. Faiza said her husband would come to dinner with her, but she couldn't tell him who I was, so that he wouldn't be able to assume my gender and impose some kind of separation, as he did with her American friend.

I was worried she might cancel on me after more than a decade of waiting to meet in person, but thankfully she didn't.

'Ed Husain.' I introduce myself and shake hands firmly with Taj-Paul as we enter the Indian restaurant.

'Brother Mahbub,' insists Faiza, using my middle name.

She doesn't make eye contact with me, nor does she shake my hand. In a text message earlier, she informed me that she wouldn't. I was warned not to hug her or greet her by kissing her on the cheek.

'He won't like it. You know the religious reasons,' she texted.

'Yes, but those rules forbidding physical contact were designed for the Arabian desert in the seventh century!' I responded. 'They were taken from the Jewish moral codes laid down in ancient Egypt to prevent rape and keep women safe!'

'Sorry, but we disagree. My husband and I do what Allah asks of us.'

'Do you really think God, creator of the cosmos, cares about kisses and handshakes?'

'Yes, He does,' she wrote back.

'I find that a very small view of God,' I replied.

'So you've been to India?' I ask Faiza's husband, based on his choice of the Indian restaurant.

'He's been all across India,' she says, anticipating his response. 'He was a hardliner with the Tableeghi Jamaat and I rescued him with my Sufi teachers,' she adds, laughing.

He clearly doesn't find this funny, but he smiles and nods at me.

'Where in London are you from?' he asks.

'The East End,' I say. 'Born near Brick Lane. That was my local mosque.'

'Do you know the Markaz on Christian Street?' he asks.

'Yes, I certainly do!' I say.

As our lamb chops, daal and naan bread arrive, Taj-Paul and I realise that we have been on similar journeys.

'Have you been to Nizamuddin in Delhi?' I ask.

'I was always in Nizamuddin,' he says with pride.

Faiza is now silent, and I look at her.

'I can't imagine you at Nizamuddin,' says Taj-Paul.

'Why?' I ask. 'It's a tough part of town, but once you're inside people are welcoming; and the history, and spirituality, and the sleepers in those graves still radiate an energy that I could feel,' I try to explain.

'No,' says Taj-Paul, confused. 'There's only one grave, and it has been covered and hidden away, because the Saudis who joined us in Tableegh opposed it. So the Indian Tableeghi Jamaat leadership have now hidden it away. We have no grave worship in Nizamuddin.'

I now realise we are talking about two different Nizamuddins. Taj-Paul is talking about the global headquarters near Delhi of the Tableeghi Jamaat, the Islamic organisation whose British and European headquarters I visited in Dewsbury, whereas I am recalling the bustling shrine of the great Muslim mystic and saint Hazrat Nizamuddin Awliya, after whom an entire area of historical Delhi is named; not the Deobandism of Dewsbury but the Islam of the majority of Indian Muslims: mystical Sufism. The contradictory modern history of India is coming alive in Manchester through our conversation.

Nizamuddin (1238–1325) was an Indian Sufi saint, who is popularly known to Muslims in India as Mahbub-e-Elahi, 'the beloved of God'. A scholar and a sought-after adviser to sultans, he later distanced himself from those who wanted his advice, preferring to preach among the poor and needy, distributing alms and calling them to follow him in acts of human kindness through pure love of God. His particular strand of Sufism called on people to deepen their love for the Divine and creation, and focus on eradicating the caste divisions in India that separated humans from each other. Nizamuddin, like the Sufi masters before him in Ajmer and Baba Farid, used music and dance as a means of popularising Sufism. Famous for not converting others to Islam by force or enforcing rituals on his new followers, he and his disciples gave birth to a passionate form of music, known as 'qawwali', that was pioneered by Amir Khusrow, a prominent student of Nizamuddin. In our times, Nusrat Fateh Ali Khan and his nephew Rahat have continued this qawwali tradition, finding students and admirers not only across the Muslim world but also in Western singers like Madonna, Elvis Presley and Elton John, and even those opposed to organised religion like the American moral philosopher Sam Harris.

The dervishes who danced to this music became so widespread in India that qawwali is still popular across the Indian subcontinent at tombs, shrines, mosques and other public places. On the several occasions when I have visited Nizamuddin's shrine in Delhi, qawwali music was played on Thursday nights, songs of love were sung by both sexes, men and women danced, and the colours of their clothes and the ecstatic climaxes they reached as they whirled or clapped were deeply moving for people like me watching from the sidelines. Millions come each year to celebrate Nizamuddin's urs (wedding night), the anniversary of his death and the night Sufis believe his soul merged with the Divine. Even the death of this great Sufi was memorialised as a celebration, a feast, not as a cause for innate sadness.

Nizamuddin's grand master Moinuddin Chishti, from Ajmer on the outskirts of Delhi, had set out the parameters of medieval Indian Sufism a generation earlier. It was he who sang songs of love and interacted with the Hindus and other 'pagans' of India with love and respect, not with judgement and the force employed by early Muslim conquerors such as Tariq ibn Ziyad, the eighth-century Umayyad general who captured much of the Iberian Peninsula from the Visigoths. For 600 years, until the rise of the anti-imperialist and Muslim revivalist Deobandi movement and its subsequent turn towards puritanism, Sufism was the mainstream form of Islam in India.

These lines of poetry, often recited by Sufis in India, are derived from ancient traditions inspired by Chishti and Nizamuddin, and they exemplify the spirit of the subcontinent's Sufism:

> Love all and hate none.
> Mere talk of peace will avail you naught.
> Mere talk of God and religion will not take you far.
> Bring out all the latent powers of your being
> and reveal the full magnificence of your immortal self.
>
> Be overflowing with peace and joy,
> and scatter them wherever you are
> and wherever you go.
>
> Be a blazing fire of truth,
> be a beauteous blossom of love
> and be a soothing balm of peace.
>
> With your spiritual light
> dispel the darkness of ignorance;
> dissolve the clouds of discord and war,
> and spread goodwill, peace and harmony among the people.
>
> This is your mission, to serve the people …

It was in remembrance of these great Sufi masters that Faiza was wearing her orange shawl, but that wasn't what Taj-Paul was referring to. Shawls like these were popular among the wandering Sufis. As they roamed the land preaching divine love, they used them as blankets at night. Upon their deaths, their shawls would be used to cover their graves or shrines. Visitors regularly buy a shawl or *chador* as a gift to place over a shrine.

It was in opposition to this folkloric, mystical Islam of the Sufis that the Tableeghi Jamaat was founded by Muhammad Ilyas

Kandhlawi nearly a century ago. The grave that Taj-Paul was talking about that had been covered up, in his Nizamuddin, was that of the founder of the Tableeghi movement himself. The Saudi-Wahhabi influence within the Tableeghi Jamaat is totally against the idea of mystic remembrance of important figures, again in opposition to the real shrine of Nizamuddin.

'I now work for Oxfam and another Christian charity,' he says to end the silence, as we both realise we were recalling different parts of India, and indeed Islam.

'Have you ever visited the actual shrine of Nizamuddin?' I ask, returning to a subject he is clearly trying to avoid.

'No,' he says. 'We were not allowed to, as it was understood to be full of *fitna*.'

That word again, the same word the student in Dewsbury used to describe the sexual freedoms permitted in Spain.

'Yes,' I persist, 'the saint sleeps there, as does the writer and poet Khusrow. But Faiza will be happy to know that the Mughal princess Jahanara, inheritor of the Taj Mahal, also lies buried there beside Nizamuddin. You'd love it, Faiza.'

Taj-Paul perks up and looks at his wife. 'We should both go, soon,' he says.

Faiza looks at me, unconvinced. Something, it seems, is not quite right.

It is now almost 8.40 p.m. and time for the *maghrib* prayer. As a traveller, it is permissible for me to pray later, but Taj-Paul points to the first floor of the restaurant, visible to us through its glass partition, where there are already several Muslim women praying.

'Do you want to go and pray?' he asks Faiza. She shakes her head and says she will pray later. He seems to want some time alone with me.

I quickly move the conversation to where they live, asking about their home in Cheetham Hill. 'Next time, come and visit us,' Taj-Paul says.

'That's very kind of you,' I say. 'Tell me, what's it like being a Muslim in Manchester?'

Faiza is keen to answer.

'Only this week at work I reported three of my colleagues to Human Resources,' she said. 'They think I'm an extremist because I wear the hijab and don't mix with them outside work. I heard them talking against me, so I went and told HR.' She goes on before I can ask any further questions.

'The bombing was terrible. The imams at all the mosques here condemned it, and we joined the protests against it in the city centre, but we are still treated as suspects.'

'The bombing?' I ask.

'At the Ariana Grande concert, in 2017,' Taj-Paul puts in.

'One of the suicide bombers, Salman Abedi, was from a mosque in Didsbury, here in Manchester,' Faiza explains, adding in exasperation: 'We have almost seventy mosques in this city. Yes, twenty-nine innocent kids died. And over a hundred were injured. For what crime?' she shrugs. 'One suicide bomber – one Salafi extremist – caused the incident, but what about the hundreds of Muslim taxi drivers who immediately took the injured to hospital? The drivers didn't charge for this, but just offered their compassion and help. And why do we forget all the Muslim doctors and nurses at the hospital?' Faiza is speaking passionately but also intelligently.

After this, we speak a little about India again, then about Muslim scholars in Britain, until it seems time to end the evening.

I ask for the bill and pay, but Faiza protests that her husband should pay instead. In most Muslim settings, paying for food is an honour and hospitality is a virtue. She wants the honour for her family, but her husband seems reluctant.

As we walk out, they point out nearby one of the University of Manchester's two prayer facilities for Muslim students, which they say is dominated by a Salafi extremist preacher and Arab students, though there is a much larger congregation at the city's Central Mosque.

'Perhaps we will meet tomorrow at the mosque,' I say.

'We hope so, *in sha Allah*,' Taj-Paul says. He shakes my hand, but Faiza does not. We part ways by around 9 p.m.

In the morning, I return to Manchester Piccadilly station. On the first floor of the station is a Starbucks, and over a skinny muffin and latte I speak with Mahfuz Alimain, a senior official at Manchester Council who is also a board member of a mosque here in the city. A father of two children at universities in Manchester and Huddersfield, he is well aware of the dynamics between communities and generations at council and institutional levels. He kindly pays for my breakfast and we sit watching the platforms, the people coming and going, during the hour we have together before dashing off to different mosques to perform our respective Friday prayers. He goes to one somewhere near his office; I plan to head for the largest mosque in the city. He is precise in his observations of Muslims and others, and in our hour of conversation he tells me the following.

'Didsbury is a wealthy area here in Manchester. The mosque management reported Salman Abedi, the suicide bomber, to the authorities six times before the concert bombing. We didn't know how to act and had no real follow-up. We get tip-offs like this all the time, but this was one that my colleagues should have taken more seriously.'

I had not been aware of this. Alimain then explains how Manchester has attracted Arab immigrants from Syria, Libya, Palestine and Iraq in recent years. Sitting serenely above the platforms of this major British railway station, he points down at the rushing commuters and says, 'These guys who come from war zones are not like us, not like all these peaceful people.'

'What do you mean?' I ask, taken aback.

'Syrians and Libyans, Yemenis and Palestinians who come to British mosques have seen bombs and destruction daily. Killings are normal for them. The Arab Spring went horribly wrong. They find it hard to adjust here in Manchester.'

My silence intrigued him.

'We diagnose PTSD in our soldiers who have been in war zones, and we fight on behalf of governments,' he elaborated. 'These refugees and others in our mosques have come from war-torn countries, often fighting against their own governments, killing soldiers, killing other citizens. Peace in Manchester troubles them; they feel they need to seek revenge and justice for the wrongs done to them in their countries. We see it in their ways in the mosques, and in their constant agitation against stability at every level. If the imam speaks in his sermon about peace, an Arab asylum seeker will accuse him of selling out and not opposing the dictators in the Arab world. But that is not our fight. They don't understand. Britain is different. We don't have to attack the Arab leaders in every sermon.

'Our younger generation encourage this instability and trouble. I am always being stopped at the mosque by younger Muslims born and raised in this country who are opposed to Israel. When I meet with Jewish leaders, the younger Muslims complain about us normalising Zionism. The elders understand the need to work with everyone, while the complaints of the younger ones then draw the attention of the war-torn Arab newcomers.

'Younger Muslims in the mosques make common cause with the refugees in a way that the elders feel is unnecessary. There is a worrying division in our congregations.'

Did the Brexit vote play a role in this young-and-old divide?

'I'm not sure,' he says. 'But those Muslims and other immigrants in the north who voted for Brexit did so partly because of organised campaigns by Polish gangs who targeted Asian homes for gold. They knew we often have gold from weddings and gifts at home, and there was an organised campaign. It made a lot of Asians want to avoid being in the EU, to stop this mass theft that was happening as a result of European immigration.'

* * *

It is time to head to Manchester's Central Mosque for Friday prayers, the weekly congregational act of worship. I hail a taxi from outside the station. My driver this time is a Sikh, judging by the surname 'Singh' on his displayed ID, and he knows exactly where to go. I walk the last 200 metres or so through the large car park to the mosque's main entrance, where two men in high-visibility jackets direct traffic and keep an eye out for any suspicious activities. This placing of guards outside mosques is new, but since the attack on a mosque in New Zealand earlier in 2019, which saw more than fifty worshippers killed, there is still fear in most mosque congregations in the West.

The red-brick building is a purpose-built mosque, similar in construction to the one in Dewsbury. It stands out, with white paint tracing parts of the minaret and windows. Here, too, it is surrounded by largely modernist architecture and older residential properties.

I go inside and up some stairs, where I remove my shoes and put them in the Hatchards bag I have with me, and walk into the prayer hall wearing chinos, navy cotton socks and an Oxford shirt. The scent of incense and Arabian oud, carried by smoke from some small charcoal burners, fills the large hall. The golden chandelier in the centre is lit up, and Islamic calligraphy circles the inner walls of the dome.

The words in Arabic calligraphy engraved within the dome are verses from the Quran. Like much else in the Quran, they record an inspired address from God voiced through the Angel Gabriel to the Prophet Mohamed. In translation, they read:

> O thou folded in garments!
> Stand (to pray) by night, but not all night,
> Half of it, or a little less,
> Or a little more; and recite the Quran in slow, measured, rhythmic tones.
> Soon shall We send down to thee a weighty Message.
> Truly, the rising by night is most potent for governing (the soul), and most suitable for (framing) the Word (of Prayer and Praise).
> Truly, there is for thee by day prolonged occupation with ordinary duties,
> But keep in remembrance the Name of thy Lord and devote thyself to Him whole-heartedly
> He is Lord of the East and the West: there is no god but He: take Him therefore for (thy) Disposer of Affairs.

The vast, open space on the ground floor could hold 3,000 worshippers, I should think, with a space above for women to pray in, out of sight of the men. The women have windows and television screens through which they can watch the imam preaching from the main pulpit, or *minbar*.

In the earliest days of Islam, during the lifetime of the Prophet Mohamed, women were permitted inside the main part of the mosque and were involved in the running of the mosque on an equal footing with men.

Decorated in gold, the mosque is open and spacious. A young man holds the microphone at the front of the mosque as I enter. There are about 200 other people here in the male section, and others are slowly arriving, making *wudhu* (the ablution before prayers) downstairs, and then entering the hall.

I can feel the soft carpet under my feet, and smell the oud wafting through the air, as I hear a popular Muslim hymn being sung by the young man at full volume from the *minbar*:

Ya akram al-khalqi, ma li man aludhu bihi
Siwaka 'inda hulul il-hadith il-'amami

O most noble of creation, I do not have anyone to take shelter in except you at occurrence of widespread calamity

Ya rabbi bil Mustafa² balligh maqasidana
Waghfir lana ma mada ya wasi' al-karami

O Lord! Fulfil our intentions and forgive us what has passed for the sake of your Chosen One, O Most bountiful

The uplifting tune and the melody of the couplets under the ornate dome feel like a very warm welcome to what Muslims call the house of God. The Arabic word for a mosque, *masjid*, is derived from *sajda* (prostration), being the place where Muslims prostrate themselves before God. The European word 'mosque' is a corruption of the Spanish '*mezquita*', from the time when Muslims in Spain during the Inquisition were regarded as 'mosquitoes' that deserved to die.

The hymn being sung is a call to love from a famed lover of the Prophet Mohamed, and is known as the *Qasida al-Burda*, or 'Ode of the Cloak'. I grew up singing it in mosques, and it brought back memories of my visit to the tomb of its writer, Sharaf al-Din al-Busiri, in Alexandria.

Al-Busiri was a thirteenth-century master calligrapher and scribe who later in life became administrator of the Sharqiya area of the Nile Delta. Troubled by his colleagues and staff, along with the corruption and intrigue, political games and conniving that he witnessed, he retreated into the teachings of his Sufi master Abul Abbas al-Mursi, himself a student of the great North African mystic and Muslim scholar Imam al-Shadhili. In the company of the Sufis and their quest for purity of the soul through love of the Divine, al-Busiri found his true calling. However, during his retreat he fell ill and became paralysed from the waist down. In that state of illness and helplessness, he recalled his life's work of praising monarchs and governors and, remembering his own shortcomings, he took up his pen to write one last *qasida*, or ode.

The poem's literary appeal and spiritual sincerity, and the ease with which the couplets could be memorised, made al-Busiri's *Qasida al-Burda* a popular hymn across the Muslim world. But there is more to his story. Once al-Busiri had completed all ten sections of his ode, he sang it alone in prayer and fell asleep with the text of the hymn on his person. The lines all praised the Prophet Mohamed, expressing love for the God who had sent this Arabian man to the people of the region to turn them back to worship of the One God, and calling on the Prophet for help in this life and the Day of Judgement in the next.

In a dream, al-Busiri saw the Prophet Mohamed come to him, smile, remove his *chador*, or cloak, and place it on, and wipe it over, al-Busiri's paralysed body. When al-Busiri awoke, the room was filled with the fragrance of rose musk, a favourite of the Prophet, and the *chador* was still on his body. Healed from his paralysis, al-Busiri walked to the marketplace, where the dervishes and mystics detected that a holy miracle had taken place. One of the Sufis asked him to share his miraculous poem with the wider community in Egypt. Thus began the power of the *Qasida al-Burda*, which has spread for the past 700 years and is now being sung in Manchester's Central Mosque, welcoming worshippers before the Friday sermon.

The singer now intones the *adhaan*, or call to prayer:

Allahu Akbar.

God is Great.

Ash-hadu an la ilaha illa Allah.

I bear witness there is no god but the One God.

Ash-hadu anna Muhammadan Rasul Allah.

I bear witness that Mohamed is the Messenger of God.

Hayy 'ala-s-Salah.

Hurry to the Prayer.

Hayy 'ala-l-Falah.

Hurry to Salvation.

Allahu Akbar.

God is Great.

La ilaha illa Allah.

There is no god but the One God.

More people have gathered in the mosque now, many in Western clothes. At the front of the mosque there are bouquets of flowers: roses, lilies, daffodils. Each time the Prophet Mohamed is mentioned in the *adhaan*, the imam and the congregants kiss their thumbs and wipe them over their eyelids. My teachers taught me to do the same while whispering the prayer:

Qurrat 'ayni bika, ya Rasul Allah.

Solace of my eyes are you, O Messenger of God.

This emphasis on love and longing was ever the Sufi way, and it is all around me now at Manchester's Central Mosque. The practices of Ajmer and Delhi, and the *qawwali* singers, would be welcome here. The imam is a young man, wearing the red fez cap surrounded by a white turban that signifies that he has trained or studied at Egypt's ancient and prestigious Al-Azhar Islamic seminary. He speaks English fluently, but delivers his speech in the manner of Pakistani politicians: loudly, with waving hands, poking his index finger for emphasis, and swaying from side to side.

'The Quran calls us to improve ourselves,' he begins. 'Whether you are a parent, a child, husband, wife, religious leader, political leader, you must change.'

It is a hot day; the air-conditioning units sealed inside the wooden works of the mosque carry the smell of the fresh flowers and the incense. In front of me sit men in Levi's jeans and polo shirts. Beside me, on my right, is an elderly gentleman with a Rolex watch and cuff links, in jacket and trousers. On my left is a man in Pakistani attire, the *s*alwar kameez, and bare feet, with his thick toes showing. There are also some men in the congregation wearing turbans in red, black, yellow and green. But most seem to be dressed in Western clothes, and while some have trimmed beards, many are clean-shaven, too. Another man, two rows in front of me, is wearing a Gap hoodie. There are students clutching folders, professionals in suits, taxi drivers with their identity badges, and what look like wealthy business people.

'A Bedouin came to the Prophet of God,' shouts the imam, getting my attention once again.

' "When will the end of the world be?" asked the Bedouin.

'"What have you done to prepare for the last hour?" asked the Prophet in turn.

'"I am not one to worship much," said the Bedouin, "but I love God and you."

'"Then worry not," said the Prophet. "You will be with those you love."'

The imam continues to develop his theme of the need to change and improve ourselves based on our love for the Prophet. He encourages us to study the life of the Prophet Mohamed and see how he acted towards people, even his enemies. Each time his name is mentioned the congregation again kiss their thumbs. The imam talks about the Prophet's compassion, his kindness to his enemies, his message of co-existence with the Jews, Christians and pagans in seventh-century Medina.

'Are we such model citizens? Do we make our Prophet proud?' he asks rhetorically, raising his hands with an exaggerated shrug like an Italian.

He quotes:

'*Qad ja'akum nur.* Certainly a light has come to you.

That light is the Prophet and the Quran,' asserts the imam. 'Are we radiating this light? Do our neighbours and friends in this country see us as carriers of love? The Prophet is *shifa*, he is healing. Has he healed our lives?'

The imam then makes the *adhaan* call to prayer again, and by now the downstairs hall is packed. My phone buzzes, but I avoid looking at it. The imam delivers two very brief sermons in Arabic mentioning the order of the caliphs and calling for peace in this life and the next, then we begin our short prayers. We all raise our hands together and the imam leads us in a collective prayer, after which we again pray individually. The mosque remains full throughout the service.

A middle-aged man takes to the *minbar* and is given the microphone. Seeing him there, all members of the congregation stand up. A few traffic wardens and taxi drivers leave, as they have to go back to work, but most stay and join the man in belting out this chorus in Urdu:

Mustafa jaan e rahmat pe laakhon salaam,

Sham'ey bazmey hedayuat pe laakhon salaam.

A hundred thousand blessings of peace be upon Mustafa, the epitome of mercy, A hundred thousand blessings of peace be upon Mustafa, the candle of the gathering of guidance.

Jis taraf uth gayee dam mein dam aagaya, Uss nigaah e inaayat pe laakhon salaam.

Wheresoever it fell, Life itself was revived, A hundred thousand blessings of peace be upon that life-bestowing gaze.

Kis ko dekha yeh Musa se pooche koyi, Aankhon walon kii himmat pe laakhon salaam.

Whom did he see? Let someone enquire of Moses, A hundred thousand blessings of peace be upon the courage of one with such eyes!
Uski baaton kii lazzat pe laakhon durood Uskay khutbay kii haybat pe laakhon salaam!

Countless blessings upon the pleasure of his words! A hundred thousand blessings of peace be upon the majesty of his sermons!

Dil samajh se waraa' hai magar yoon kahoon: Ghuncha e raaz e wahdat pe laakhon salaam.

Your heart is beyond my knowledge but I shall say this: A hundred thousand blessings of peace be upon the bud holding secrets of Oneness!

Between the couplets, we sing the first chorus together with profound joy. These are the words of another, more recent, Sufi master from India who was likewise deeply in love with the Prophet Mohamed: Ahmad Raza Khan (1856–1921). Also known as Ala Hazrat, Khan was the founder of another great Islamic movement that has hundreds of millions of adherents in South Asia, known as the Barelwis. Their name comes from Ahmad Raza Khan's birthplace, Bareilly in northern India. The group draws inspiration from the traditional mysticism of the Sufis and was formed in the late nineteenth century in opposition to the reformist Deobandi movement. After the Deobandis, the Barelwis are Britain's second largest Muslim denomination, controlling around 45 per cent of Britain's mosques.

Unlike the Sufis of old – the *qawwali* singers and dancers, those who accept Jews, Christians, Hindus and Sikhs as believers, and who judge none and love all – the Barelwis in Britain are the sworn enemies of the Deobandis. And since Dewsbury is the headquarters of the Deobandis and their Tableeghi missionaries, the proliferation of mosques in Dewsbury is all too often, beneath the surface, partly to do with Barelwis vying for influence and support from British Muslims.

The mystical focus of the Barelwis is attacked by other Islamic movements, too, including by the literalists, the Salafis. The Barelwis are accused of polytheism on account of their veneration of saints; because of their many holy shrines and their allegiance to spiritual leaders, they are said to worship others besides Allah. Barelwis contend that the Prophet Mohamed is both human and light (*nur*), another aspect of their beliefs that is attacked by literalists.

Then everyone stands up, here in this mosque in Manchester, expecting to receive the spiritual presence of the Prophet. Some fold their arms in humility, and most have their eyes closed in spiritual dedication. Once the singing comes to an end there is another quick prayer, in which the imam again asks for peace in this life and the next with a quotation from the Quran. The service is over.

As the crowd departs, many of the worshippers stop to hug each other and ask after each other's families, jobs or studies. There are smiles and joy in abundance.

I check my phone as I approach the exit. Faiza has sent me pictures of the packed women's section of the mosque on the second floor.

The imam walks past me.

'Thank you, Shaikh, for the prayers and *khutbah* [sermon] today,' I say.

'You're welcome, brother,' he says affably. 'We haven't met before, have we?'

'No, I'm a friend of Imam Qadiri.'

'Oh, *ma sha Allah*! All this is his creation, he's our teacher,' says the imam.

'I'll be seeing him later this evening, in Rochdale,' I add.

'Please say "*salam*" from us all in Manchester. We look forward to seeing him again at the weekend or next week.'

I pass the mosque library and see from the titles that the books are mostly in Urdu; the few in English are about rituals and prayers. There are no books on women, politics, jihad or sexuality. The focus here is purely spiritual. But the things I heard about the mosque at Didsbury in my conversations last night and this morning have stuck in my mind. I order an Uber to take me there, as it is only a few miles away.

My driver, Ahmed Jaan, is a Muslim, and he's keen to show me Manchester as he takes me to Didsbury. We drive along the 'Curry Mile' again, and this time I notice that the two pubs we pass, the Huntsman Inn and Hardy's Well, are boarded up, with metal grates across their doorways.

'Why have they closed?' I ask.

'The white people drink in town now,' Ahmed replies.

This time, too, in the daylight, I can see an array of global cuisines and cultures represented by the shops and restaurants we pass. Signs flash by: Islamic Life, Al Jazeera, Araby, Mughli Restaurant, Antalya Café, Al-Madina, Afghan Cuisine, Al Zain Shawarma, Jafra Palestinian Cuisine, Beilul Lounge East African Restaurant, Syrian Sweets, Marmara Grill, Manchester Super Store.

As we turn on to the high street in Didsbury, I can see a redbrick church in the distance near a set of traffic lights.

'This is the mosque,' says Ahmed. The small church, now converted into a mosque, is a sight to behold. I get out and take a good look at it. A minaret has been constructed alongside it in the same red brick, with pointed arches that match the neo-Gothic windows of the original church building.

The contrast with Manchester Central Mosque is immediately visible. Women can clearly access this mosque, as I can see them carrying banners and Palestinian flags in from a minivan. Outside, on the walls of the mosque, are billboards advertising 'We Love MCR', a Manchester charity.

At the entrance to the mosque there are plastic bins for clothes donations and recycling, alongside posters for Islamic Relief. Already this mosque, with its organised charity appeals and banners, strikes a much more activist note than the Central Mosque with its more contemplative, mystical feel. I recall that this is the mosque where the suicide bomber of the Ariana Grande concert worshipped.

The building was purchased in 1967 by Syrian Arabs and stands at the edge of a prosperous, leafy suburb. Wealthy, white middle-class couples walk past me, nodding politely, as I walk around the mosque's exterior. A friend of mine who is a student in London but prays regularly here meets me and leads me inside the building.

'Good to see you,' he says.

'And you!' I reply.

As I remove my shoes, I hear people talking from a room labelled 'Main Hall'. There is a group of men discussing the American Embassy being moved to Jerusalem a couple of years ago.

'The Saudis will not accept this!' says a voice with an Egyptian accent.

'But the Iranians don't see it as part of their creed,' says a Syrian one.

'Jerusalem and the mosque is not to them what it is to Sunni Muslims. It is Sunni creed,' says another.

'The Zionists will not be accepting these things either,' states the Egyptian.

I don't understand why they conclude every power in the region rejects an American decision: analytical logic is missing, but I don't question why Israel and America are subjects of conversation after Friday prayers.

I take a moment to message Faiza: 'Didsbury feels so much more activist and politicised.'

'That sounds right: we pray and are patient, they protest and organise,' she texts in reply.

My friend takes us down a corridor. A sign on the wall points the way to the main prayer hall. Directly above it, a notice reads: 'Social, Educational Events, Functions, Quran circles, Group Meetings, Gatherings and Debates of any kind that are held in the Manchester Islamic Centre and Didsbury Mosque <u>shall require mandatory written permission in advance from the Management</u>. Failure to obtain such permission will result in the immediate eviction of the group concerned, and we shall reserve the right to take legal action against such violations. Thank you for your co-operation.'

It is signed by the Chair and Management of the facility.

Inside, the hall has a vaulted wooden ceiling and still looks like a church. Yet the pews have gone and the floor is covered with green carpet. The plainness of the mosque, using the space of a church without any of the furnishings, feels incongruous. And with room for about 500 worshippers, it is much smaller than the Central Mosque I have just left.

'We held a special prayer for the old Egyptian president, Mohamed Morsi, after he died a few weeks ago,' my friend tells me.

'What do you mean?' I ask.

'I'd never done it before, so I didn't know what it was, but the imam said we were doing a funeral prayer for Morsi.'

'You mean a *janaza gha'iba*, an absentee funeral?' I ask.

'That's it,' he says. 'It was to show solidarity with him and the Muslim Brotherhood in Egypt.'

'What about Lord Patel, Britain's leading Muslim peer?' I say. 'He died this summer, too. He did a lot for Muslims in this country, to make Hajj easier with the British government, getting FCO support for pilgrims and so on. Were there prayers like that said for him as well?'

'As I say, it was my first time at such a funeral prayer. Nothing was said for Lord Patel. I guess he's just too local. People here feel more connected with politics in Egypt and the Middle East.'

So within five minutes at the Didsbury Mosque I had encountered politics, activism and even prayers held in the mosque for a deceased Islamist president. No mention was made of such things at Manchester Central Mosque, where the focus was on the Quran, the word of God.

My mind wanders off to how this hall, these walls, this wooden ceiling and those elders commenting on Israel had, in years gone by, prayed beside Salman Abedi, the suicide bomber who attacked the Ariana Grande concert.

'Didn't the brother of Salman Abedi pray his nightly prayers here during this Ramadan, only four weeks ago?' I ask, remembering something Taj-Paul mentioned to me last night.

'Yes. Some of the congregation complained, but we can't ban the brother of a suicide bomber just because he's a relative,' he replies. I can't argue with that: the principle of presumption of innocence, even for the brother of a suicide bomber from this mosque, must be upheld.

I walk out of the prayer hall and notice a signboard pointing to the 'Sharia Department' down the corridor. I see a man coming out and ask him what goes on in that department. My friend answers instead. 'That's for divorces and marriages, and any disputes and other issues that Muslims want to take to sharia,' he says.

'Is that not a parallel legal system to the one we already have in Britain?'

'Well, it could be,' he replies, 'but it upsets the mosque if we question it too much. Those who need it use it, and most of us don't interact with it.'

Sharia courts or councils are on the rise across Britain. They are where women turn when they need clerical approval for marriage or divorce; men use them for sanctioning their marriages. From 'one-man courts' to establishments as sophisticated as the London Sharia Council, they charge fees to provide divorces or conduct marriages. Much like mosques in Britain, these are unregulated spaces.

I walk towards the main hall and can still hear Arab men talking politics. I hear the accents of Egyptians, Palestinians, Sudanese, Syrians, Libyans and others. The words of the council official I met earlier today still echo in my mind. These activists are surrounded by something abnormal to them: peace.

A worshipper from this mosque went on to kill and maim lovers of music in a suicide bomb attack. And here in the mosque men are still talking Middle Eastern politics and issuing Islamic divorces. Outside the main hall is a small shop selling honey, dates and *miswak* twigs with which to clean one's teeth before praying.

'What was the sermon about today?' I ask my friend.

'It was about remembering the lessons of Ramadan and staying steadfast in faith.'

As my friend explains the imam's message, I see several books beside the entrance to the prayer hall. One is a translation of the Quran into English. Another is *Manhaj al-Tarbiyya al-Islamiyya* (*The Method of Islamic Education*) by Muhammad Qutb, an ideologue of the Muslim Brotherhood and brother of its founder Sayyid Qutb. This book changed Saudi Arabia's education system in the 1970s, while his other works shaped the worldviews of Osama bin Laden and other members of al-Qaeda. The works of the Qutb brothers are banned across the Middle East because of their calls to violent jihad and claims that all Muslim – yes, Muslim – governments today are pagan and should be overthrown by force to ensure a return to the Islam of seventh-century Arabia.

The third book on display is by Khurshid Ahmad, an ideologue of the Jamaat-e-Islami and other Islamist groups in Pakistan who has advocated for the creation of an Islamic state. He has referred to members of al-Qaeda as 'brethren' and refused to acknowledge their role in the 9/11 attacks.

I take some photos with my phone, and my friend asks, 'Are you sure they're a problem? They're always here, these books.'

'I'd love to spend more time with you discussing why these are a problem, but let's do that some other time,' I say.

I have to dash. The main imam of Manchester Central Mosque, Imam Qadiri, is waiting for me in Rochdale. My Uber driver this time is a Muslim from Somalia. He's listening to Radio 4. I tell him my destination and have a quick siesta. Within forty minutes, I wake up to see one of the main roads in Rochdale, on which there are three mosques. I ask in a sweet shop for Imam Qadiri, and the men there fetch a travel agent who shows me to the main door of one of the mosques. The narrowness of the street, and the bustling Asian shops, halal butchers, travel agents specialising in trips to Mecca, Pakistan International Airlines booking offices, Afghan sweet shops and ethnic clothing stores, make it feel like a strip of Lahore in Pakistan, along with the smell of basmati rice, the sound of Punjabi being spoken and the relative absence of women.

Once inside the mosque, I remove my shoes and go to see the imam on the second floor. He is sitting on the floor with three advanced students, teaching them Quranic Arabic. Upon seeing me, he stands up and gives me a long embrace: we have not seen each other for about five years. I sit opposite him on the floor in emulation of the Prophet Mohamed, who sat on the earth in order to be close to nature, and also to avoid the arrogance of the Persian kings on their thrones. The practice continues to this day. However, the imam insists I sit on a pile of cushions with armrests. 'You are our guest,' he insists.

He asks the students to leave, then he and I start to talk about my experiences of the Central Mosque and the sermon I heard there this morning. Within minutes we are interrupted. An Irishman appears at the door and asks to see the imam in private. I leave the room, but am soon invited back in by the imam. The gentleman wanted £40 to travel home and asked if the mosque could help. The imam has found a solution and refuses my offer to pay, again saying, 'You are our guest.'

Changing the subject, he makes a different request. 'In a few minutes we have an assembly for the children who attend our Quran classes,' he says. 'It'll last for thirty minutes, and we'd be honoured if you would speak.'

'But I'm here to learn from you,' I assert politely. 'Speaking at mosques and addressing children wasn't part of my plan.'

'We plan and Allah plans,' he says, 'and Allah is the best of planners.' He is citing a verse from the Quran.

'What would you like me to say?'

'Say anything you'd like to inspire them with. We have a hundred and twenty children, split evenly between boys and girls, all under the age of twelve, so roughly upper primary school age. Share your travels with them and take questions. We would be grateful.

'After that we can sit and talk, and then go for tea and dinner.'

I politely decline the offer of dinner, as I have already arranged to meet two of my wife's friends back in Manchester. He is genuinely disappointed.

We go down to the main hall of the school on the ground floor of the mosque, as 120 children and several teachers walk in. Some of the teachers sit on chairs, as do several of the students, but most of them sit on the floor cross-legged. The girls are wearing black robes and headscarves, some of them coloured. The boys are wearing white caps and long, flowing white shirts.

The imam calls for silence and stands up. I have only ever seen him in a business suit before, but here he is in a turban, flowing *thawb* and spectacles. Yet his English is from these parts, and he would be as comfortable in a pub having an orange juice as he is here in the mosque. He asks me to sit on a chair beside him, closes his eyes and starts to recite couplets from al-Busiri's 'Ode of the Cloak'. The students join in:

Mawlaya salli wa sallim da'iman abadan
'ala habibika khairil khalqi kullihimi
Huwal habib ulladhi turja shafa'atuhu
likulli hawl min al ahwali muqtahimi

Remembering the Prophet and chanting the *Burda* together brings a harmony into the hall.

The imam introduces me as a friend and a guest from afar: 'He has travelled all over the world and written two very well-received books, and he's a writer in some of Britain's leading newspapers. We met after 7 July 2005. Who knows what happened then?'

There is silence in the room.

'Who was born in 2005?'

Nobody raises their hands. All these children were born after that horrific terrorist attack in London. It doesn't form part of their collective memory or knowledge of Britain's history.

'Four evil men killed themselves and murdered fifty-two people on the London Underground in the name of religion. But that same group of people has grown. Their evil is still with us. Who knows what ISIS is?'

Several hands go up. The imam calls on one boy.

'They are terrorists,' he says with conviction.

'That's right,' says the imam. 'Our guest and I, you and your parents, all our teachers, we want a better world, free from this evil and where everybody lives freely. Our guest will speak for a few minutes and then you can ask him questions about his life in America, the Middle East or London.'

Over to me.

I remember Cicero's rule of three when speaking, and start with a prayer in Arabic before I begin:

'I have three things to say to you. Firstly, you are all blessed to have a teacher like Imam Qadiri and his father before him. When I was a child, like you, I went to a Quran class in Brick Lane, and even though I didn't always understand my teachers, because they didn't speak English, I felt their love for God and the Prophet, and for Jesus, Moses, David and the other prophets, too. You are blessed to have a teacher like Imam Qadiri. That love will stay with you in life.

'Secondly, never forget that you are children of this soil. You were born here and you belong here. Let nobody tell you otherwise. Muslims serve in Her Majesty's Armed Forces and are present in every aspect of life here. Serve your country and your faith, and know that there is no contradiction between the two of them. Those who say we must choose between them, one or the other, are wrong. It's like asking us to choose between our mum and our dad. Our religion tells us to serve our country, and our country gives us the freedom to be religious in a way that China or Russia does not.

'Finally, dream big. Think big. We need you to continue to help people, love creation, give back and serve in whichever realm of life you choose to excel in: teaching, medicine, government, business. We are here to help you. But come to your chosen ambition with love for God and country, and the confidence of knowing you are children of this soil.'

As I finish, the imam takes out his mobile phone and at the same time asks the children if they have any questions. Several hands shoot up. A girl asks the first question, and after that they come thick and fast.

'How many countries have you visited?'

'Which is your favourite?'

'How do you write a book?'

'Which shop sells your book?'

'Who's the most famous person you've met?' – to which I answer: 'The Pope.'

'Have you met Donald Trump?'

'Where are you going next?'

One by one, I answer their questions.

The imam then reads out a letter from his phone that he's pulled up while I've been speaking.

'As our brother was speaking, I was reminded of these words from just this week. Who is Sajid Javid?' he asks the children.

'The home secretary and a member of parliament!' answers a boy to whom the imam says approvingly, 'You know your politics!'

He then reads the short letter, written by the former home secretary, who was born in Rochdale (the imam reminds them) and from a Muslim background, on being eliminated from the Conservative Party's recent leadership contest:

'If my ambition and conduct in this contest has set an example for anyone, then it has been more than worth it. This is my message to those children growing up as I did. To kids who look and feel a bit different to their classmates. Those who don't have many toys or private tutors. Those who feel like outsiders and wonder whether "opportunity" is just for other people ... Work hard, have faith in your abilities, and don't let anyone try to cut you down to size or say you aren't a big enough figure to aim high. You have as much right as anyone to a seat at the top table, to be ambitious for yourself, and to make your voice heard. So seize every opportunity that this wonderful country presents to you with both hands. Your – and our – best days lie ahead.'

Mothers gather outside the mosque to collect their children. Most are not wearing headscarves, and they speak to their children in English.

'Have you got your books?'

'Did you pay the mosque?'

'Where's your friend?'

The questions keep coming, and then within minutes the noise disappears.

The imam and I speak alone. He thanks me and introduces me to his brother and other colleagues. We agree to meet again soon when he is in London or I am in Manchester, but I still have one niggling question on my mind.

'The love and peace here in your mosque and in your school are absolutely brilliant, and bode well for our country. But what are your thoughts on how the concept of "killing the *gustakh-e-Rasul*" is gaining popularity?'

A Persian expression, popular in Urdu, '*gustakh-e-Rasul*' is a pejorative term among Barelwis and Deobandis for anybody who is 'an insulter of the Prophet'. In the year 622, when Mohamed migrated from Mecca to Medina with the early Muslims who formed a political city-state, later viewed as 'the Islamic state', insulting Mohamed was deemed to warrant death. The caliphs who came after him did not allow any mocking of Mohamed, and thus a key tenet of caliphism is that the state, led by the caliph, must uphold the honour of the Prophet Mohamed. The demand for any *gustakh-e-Rasul* to be killed is explained by the caliphists as *wajib-e-qatl*, a duty to kill, or mandatory killing.

No verses in the Quran call for the killing of Mohamed's opponents. On the contrary, several verses highlight how, when Mohamed was ridiculed, God commanded him to be patient. His wife Ayesha regularly teased him for receiving revelations that suited his purposes, and Mohamed was known to have borne such mockery with a smile. The thirteenth-century Sufi philosopher Molla Nasreddin Hodja readily laughed at and mocked himself. But the practices of the political entity in Medina, the model caliphate, as explained in the ninth-century *hadith* collection of Bukhari, bind today's caliphists to the command to kill those considered to have scorned the Prophet.

The call in 1989 to kill the British author Salman Rushdie, and Iran's offer of legal support and a financial reward of several million dollars for doing so, were directly descended from this historical caliphist idea of *gustakh-e-Rasul* cleansing. Rushdie's Japanese translator was killed. Rushdie himself went into hiding. His books were burned in Bradford and London. A founder of the Muslim Council of Britain, subsequently knighted, declared that 'death was perhaps too easy for Rushdie'.

Turkey has sought to bring back blasphemy laws across the world by lobbying the United Nations to introduce international legal mechanisms to prosecute blasphemers. The desire to enforce the laws of the early caliphate is widespread and vibrant, but the failure of governments to enforce the laws and practices of the early Islamic empire means that every so often individual caliphists will act on their own initiative and implement the perceived duty to kill. In March 2019, a student in Pakistan killed his teacher because he had allowed male and female students to mix. This was seen as mocking the ways of the early caliphs of Islam and the teachings of the *hadith* compiled by Bukhari.

Almost everything and everyone can be targeted as *gustakh-e-Rasul*, 'an insulter of the Prophet'. Love for the Prophet is so strong that insulting him or his perceived teachings, as documented by Bukhari's writings, can result in death.

In 2011 the governor of Punjab, Salman Taseer, was killed by his own police bodyguard, Mumtaz Qadri. Instead of facing universal condemnation, Qadri became a national hero and it was the judges who sentenced him to death who were condemned for punishing him. In Islamabad a shrine to Qadri was developed into a huge mosque complex with his marble tomb inside it, and hundreds of thousands of people visited it to pray on the anniversary of his hanging. The Dawat-e-Islami, a caliphist group loyal to the Barelwi movement, consider Qadri's murder of a *gustakh-e-Rasul* a right and brave action.

'What do you think of Mumtaz Qadri?' I text Faiza. I want to know what she thinks of this issue, too.

'What do you think?' she answers.

'Murderer. Criminal. Sinner. Do you agree?' I respond.

Silence from her end.

'Do you condemn him, Faiza, for killing an elected governor who defended Christians?'

'I have to ask a scholar,' she replies.

'But what do *you* think?' I persist.

Silence again.

In Britain, supporters of the murderer Mumtaz Qadri gathered in many of even the more peaceful mosques. 'What should Muslim leaders from this mainstream background say?' I ask the imam. 'They condemn ISIS, they condemn Deobandis, they condemn the Islamists, but what of this beast growing in their midst?'

'We cannot take the law into our own hands.'

'But must the law be changed to accommodate dealing with blasphemy?'

'We are consulting other, senior and wiser, scholars and will have a decision on this soon, but it's an important issue you have highlighted. Thank you for raising it – we do have to address it. There's also the issue of the teaching about homosexuality and protests outside schools in places like Birmingham. We're not thinking about these things enough and issuing judgements as scholars. We will discuss this more with our scholars and lawyers.'

He's taking extensive notes. My time is coming to an end, and I order my car.

The imam comes out with me and asks the Uber driver to wait. He takes me to the Afghan shop and orders tea. As I get into the car, he asks the driver to wait another minute, and then returns with a large box of Indian sweets. The brown *gulab jamun*, white *rasgullah* and yellow *laddus* make my attempt to abstain from sweets a failure. The driver and I share the tea and sweets on the way back to central Manchester. A Muslim driver from a Bengali background, he points out the areas of Salford and Prestwich, a Jewish community, and other areas as we drive. There is no trace of animosity in his matter-of-fact highlighting of Orthodox Jewish families walking on the pavements.

Back at the Radisson Edwardian, my wife's two friends are waiting. Shelly and Simla are both lifelong friends of hers. They were with my wife and me at Newham College in London, where we studied for our A levels, but they have both found themselves married to Muslim men in the north. They enter the hotel with me and both shake my hand willingly, naturally.

I offer them dinner, but they don't want to eat, so we settle down with mint tea and lattes.

'So what brings you here?' asks Shelly, a small-business owner and mother of three teenagers. She wears a headscarf and is relaxed and interested when I say I am researching mosques and ordinary Muslims in Britain and their concerns.

'That's really interesting,' says Simla, a lawyer who lives on the outskirts of Manchester and who no longer wears a headscarf. I remember Simla at college as being Sikh or Hindu – certainly not Muslim. But it wasn't due to our presence on campus or in the wider community that she had converted.

'Why did you actually convert?' I ask her now.

'All my friends were Muslims, and it seemed like the right thing to do.'

'But I remember you wore a headscarf, then the black *abayah*, or *thawb*, and then a face veil, and ultimately a pair of black gloves, too.'

I want to understand better why she became such a Salafi Muslim woman, but she would rather talk about that in private.

'Come back again and I will show you Bolton. You can't understand the Muslim problems here without coming to Bolton.'

'Yes,' says Shelly. 'I pray at the mosque here in Manchester, and we sing songs. When I tell that to my cousins in Bolton or Blackburn they are utterly disgusted and insist I shouldn't do such things.'

'But why? Why, if you can work and drive and go to university and school, can you not pray at the mosque?'

'But that's just it,' says Shelly. 'In Bolton, Dewsbury, Blackburn, Preston, it's a different universe. Women don't work. Most of my cousins are at home looking after their husbands, who are taxi drivers or postmen. The mosques there don't allow women to pray.'

'It's worse than that,' says Simla. 'We paid for the building of the mosque. They asked us to sell our gold to build the Zakariyya mosque in Bolton, and now they refuse to let us in.'

'Can I come and see?' I ask. 'I was worried when I visited Dewsbury and saw the absence of women in any part of the mosque or madrasa.'

'You went to Dewsbury?' asks Shelly, mildly shocked.

'Yes.'

'That was brave! I'm impressed. I wouldn't go there unless I really, really had to visit. They behave badly in Dewsbury and maintain a lifestyle from the Gujarat region of India, or 1960s villages in India. Even in Gujarat, now women are modern and free, and study at school and colleges. But not in Dewsbury.'

'But why are local politicians silent about this?' I ask.

'Because the councillors are from the same clans and tribes, and the Lords and MPs are elected by these same groups too. So there's little to be gained by speaking out.'

'Even here in Manchester, the MP Afzal Khan has his meetings and surgeries in a massive place called the British Muslim Heritage Centre. There's something not right about that place,' says Simla.

'Where is it?' I ask.

'About fifteen minutes' drive from here.'

I make a mental note to visit it tomorrow morning,

'In Blackburn you'll see row upon row of houses, all facing each other and back-to-back, where everything a woman does is known: who she meets, where she shops, if she's pregnant. They all cover their faces, but the men know from their height and way of walking who they are.'

'What?!' I say.

'Come and see some time.'

'But their men aren't faithful,' says Shelly.

'My husband tells me he sees groups of three or four men leaving Bolton, saying they are going to Tableegh or on a boys' trip, and it's always to Morocco! And there, in Morocco, many of them have second wives and families – the arrangement is to visit every three months. So having Tableegh or a boys' trip as a cover story reassures their wives here that the men from Preston, Blackburn and Bolton are going as friends, and thus wouldn't do anything untoward together.'

***

My Muslim Uber driver, Selim, steers the car towards a vast nineteenth-century building complex. The British Muslim Heritage Centre[3] is designed like an Oxbridge college, country house or vast church in light Bath stone. I ask him to stop near the pathway, and I walk up to the main entrance, then up some stairs to a reception area. Displayed on the walls are awards won by the centre, including the Queen's Award for Voluntary Service, Manchester's coat of arms, and an award for Enduring Support to HM Armed Forces. There is also a plaque from April 2019 that celebrates ten years of the centre 'supporting and developing diverse communities'. It was unveiled by HRH The Prince of Wales. There's also an advertisement for a Heritage Radio show entitled 'The Two White Muslims'.

I ask at the desk if I can look at the exhibition that is advertised outside, entitled 'House of Wisdom', about Muslim inventions and achievements throughout history. Three rooms full of photos and artefacts convey the clear message that Islam was once a great civilisation and could be one again.

In the long corridor outside, two men and a woman walk past me, all dressed in black robes, the men with beards and skullcaps. Is this a Deobandi institution? It doesn't feel like it, and surely it can't be if the local MP holds his surgeries here. I hear a voice coming from a room further along and walk towards it. 'Approachable Parenting' says the notice on the door, and I see cameras on the corridor's ceiling. I can hear a voice from inside the room. There is clearly a meeting of several people under way. Deciding there's nothing to be lost by eavesdropping, I listen to what they are saying.

In a Scottish accent, someone makes the case for raising more money.

The voice I've already heard responds with speed and energy.

'No, you must raise money from your local community. ISB Central [Islamic Society of Britain] can't give you any more money.'

'But we gave you the money from ...'

'Hold on!' says the energetic voice, now shouting. 'Hold on. The government has no money. We can't get new cash, so you have to be entrepreneurs and find ways to increase what we gave you last year.'

Another man in a black *thawb* walks past, and I feel the need to leave: I don't want to be seen to be listening to this meeting. But I definitely recognise that last voice. I heard it most recently on *BBC Newsnight*, telling presenter Kirsty Wark that 'Islam forbids gay relationships' as a matter of ethics. This was my old friend Imam Ajmal Masroor, a Londoner whom I first met twenty years ago at the East London Mosque, where he was a leader of the Islamist movement.

Masroor was recently expelled from a mosque in London for criticising the Saudi government. He has also expressed sympathy on social media for the Muslim Brotherhood's Mohamed Morsi, the ex-president of Egypt. Saudi Arabia and Egypt are increasingly working towards removing all forms of political Islam and caliphism in their midst. And here is Masroor at a meeting of activists in Manchester at the self-styled British Muslim Heritage Centre, the place where Simla told me 'there's something not right'.

Simla and Shelly are maybe right to be concerned. I decide to follow their advice. To understand the problem properly I need to head to Blackburn.

3

Blackburn

I arrive on a rainy, windy Friday morning in October. There are no direct trains from London to Blackburn, so I disembark at Preston. A sign reading 'Welcome to Lancashire', with the image of a red Lancaster rose, stands above the exit. Station information screens indicate that the next two trains to Blackburn have been cancelled. The next available train is in an hour, but the official at the information desk tells me it could also be cancelled.

Beside the information desk is a war memorial, recording the deaths of local soldiers in the First World War. Every railway station I have passed through so far has had this visible connection to the past, the sacrifices the men and women of these mill towns made to keep this country and the world free.

I head outside to find a taxi, as Blackburn is only ten miles from Preston. I find a lone Asian taxi driver and no queue. The sky is dark and feels oppressive, with low banks of clouds along the horizon.

'To Blackburn Central Mosque, the Jaame Masjid, please,' I say.

'Cumberland Street?' he asks.

'Yes, that's it. I need to get there as quickly as possible, please.'

'You want the quick way or the cheap way?'

'The quick way,' I answer.

It is cold in the back of the cab. I am wearing a navy Barbour jacket and a thick wool cardigan, jeans and Chelsea boots. I thought

I was ready for the Lancashire elements. In London, when I press a button in the back of a cab a heater comes on. The buttons don't seem to work here.

'It's very cold. Please will you put the heating on?' I request.

'Close the window, my friend,' replies the driver.

The window doesn't close, the heating doesn't work, and the rain splatters on my face as the car picks up the pace on the motorway to Blackburn. My options are limited.

Blackburn, one of the former great mill towns of the north that most people largely ignore, is today another global hub for the Deobandis and the Tableeghi Jamaat. Their annual congregation (or *ijtema*) in the summer of 2019 saw over 12,000 men attend. The town has had a significant Muslim population since the 1960s, when migrants from the subcontinent arrived to work in the dwindling textile industry.

Although Blackburn has avoided instances of racial rioting such as were seen in 2001 in much of the surrounding region, it is a deeply divided town. A 2007 *Panorama* documentary interviewed Ian Goodliffe and Mohammed Nawaz, two taxi drivers who worked for firms from different areas of the town. Both commented on the stark social segregation affecting many in the town, with Nawaz commenting, 'We're living two different lives here, aren't we?' Ten years later, a second programme revisited the issue to see if anything had changed. Goodliffe and Nawaz met again, even more pessimistically than before. According to Goodliffe, the Muslim and white communities were 'integrating even less than we were before'.

The borough of Blackburn with Darwen has the highest proportion of Muslim residents in the UK outside London. Dame Louise Casey, commissioned to carry out research into social cohesion, found in her report of 2016 that in a number of wards in Britain a minority faith community had become a local *majority*; two of the five areas of highest concentration were in the Blackburn with Darwen authority area: Bastwell (85.3 per cent Muslim) and Shear Brow (77.7 per cent).[1] Blackburn's total population in the 2011 census was only 117,963, with around 49,460 British Asian residents (34.3 per cent), but this is estimated to have grown significantly. The town has an unemployment rate of 6 per cent, notably higher than the national average.[2] Although the Muslim population are represented on the borough council, with seventeen out of the fifty-one councillors elected in May 2018, all but two of those representatives are male, and before that the borough had never had a Muslim woman on the council.[3]

Former home secretary and later foreign secretary Jack Straw was the Labour MP here for thirty-six years, from 1979 until the 2015 election. Straw famously supported the Iraq war and tried to make peace with Iran, but what of his relations with his own constituency? In the late 1980s he called for private Jewish and Muslim schools to be granted public funding, despite their separation from the state school system. In 2006 he commented in the *Lancashire Telegraph* that the wearing of the niqab by Muslim women in Blackburn enforced societal divisions and hindered discussions on such issues. His comments were sensationalised and a debate followed over the place of the niqab in British society.

As the taxi enters the town of Blackburn, visible on my left is a large mosque complex with a dark red dome, the Masjid-e-Saliheen. It looks as if old council flats have been combined into one mass. To my right is a brick office block called the Blackburn Enterprise Centre, and beyond it there are the green tops of hills. I can see another mosque dominating the town centre; its green dome and minaret are distinctive, and my eye is drawn to it.

The first person I see on the pavement is a lady in a long burgundy skirt and black face veil pushing a pram with a child. A hundred yards later, we pass another woman, white-skinned and wearing jeans and a fleece jacket.

Blackburn Central Mosque's website says that Friday prayers take place at 1 p.m., and the time showing on the taxi's dashboard display is 12.56. The streets around the mosque seem empty, which strikes me as odd. I pay the driver £40 and dash out across the car park.

Jaame Masjid is a huge brick building, with a band of dark red around the bottom quarter of the façade and yellow brick above. Massive, pointed windows cover the surface, and a pointed, tiled green dome sits on top. Twin minarets on either side of the main entrance contain square blocks of glass with pale yellow stone twisting upwards to ornamental toppings of smaller green semicircles that echo the dome. I see signs for the attached Islamic school for boys and girls, the Madrasah Ta'leemul Islam.

It is still raining. An older man wearing a white *thawb* and an upturned white cap, a shorter version of a chef's hat, approaches me. He's wearing light-sensitive glasses that are slightly darkened and contrast sharply with his white beard and hair.

'*Salam alaikum*, Uncle Jee.' I greet him with a term of endearment from the Indian subcontinent. 'What time is *jum'a*? Am I late?'

He smiles, comes closer, touches my right arm, and tells me that prayers are at 1.30 p.m., so I am early. He asks where I am from; I tell him London. We walk towards the door and he opens it for me, but I insist he enters first.

'This was the first mosque in Lancashire,' he says with pride. 'The first one was in some houses bought in 1962.' And then he asks, 'What brings you here?'

I have a meeting with a local councillor soon afterwards, but I am not sure if disclosing such details is sensible. This is a small town, and people are bound to talk. I simply say I have a meeting.

As we enter, the warmth is welcoming after the cold taxi ride and the drizzle outside. He indicates the *wudhu*, or washing area. I remove my boots and place them on a nearby shelf.

Uncle Jee is wearing an oil perfume that is strong and overwhelming. Others in the mosque seem to use a similar type of strong perfume oil, as the whole place smells of it. The floor of the *wudhu* area feels warm under my feet, even though I do not remove my socks. It feels wonderful after the cold outside. Over on the far side several men are making their ablutions, and before too many more arrive I quickly do my own ablutions to avoid being questioned on why I am not wearing the typical leather socks, and then head into the prayer hall. There I pray two units of thanksgiving prayers and sit down to admire the light-filled space. The white ceiling is decorated with geometric reliefs, and the central atrium is ornately decorated in a complexity of patterns that reminds me of Moroccan mosaics. The niche in the wall at the front of the hall, the *mihrab* indicating the direction we should face when praying, looks to be made of marble.

Uncle Jee is in the first row. I am towards the back of the hall, though it is still mostly empty. I sit on the floor, cross-legged, as other elders arrive one by one; many sit on chairs placed along the sides of the hall for the disabled and frail who cannot reach the floor. My Egyptian prayer beads in hand, I look around me, noting the varied collection of white robes, black turbans, white turbans with two long pieces hanging at the back, men with long beards, and others with trimmed moustaches. The presence of many Indian elders in Gujarati cultural attire, similar to that I saw in Dewsbury, suggests to me that this is another Deobandi mosque.

There are no obvious facilities for women at this mosque, either. Slowly the mosque fills up. Within twenty minutes of my arrival there are around 2,000 worshippers – all men, mostly in beards, mostly in traditional Indian or Arab clothes. It feels much like the Dewsbury austerity, and I can hear the Hanafi prayers of those gathering. Neither the lyrical singing of the Barelwis nor the modern style of the English-speaking, jeans- or suit-wearing Islamists of the British Muslim Heritage Centre in Manchester is detectable here at Blackburn's Central Mosque.

The carpet beneath me is thin, but on a cold day like this it feels warm. I feel around me and realise there is underfloor heating here, too. Amidst the autumnal gloom of this and other mill towns of the north, these vast, luxurious and warm mosques stand out as the meeting places of Muslim elders and youth.

Uncle Jee spots me and comes over. 'How are you?' he asks.

'Very well, thank you,' I reply, suddenly realising I've spoken a little too loudly, as others turn to look at me.

'Do you need anything?' he asks warmly.

'No, I'm fine, thank you, Uncle Jee.'

'Please have lunch with me afterwards.' Unsure whether he is just being polite, or acting on the instructions of the Prophets Abraham and Mohamed to be hospitable to guests, I thank him and politely decline. Another elderly gentleman joins us, clearly curious about this newcomer.

'Where is your meeting?' Uncle Jee asks. I am actually unsure, but say it is near Asda.

'Please rest in the mosque before your meeting,' says the other elder. I stand up to thank them and shake their hands and reassure them that all is well. They hold my hands with theirs in a moment of warmth and head back to the front row to pray.

A bearded man in a white *thawb* and plain turban walks towards the prayer niche and takes the microphone. He looks like the Indian elders of Deoband – no colourful turban, no symbol of the blessed sandals of the Prophet anywhere about his attire, no songs for the gathering. As more and more people arrive, some in tracksuit bottoms and almost all with some form of head covering, the imam starts to speak, opening with prayers in Arabic and then in an Urdu-Hindi combination. He does not raise his voice or give an angry or emotional delivery, but speaks in dry and pointed manner.

'I seek refuge in God from the accursed Satan. I begin in the name of God, Most Compassionate, Most Merciful,' the imam begins in Arabic. He recites a Quranic verse: 'O you who believe, be cognisant of God and be with the truthful.' Then in Urdu he recites prayers for the Prophet Mohamed, starting with those suggested in the *hadith* literature.

'Scholars, elders, friends, brothers,' he says, after finishing the prayers. I notice that this imam omits 'sisters', 'ladies' and 'daughters' in his address. 'God has created us, and in the hearts of our youth we must place the love of God,' he continues in Urdu. 'In the Messenger of God we have the best example of how to love God.'

The imam implores his audience to abstain from worldly sin. 'The *dunyah* [earthly world] of temptation, confusion, must be avoided. You must think about your own faith, your actions, prayers, the character of your children, your words and truth. Are your words, your behaviour hurting anybody? Think about these things and then raise your children with noble character. If you concentrate on you, then your children, relatives, neighbours and the whole ummah will have good character. They will pray, they will come to the mosque, and then they will go out to call others to the mosque and path of God. May God make more of us people of prayers and deeds to call to God and the mosque.'

He is referencing the crucial aspect of the Tableeghi movement: proselytising.

'May God save us from the world. May God save us from being busy only with worldly activities. Don't focus always on making your children a success in this world, but focus on their graves, their afterlife. What will happen after their death? Will they be found on the Day of Judgement with faith? Think like this for your children.' The imam then speaks in more detail about the importance of encouraging strong faith in our children to protect them against the world, and of patience and prayer in the mosque.

He then highlights the half-night of blessings promised if a Muslim prays in the mosque at night prayers and early morning prayers, explaining that while the believer is asleep the angels are writing their good deeds in their book of records for the Day of Judgement. He says that whenever the travelling group of Tableeghi evangelists go to Manchester or Bolton they will pray in the mosques there, and that travelling and praying together in a *jamaat*, with the Tableeghi group, brings even more blessings from God.

The imam does not speak with any melody or emotion, but in a dry and didactic tone. Before he can bring his *bayan*, or sermon, in Hindi-Urdu to an end, the call to prayer goes off. He rushes to an inaudible conclusion. Then he opens a book and delivers an Arabic sermon from its pages. In classical Arabic, perfectly pronounced, he declares to his audience, most of whom are not Arabic speakers:

'Prayer is the pillar of faith, O believers, head of sustenance, and fruit of all obedience.'

He then continues to cite, in Arabic, alleged sayings of Mohamed, *hadiths*, on the dangers in the next life if one does not pray. This part of the sermon has more scriptural citations; the Urdu-Hindi *bayan* was just a summary of the Arabic sermon for the benefit of the masses. This clerical, priestly distinction between the mullah and the masses is amplified through the use of Arabic – which few understand – and what is supposed to be a 'local' language, but rather than English is a blend of two languages from the Indian subcontinent. Only dedicated students of sharia, and anyone in the audience who happens to be an Arab refugee from Syria, will understand the main address.

The imam has now finished delivering his sermon, and suddenly the mosque hall erupts into calls of 'amen' as the familiar words 'God protect the Muslims, honour the Muslims, strengthen the Muslims, and humiliate their enemies, destroy their enemies' are spoken.

The prayers are led by the same imam who gave the sermon, now in melodious recitation. Then, unlike in the Dewsbury mosque, where the similarities with Saudi literalism seemed stronger, the imam here raises his hands to the heavens and prays for the poor, the ill, the needy and places of conflict.

I glance around me. There is nobody on the first-floor balconies around the main space, and even the central hall on the ground floor isn't full, perhaps only two-thirds of its full capacity. This is the first time in my travels so far that I have found myself on a Friday in a mosque not packed to the brim with worshippers.

After the prayers, I perform some optional prayers by myself and then leave the main hall. There are several posters on the wall immediately outside, and a particularly colourful one catches my eye. It is for an event hosted by the READ[4] Foundation on the topic of 'Fundraising for education and building schools for orphans and needy children'. It advertises a three-course dinner and 'fully segregated events'. The speakers are Shaykh Muhammad Vanker and Qari Ziyaad Patel, two Islamic scholars from South Africa, and Shakil Malji, the CEO of a London charity.

Next to Vanker's poster on the noticeboard there is an empty space.

I notice five young Muslim clerics, bearded, in Arab clothes, heads covered, speaking to worshippers in the entrance to the *wudhu* area and clearly seeking financial support. They are registering those making contributions to the *jamaat* and advertising for donations to Islamic charitable organisations.

'I'm not scared of you!' shouts a young man suddenly. He is slightly chubby, in his early thirties and wearing a grey *thawb*. 'Put my poster back up there!' he demands.

The five men all ignore him as he angrily thumps his fist on a table. The men are all clerics, so the worshippers continue to walk by, choosing not to get involved. The man says again to the five youths, 'Others are scared of you, but I am not!' and he thumps the table again. 'This is about my *izzat* [honour]. I will not let you destroy my *izzat*!'

More shouting and interjections from the five youths follow:

'Leave us alone!'

'Go away!'

'Get out!'

And then a man from among the five, clearly their spokesperson, who is leaning on the desk, shouts loudly back at the first man, 'You can't do *ruqya* properly, your poster shouldn't be here!'

'I challenge you to do a *ruqya*,' says the grey-*thawb* man again. 'All five of you against me, and let's see who can do *ruqya* best!'

Ruqya is the practice of Muslim exorcism, performed by *raqis*, men who recite specific verses of the Quran to rid the subject's body of jinns, or evil spirits. Today the practice is widespread in many Muslim communities across the UK.

At this point, Uncle Jee appears and orders the protesting man to go into the hall. Uncle Jee's focus is on me. He turns to me to say he can give me a lift to my meeting in his car. I'd been wanting to ask him why there are no women in the mosque, but now that I know the practice of *ruqya* goes unquestioned here, I merely thank him for his offer and leave.

Outside, I briefly check Twitter for the news and see that an Emirati astronaut has returned safely to the United Arab Emirates. A video shows Hazza al-Mansouri meeting the Emirati crown prince upon landing at the airport, and then greeting his mother in the prince's presence. The returning astronaut falls on his knees to kiss his mother's hands. While Muslims in Britain are fighting over demons and jinns, Emirati Muslims are launching successful trips to space while staying loyal to traditional family values.

What has gone wrong here? I wonder as I walk past the car park, where several taxi drivers are waiting, and again note the absence of women.

On the corner opposite the mosque are the first-floor offices of the Al-Imdaad Foundation, a charity. On the ground floor, a sign for the Al Shifa Centre offers herbal products, *hijama* (cupping), *ruqya* and 'Quranic healing'.

On the opposite side of the road are a range of shops: Audley Islamic Wear, the Gift Centre, Sweet Palace, a newsagent's and some Islamic bookstores. I cross the road to take a look at the books on offer.

On the crowded bookshelves on the first floor my eye is drawn to the eleventh-century *Mukhtasar al-Quduri: A Manual of Islamic Law According to the Hanafi School* by Imam Ahmad ibn Muhammad al-Quduri. Al-Quduri's work is essentially a core textbook of madrasa education, yet some of its dictums are questionable, even irrelevant, in the modern world. It cites the following *hadith*: 'When a girl reaches puberty, it is not appropriate that any of her should be seen, excepting her face, and her hands up to the wrists.'[5] It says that 'the entire body of the free-woman is nakedness, except for her face and hands', citing the *hadith*: 'The woman is a nakedness, and so when she goes out Satan raises his glance to her.'[6] It also stipulates: 'Women's clothing should not be such as to attract undue attention to them, as with extremely bright colours.'[7]

And then I spot multiple volumes of Abul-Ala Maududi's *Towards Understanding the Quran*, published in Leicester. Maududi (d. 1979) was the first writer to promote an interpretation of Islam as a political ideology on a par with, if not superior to, communism. In *Islam and Modern Civilisation*, published in 1969, he wrote: 'I tell you, my fellow Muslims, frankly: Democracy is in contradiction with your belief ... Islam, in which you believe ... is utterly different from this dreadful system ... There can be no reconciliation between Islam and democracy, not even in minor issues, because they contradict one another in all terms. Where this system [of democracy] exists we consider Islam to be absent. When Islam comes to power there is no place for this system.'[8]

Maududi founded Jamaat-e-Islami, a political group originally based in Pakistan that called for Islamic revolution and implementation of the sharia, and promoted literalist interpretations of the Quran. His thinking lies behind Pakistan's contemporary blasphemy laws and the idea of an 'Islamic state', and had an influence on Sayyid Qutb, the founder of the Muslim Brotherhood, as well as Ayatollah Khomeini. So caliphist texts are readily available in Blackburn, too, as well as Dewsbury and Manchester.

The shop also has copies of *Bahishti Zewar* for sale. The book is a collection of Islamic jurisprudence and moral guidance, primarily aimed at women and girls. According to this book, it is a sin against the sharia to 'appear before one's brother-in-law, sister-in-law, cousins or any other strangers etc. without any modesty or bashfulness'.[9] Another major sin is to 'enjoy dancing and listening to music' and to 'like and be attracted to the customs of the *kuffar* [unbelievers]'.[10] In addition, according to this book, attending even female-only madrasas still has a 'detrimental effect' on women's morals, and if girls 'mix' with male teachers their 'chastity will be in danger'.[11] It says that because Islam has suggested the seclusion of women, allowing women to partake in 'modern education' and the sciences is 'in no way proper for women'.[12]

I leave the shop and walk down Audley Range, which has terraced brick houses interspersed with shops and industrial areas. There are more shops selling hijabs and perfume and Hajj travel agents. Much like Dewsbury, it is clear that a caliphist subculture thrives here, a separate world from the rest of British society. In R'Exclusives, a clothing shop, there is a basement where I am not allowed to go. The shopkeeper, a man, is selling women's clothes but cannot allow other men downstairs. Three girls in abayas walk past outside.

I thank the shop owner for his time, and he says, '*Jazak Allah*'.

A chippy next to the mosque offers kebabs, so I go in and order lunch. The Quran is being recited on a radio in the background.

Only half a mile from the Central Mosque, and visible behind the brick terraced houses, is another vast complex of yellow brick and brown marbled stone with a dome, two minarets and a large car park: Masjide Noorul Islam. There is a madrasa, Al-Islah Girls' High School, opposite it. I head towards the mosque, and a gentleman opens the door for me. I thank him, and he too responds with '*Jazak Allah*'.

I sit near the shoe shelves and charge my phone as worshippers pass me for the 3.30 p.m. prayer. Again, it looks like only men are allowed in this mosque. Almost all those coming in are wearing Arab robes and have big beards. One of them walks slowly, apparently not in as much of a rush as the others, and I say '*salam*' to him.

'Why are there no women in the mosque, brother?' I ask.

He smiles. 'You're from London, aren't you?'

'Yes.'

'You guys let your women in the mosques, I hear, I haven't been for a long time. But you're spreading *fitna* by letting women out.'

'Out?' I query.

'You should seek more knowledge, brother,' he says. The chap assumes my understanding of Islam is so basic that I don't understand the concept of *fitna*. I cast my mind back to the boy I met in Dewsbury who had left Spain because of his family's aversion to *fitna*. *Bahishti Zewar* echoes this same sentiment, discussing *purdah*, or the seclusion of women within the home.

'Tell me, why is there another mosque here so close to the Central Mosque? Is this one a Barelwi mosque?'

'No,' he replies, 'we just grew organically. I know in London you have planning rules and limits on mosques. Here we just build them organically. We're mostly Deobandis.'

'And this is Gujarati and Indian, too?'

'Yes, but we have diversity among the people – Bengalis, Pakistanis, Indians …'

'But no women,' I interject.

He laughs. Diversity has a different meaning in Blackburn.

'We do have Jack Straw come sometimes, and his representatives are also here. Salim Mulla is a councillor who prays in the Central

Mosque, and others pray here. We like Jack Straw, and his people help us with new mosque applications to the council. Most mosques started from Lambeth Street,' he tells me.

The current MP, Kate Hollern (first elected in 2015), has clearly not yet registered in the collective consciousness of Blackburn.

I leave the mosque and walk down Dundee Street towards Chester Street. Back on Audley Range, the William Hill betting shop is closed and there are no pubs. I pass more Islamic charity offices, this time for the Global Rahmah Foundation, as well as a halal butcher's, a launderette and a travel agent offering Hajj package tours for £4,495. There is a Queen's Park FC building. It is closed up and derelict. I knock on the doors of two nearby houses to ask why, but nobody answers.

Shanwaz Barbers on the corner is busy. Dickens Street is ahead of me. Azad Video, now a corner shop, is a reminder of the pre-Netflix past. Passers-by and those walking around are all wearing hijab or robes, the men bearded.

Further along, near the corner of Cromwell Street, I can see another mosque being built. Set on a small hilltop, there is a metal dome and infrastructure waiting to be filled in with bricks and mortar.

Some teenage girls on a street corner are talking to boys on a video call. I can hear behind me: 'You fucked up. You did shit to me. Karma back to you.'

A young woman in hijab is wearing a school uniform: miniskirt with black tights. Another, in her late teens, with no hijab, smiles at me as she goes by.

A group of teenage boys are on their way to the mosque. Others are gathered on the corner of Copperfield Street.

'Looking for something?' asks one of the teenagers, a boy in a white *thawb*. He has clearly spotted me as an outsider, a lost stranger.

'Are there any white English people's houses around here?'

'Two, three houses over there.' He points to a row of terraced houses.

I pass Durham Close and then reach Audley Junction. I knock on the doors of several houses I pass, curious to gauge the mood of the community here in greater depth. Again, no answer. Some of the houses display the name of the Prophet Mohamed. One has amulets to protect against evil spirits. Several have stickers praising God and Mohamed.

My meeting with the local councillor is due soon, so I head towards Asda.

I walk past a roundabout and over a bridge and see a park beside a canal. Two white men are standing there talking, the first white folk I've seen in several hours. I walk over to them.

'Excuse me, please, can I ask you a couple of questions?'

One of them is bearded, slightly rotund, the other very thin. 'Are you guys from around here?' I ask.

'Yes, born and bred, mate,' says the chubby fellow.

'I just wanted to ask you, where's the nearest Asda?'

They give me directions, both men keen to help and very friendly, pointing out the turnings and routes I should take. Then I put my second question to them.

'I also want to ask you something else. I've just prayed at the Central Mosque and then walked up this road. There are two large mosques in just a short space – how do you feel about that?'

'There are about thirty mosques in Blackburn,' says the chubby man.

'Over there, look, they're building another one,' says the thin chap.

'That's only been stopped because the houses at the back have collapsed,' says the chubby man. 'They've all caved in. But we're just waiting for it to go up. I've always said that once that goes up, I'm going to move away from Blackburn.'

'Too many mosques in Blackburn, mate, too many,' adds the chubby man.

'Too many,' echoes the other.

'The Asian population of Blackburn,' says the thin man, 'it doesn't warrant that many mosques.'

'Full disclosure,' I say. 'I prayed at the first large mosque, and it was empty at the back.'

'You've got mosques here that'll take three or four thousand people,' says the chubby man.

'Why is all this happening?' I ask.

'I don't know,' he replies.

'We've been saying it for years,' says the skinny man, in his strong northern accent. 'It doesn't need it, mate. It doesn't need it in Blackburn, nah. It doesn't. Nah. They just got a new Muslim school in Blackburn now, again. Muslim school for eight hundred boys. How does it warrant it? We just had a new academy for kids built just here.'

'You said you'll move away?' I asked, returning to an earlier theme. 'Where would you move to?'

'I don't know,' says the chubby fellow. 'I'll probably move to Oswaldtwistle. Just near Accrington. Oh, I have seen changes, all right. Too many. That's why there's so much division in this town. They got white areas. There's a place called Mill Hill. People don't pay attention to towns like this. They don't know, they don't see what goes on. They don't see what goes on ...'

I interrupt by asking about the worst things they have seen that outsiders don't hear about.

'Well,' says the thin man. 'My son's been jumped five times, they were all Asian. Five times.'

'You mean Asian kids?' I try to clarify.

'No, Asian men!' he says, with emphasis. 'Eighteen- and nineteen-year-olds. My lad's only twelve. They battered him in broad daylight here.'

'For what?' I ask, astonished.

They don't look happy at my questions, and they both go quiet.

'For being white,' he says, slowly and deliberately. 'Wrong area!'

'No!' I say, unable to stop myself.

'Yes! Yes!' he says.

'You get it in Blackburn, mate. You go to certain areas of Blackburn, they're no-go areas ... no-go areas,' says the larger man.

I still can't believe them.

'Look, this is what the media guys say, but is it really true?'

'That is true, yes. There are no-go areas in Blackburn, mate, yes.'

I am shocked. How can it be 'no-go'?

'So what will happen?' I ask.

'If we go to Whalley Range, like, him and me at night-time, we're guaranteed to get jumped. We won't walk out of it. We won't walk to the other end of the street.'

I am still looking puzzled. They pick up on my evident disbelief.

'It's just the way it is in Blackburn. Just the way it is. And Westminster and that, they don't realise. They just see the town centre. Whalley Range is like, the Asian community. Mainly Asian. Yeah, it's an Asian community.'

I have to open up now. So I do. 'I've walked along here, and there are no pubs, no major chains or brands.'

'All the pubs are shutting,' says the chubby chap. 'There's no diversity. The reason why the pubs are shutting is so many Muslims coming into Blackburn now. There are no whites coming into these places.'

'We call this the Khyber Pass,' says the thin man, pointing to the bridge and the roundabout I have just crossed. 'We always called it the Khyber Pass, we did. 'Cause the Asian community and that, yeah, are on the other side.'

'Was it always like that?' I ask. 'In the past, when the mills were here?'

'No, it were diverse,' says the chubby man. 'Peopled mixed, we were diverse. The young Asian lads, the way they're brought up now, because they become more Westernised, they think, "Oh, yeah, we do what we want."'

'But being Westernised is to be integrated!' I protest.

'No,' they both say at the same time.

'They're not integrating!' says one.

'You come along here at night, you get ten to sixteen Asians in groups everywhere, all drinking and smoking weed. And you can't even walk through. If you're a white lad, you can't. They control the drug trade and businesses in this town.'

'You don't need to wait,' says the thin man. 'You wait ten minutes at the bottom of my street, an Asian guy will pull up: "You waiting for drugs, guv?" They got this, got that, you'll get everything.'

'How does that make you feel when you can't speak out against crime?' I can't complete my thoughts.

'It's racism against us white people!'

'Then what happens?' I ask.

'Well, that's the thing. I don't think there'll be a white man in this town in twenty years.'

'No, no,' says the thin man, in full agreement.

'What about your kids?' I ask them, shocked.

The chubby man answers. 'Well, I've got four lads and a girl. I can imagine two of the lads staying in Mill Hill, it's a white area, but my son and daughter, I can see them flying out. I've told them not to live here.'

As we speak, a Muslim man walks past in an Arab *thawb*.

They look at him.

'What are you thinking?' I ask.

'We're so used to seeing it now,' says the thin man. 'We just call them pyjamas!' They laugh. 'We don't care if they want to wear that to the mosque, like. They're comfortable. It's traditional, and going to the mosque and all that lot, we don't mind that. But not every day, mate.'

The chubby man interrupts. 'Besides, what I don't like, they got all these mosques, and then they start praying loud on the microphones outside, but if we do that, we get pulled up. You're not even allowed your Union Jack flags around here.'

'You're not allowed England flags, no,' says the thin man.

'I haven't seen any,' I confirm.

'No, you won't,' the thin man insists. 'Blackburn with Darwen, the council and all that, will threaten you with eviction if you fly the English flag. They say we're racist.'

A sigh. They fall silent. I sense that they have said the unsaid, and I have heard the unheard. We look at each other.

'I've stopped you, two random men, and heard how you feel so strongly about this.'

'Yeah. Yeah, we do.'

I thank them for their time, and they say I should report back to the politicians in London so that they pay more attention and spend more money to end the separation, mix up the different populations, and come to their town to see the situation. They insist on shaking my hand and thank me for listening to them.

Bewildered, I head to Asda to find the Costa Coffee where I am meeting a local councillor. Inside the Asda, my first encounter is with a young Muslim woman. When I ask her about integration in Blackburn her response is: 'If we don't integrate, they call us layabouts. If we work and integrate, they say we've taken all the jobs. We want to do well for ourselves,' she says, 'and not because anybody else wants us to. We work together here in the town centre, but then we live in different parts of the town at night.' I'd like to continue my conversation with her, but I see that it is now 5 p.m. and my meeting is due to start.

I go into the coffee shop, order a skinny latte and sit down to wait. It's started raining again. The councillor arrives and says animatedly, 'Sorry, I'm soaked!' We shake hands. She is immediately approachable, and clearly open to any questions.

Saima Afzal is one of the first two British Muslim women elected to Blackburn with Darwen Council, in May 2018, after eighteen years of local Asian men ensuring that no Asian women could succeed as politicians. She has experience as an activist and police adviser, focusing on women's rights and religion among the minority ethnic communities of Lancashire. In 2010 she was awarded an MBE for her work.

The victim of a forced marriage at a young age in Pakistan, Saima refuses to acknowledge the validity of that union, referring to the man involved only as her 'abuser'. This experience cemented her commitment to helping others, and since then she has campaigned on issues relating to forced marriages, so-called honour-based violence, sexuality within Islam, female genital mutilation (FGM), children's rights in Islamic marriages, child sexual exploitation and many other issues prevalent within communities where human rights and religious beliefs are often irreconcilable. She runs two organisations, Saima Afzal Solutions (SAS) and SAS Rights, which provide both aid and advice to victims and raise awareness of issues facing women within communities where religion plays a major role, whether Sikh, Hindu, Christian or Muslim. Saima has said in a previous interview that 'religious mantras, or distorted and ill-interpreted variants of them, are widely utilised as a vehicle to control people – women in particular'.[13]

She has been on the receiving end of comments from both sides, Muslim and non-Muslim, about her not wearing hijab, over which, she says, her Muslimness has been questioned.

'The Indian elders wanted a Gujarati woman,' she says of her election to the council. We both understand the intra-Asian racism at play, but what of other forms of racism? And has she come across the Asian grooming gangs that I've heard mentioned in my conversations?

'Yes,' she says. 'What's worrying us professionals in the field, and what the academic studies don't explain, is why Asian or Muslim groomers are operating in gangs. White groomers often work alone. Don't underestimate for a moment that white girls are seen as "easier" and "available". But Asian and Muslim girls are also victims of these criminals and perverts. Only the Asian girls don't talk. There's more fear, shame and dishonour of the family involved.'

When she ran for local office, the hate mail and opposition she got from Asian Muslims was stronger than from any other quarter. Men posted letters to her with their semen and ejaculate, saying, 'You need a man to sort you out.'

Over the course of our long conversation, she provides me with information and insights into incidents, and many off-the-record anecdotes about her interactions with the local communities in and around Blackburn. Saima and women like her should be advising central government on the many issues on which it has gone wrong. 'Does Her Majesty's Government ever call you for advice?' I ask her.

She smiles. 'Occasionally we have ministers and officials come up here. I call them "photo ops", "tourist fashion cohesion", because as outsiders they take photos with people of all colours and pretend that all is well. All is not well.'

Saima explains how she has been rejected for several such photo opportunities and meetings by white officials because she does not wear a hijab. They prefer someone who they think looks 'more Muslim'. 'How is that different from the Asian elders who want to see a scarf on my head?' she asks.

She tells me of one instance where she was supposed to meet a local Muslim man to discuss her work on community engagement. When they met, he refused to shake her hand or make eye contact with her. She later found out that members of the Muslim Council of Britain had told him not to do so. On several occasions Muslim community leaders in her ward had refused to meet with her (or even endorse her running for the council) due to the fact that she didn't wear a hijab. They said she was 'not Muslim enough' to support.

She tells me that local government continues to empower community leaders and Muslim clerics, who then claim to speak for the entire community. There is widespread corruption in local elections, where the issue of 'Asian votes for Asians' has become widespread, ensuring that certain councillors are re-elected.

We move on to the issue of children. Saima tells me that at one Muslim school in Blackburn the headteacher withdrew young girls from swimming lessons, saying it was inappropriate for them to wear swimming costumes. Saima is currently focusing on the legalities of the *nikah*, the Islamic marriage contract, and tells me about a recent ruling on couples who are cohabiting but not legally married. Finally, she explains that racism is not a one-way street in the communities she works with. Muslim leaders often decry 'Islamophobia', yet frequently refer to white British people as '*goras*', a racist term.

I thank her for her insights into life in Blackburn and take my leave.

Several months after my meeting with her, Saima and her colleague Maryam Batan, another Muslim councillor who was also elected in 2018, were deselected by the Blackburn Labour party despite wishing to stand again for the elections in May 2020. Local sources have claimed that they were replaced by two other female candidates who are seen to be less likely to speak out against traditional gender roles within the community.[14]

* * *

Mill Hill in south-west Blackburn has terraced brick houses, corner shops, Chinese and Indian restaurants and a pub on King's Road called the Lord Raglan. Everything looks a bit run-down. I sense deprivation. As I approach the pub, two men and a woman come out to smoke. All three are white. I catch their eyes.

'Hi,' I say. 'I've just popped up from London to understand Blackburn a little better. Do you mind if I ask you something?'

'Sure you can,' says the woman.

'Would you go to the Whalley Range area of Blackburn?'

'No fucking way,' says one of the men, lighting his cigarette. 'We'd be dead meat.'

They explain that white people are not welcome in that part of Blackburn. Asian families are clearly present in Mill Hill, though, as I have seen the Indian restaurants and newsagents. It looks as if nobody minds them being here, but white people are not welcome in Whalley Range.

I thank them for talking to me and decide to head straight to Whalley Range to see what it is like, rather than going into the pub to ask more questions.

I take a taxi there, as it is on the north side of the city centre. My driver is an Asian Muslim named Abdul. I want to know his thoughts on the area, and on what the two men in the park revealed to me about the drinking and drugs culture in the community.

'Preston, Boston, Manchester, even Darwen, that's where the young people go for their nightlife. There are a couple of clubs in Darwen. Asian boys who are with English girls are going that way,' says Abdul in response to my questions.

'And do you think English boys are going out with Asian girls? The other way?'

'Err …' he says. 'Maybe, maybe. This is a very small town. Everybody talks, and an Asian girl dating will be a talking subject for every family.'

We enter Whalley Range. Suddenly the streets are more colourful, more vibrant, with flashing neon lights strung up in windows.

'Did Blackburn have a nightlife, ever?' I ask.

'Oh, yes – in 2003, when I started cabbing, Blackburn's nightlife was very, very busy! Back then Blackburn had a massive club. Very, very busy place. Then, all the people were coming to Blackburn, from Bolton, Burnley, Nelson, Preston. Oh, those days! So many people came to Blackburn! Now it is not like that any more.'

'Why?' I ask.

'Because all the clubs have closed.'

'Yes, but why?'

'I don't know. Probably because of too much fighting. In the town centre there was a fight every weekend, so maybe the council closed them. Lots of smoking happened, so maybe the council wanted to stop drugs. That is why, probably.'

Whalley Range is busier and bigger than Mill Hill, or at least it feels like that. But Abdul's answer does not convince me. There are multiple mosques and halal butchers, and all a stone's throw away from the town centre.

'Do you think the nightlife has died down because there are more Muslims here now?'

Silence follows that question. 'Maybe, yes. Maybe that is a fact. All the pubs closed down and went to Asian people for their shops. All the pubs are gone in this part of town.'

On the high street, on my left, I spot the Shandar Tandoori Restaurant. Affixed to the building is a green neon outline of the Nalain Shareef, the stylised depiction of Mohamed's sandal that is believed to bring blessings to Muslims. Next to it is a large banner with an advert for Sky 828, the Barelwi group Dawat-e-Islami's Madani Channel. It hits me like a slap in the face to find the supporters of the killer of Salman Taseer, and supporters of Pakistan's blasphemy laws, advertising their propaganda in Whalley Range. Further along, there are posters for al-Aqsa Mosque and a gathering about liberating Jerusalem from Israel. There are more shops for arranging Hajj pilgrimages, restaurants, Islamic bookshops, and a number of mosques and Dawat-e-Islami centres.

Several restaurants provide for gender separation, with signs offering 'Family Seating', something I have seen previously in Saudi Arabia.

On a wall there is a handwritten sign in Urdu, above a pointing arrow, reading 'Khab Ilm', 'Knowledge of Dreams'. This is a common sight in the subcontinent, normally an Islamic astrologer who interprets dreams for visitors to his shop.

I have the driver go up and down the high street of Whalley Range twice. There are Muslim and Asian female drivers, boys in white outfits going to school, young kids on street corners – but for all the colour, buzz and vibrancy of the area, there is not a single white face.

* * *

Twelve miles south-east of Blackburn, on a hill above the village of Ramsbottom, stands Darul Uloom (meaning 'House of Knowledge' in Arabic). It was the first exclusively Muslim school in Europe when it was established in 1973, after some difficulty in obtaining planning permission from the local authority. Its full name is Darul Uloom Al-Arabiyyah Al-Islamiyyah, though it is better known these days as 'Darul Uloom Bury', and it was partially financed by the Saudi Arabian government. The school provides GCSE education as well as Islamic teaching for students between eleven and twenty-three years of age, and was established by the Deobandi cleric Yusuf Motala, a man responsible for the founding of numerous madrasas across the UK.[15] The Dewsbury madrasa I visited was also founded by disciples of Yusuf Motala.

A Credo documentary produced in 1980, entitled *Schools for Moslems*, outlined the reasons behind the school's foundation. The father of Sayid Malik, one of Darul Uloom's first students, explained his discontentment with the 'un-Islamic' aspects of the local state school, where his son had been asked to draw pictures of angels in his religious education class, and was told to shower with his classmates after PE lessons. Mr Malik refused to appear on camera for the interview, for religious reasons. He was also opposed to his son being forced to attend music classes because, he said, 'music is against Islam'. Malik explained why he wanted his son to receive a religious education: it would make him a 'good citizen', one who is willing to serve others. 'A good Muslim,' said Malik, 'is a good person, a good human being.'

Darul Uloom's secretary at the time, Ibrahim Sayyid, was also interviewed by London Weekend Television for the programme. Sayyid, who did appear on camera, said the school focused on imparting an Islamic way of life that was missing in British state schools. He stressed the ways in which the school was striving to achieve standards of education in line with state schools for boys wishing to continue on to A levels beyond Darul Uloom.

The programme also noted the strong opposition of the education authorities in the 1970s to separate Muslim schools due to their exclusionary nature, with boys seldom leaving the school grounds. Today there are thousands of Islamic schools across the country, and these problems have indeed come into being.

My driver heads up to the school building. A purple sign outside highlights a recent Ofsted report that gave it an overall rating of 'Good', praising the academic excellence and behaviour of the students. Inside the school we come to a security checkpoint. The barrier in front of us lifts, but the driver is asked to wait. I get out of the car and go into the security cabin. Inside are seven teenage boys with beards, wearing long Arab robes and sitting on a bench. One of them, a tall, lanky, dark-skinned youth in his early twenties wearing a dark green jumper over his *thawb*, asks me why I want to visit the school.

'I've read your authors and have heard so much about this place! I was in Dewsbury recently, and now I want to see the madrasa that has produced all these thousands of imams who are responsible for more than half of Britain's mosques. This is the mothership! From here more than thirty other madrasas have been started. I'd like to see something of their history, please.'[16]

He doesn't look persuaded.

'We have to ask Mufti Amin. We'll get into trouble, he told us not to let anybody in. Because of Ofsted and the media, we have to make sure nobody sees the children.'

'I understand,' I say. It's as if he was expecting a negotiation, an argument. I walk out. 'Thank you, and Allah bless you all.'

I get into the car, and ask the driver to turn round and head down to Ramsbottom. I want to ask the locals what they think of a local madrasa run by an Islamic sect that has previously supported the Taliban and hosted jihadi speakers and now controls the majority of mosques in Britain.

As the car begins to turn, the tall student comes out of the hut. 'You can go in, brother,' he says. 'We'll take you.'

The boys are all students of the Darul Uloom, volunteering on a Saturday to keep the premises safe. I ask them to check with Mufti Amin (the headteacher, and chosen successor to Yusuf Motala) if it is OK for me to come in. One of the boys goes and makes a call and comes back to say it has been approved. Two of the boys stay to man the security cabin, a couple decide to walk down to Ramsbottom and the other three offer to show me around.

'My name's Waseem,' one of them says. 'We can't take you inside the classrooms or bedrooms, because ...' He is handsome, with a trimmed beard, and he seems both worldly and reserved.

'We have five to six acres of land here,' he says, moving on from his earlier statement. 'Hazrat Jee kept buying more and more.' It's interesting that they don't refer to Yusuf Motala by name, but call him by this Persian and Urdu title of honour, meaning 'the great one', 'the present one'.

The boys slowly warm to me as we make our way around the site. They start to smile and seem to enjoy having an adult visitor from London. We stop outside a ramshackle tin cage that smells of poultry and bird droppings. It appears alongside the path the boys are taking me down. Inside it are two peacocks. 'Hazrat Jee liked peacocks,' the boys tell me.

Hazrat Jee died recently, about two months ago, while on tour in Canada. There are no photos of the man because he was opposed to photographs, to modernity. 'To honour him, we don't take any photos together at Darul Uloom,' the boys explain.

'This is the original building,' they point out next. Apparently it was once a mental asylum, and the arch of the original nineteenth-century building still stands behind the peacock cage. Hazrat Jee built extensions above, sideways and frontwards, and crammed the building with bedrooms for residential students. Some are day pupils, but over a hundred board full-time for their GCSEs and the secondary Islamic school.

Then there are another 150 students on the *alimiyyah* course, who study in the five-year-long 16+ Sixth Form, where the curriculum is the *Dars-e-Nizami*, the same as taught in each of the forty other Darul Ulooms across the country.

The *Dars-e-Nizami* is a method of learning developed by Mullah Nizam al-Din Sahalwi Lukhnawi (d. 1748), during the time of Mughal rule, that was later adopted and developed by the Deobandi movement after the establishment of its first Darul Uloom in 1866. The focus was, and still is, fully textual, based on the memorisation of texts related to *fiqh* (Islamic jurisprudence), *hadith* collections, Arabic language and Quranic verses. Sophie Gilliat-Ray has set out what the *Dars-e-Nizami* of the Darul Ulooms would look like if specified in terms of British 'higher education terminology' and objectives:[17]

- Translate the Quran and six collections of *Hadith* from Arabic into Urdu.
- Undertake composition in Arabic, with an awareness of basic Arabic grammar and rhetoric.
- Demonstrate an understanding of the early history of Islam and the life of the Prophet (*seerah*).
- Perform correct recitation of the Quran (*tajweed*).
- Understand the principles of Islamic jurisprudence via Hanafi texts.
- Show an awareness of key texts and commentaries such as:
  ◦ Suyuti's commentary on the Quran, *Tafsir al-Jalalayn*;
  ◦ Tabrizi's collection of *Hadith*, *Mishkat al-Masabih*;
  ◦ Marghinani's *Hidaya*;
  ◦ Nasafi's text on articles of belief.

The method of teaching by rote memorisation in the Darul Ulooms has been widely criticised, especially by graduates of the madrasas. One of many such statements asserts: 'Our madrasas seem to give an education that is not to spread enlightenment at all; it is simply to reduce as many individuals as possible to the same level of indoctrination, to breed and train a standardised following, to down dissent and originality.'[18] The Cambridge Muslim College established a foundation course for madrasa graduates in 2012 covering areas of study they believed to be strongly lacking in the Darul Ulooms. Topics covered included modern science, Western intellectual history, British politics, religious pluralism, Islam and gender, astronomy and social science.[19]

The boys showing me around are all in their fifth year, and had expected Hazrat Jee to be teaching them *hadith* from the ninth-century collection *Sahih al-Bukhari*, again a major focus of study, as it was in Dewsbury. They are sad that he is no longer here. 'How do you remember him?' I ask, curious. One of the boys, Kamal, who has a fluffy beard and a slight smile, is keen to tell me.

'He was always walking around with someone, because we were on high security. We saw him a lot in the evenings and weekends. He owns the two houses outside the school, and he had other houses in Blackburn with his family. When he walked, he was always going at a snail's pace, slowly, but the people behind him were running and sweating.'

I don't understand what he means by this, but Kamal is smiling, pleased with this disclosure of a great miracle that he's conveyed to me.

Waseem explains. 'He was special and had a greater speed, so even though in our eyes he was slow, in reality he was fast, so others in the same reality had to run to keep up with him.'

'Yes,' agrees Kamal. 'He was given these powers by God. These special people have a speed to their actions. He would be at the top of the stairs while his followers were still downstairs. They were running, yet he was slow.'

I smile, but cannot make myself say the customary '*Subhan Allah*', or 'Glory be to God', as the boys seem to expect of me after this description of a miracle.

From the dormitory building, we go on ahead to a newer structure that Hazrat Jee added, still in the same pale brown stone of the earlier structures.

We walk slightly uphill towards the highest point in Bury, where Hazrat Jee built a two-storey mosque. There are boys praying inside, but my guides lead me to a large open window at the back of the building. It seems to be an entry and escape point for those not wishing to catch their teacher's eye. They push the window open further and smuggle me in to take a look, clearly confident that nobody will see us.

'Can you see the chandeliers? There are so many of them!'

I can see them, but what catches my eye is the vast open space with row upon row of little bookstands on the floor where children would memorise the Quran.

'We all pray *fajr* here in the morning.'

'You're in here at 4 a.m.?!' I ask, unable to contain my shock.

'We're here earlier, because we have to knock on the doors of the schoolboys, to ensure they're here for the prayers.'

'Guys, that must be hard,' I say. Waseem is unsure how to respond, but Kamal agrees readily.

'That is the hardest part.'

The thought of being awoken at 3.30 a.m. with a knock on the door from the senior boys horrifies me, so I make a suggestion.

'Why don't you get on-site radios, so that when the prayer call goes off here at, say, 3.40 a.m., the *adhaan* is heard in the boys' rooms, so they can wake up to the calling of God's names rather than knocks on the door from you boys?'

Waseem agrees this is a great suggestion and takes out his phone to talk to Mufti Amin. Concerned that Mufti Amin might want to meet me and question my motives for visiting Darul Uloom, I suggest they do it face-to-face later.

'In Ramadan we have lots of visitors to the mosque, the *iftar* [meal breaking the Ramadan fast] in the evening, and some stay here for ten days.'

From the mosque we walk to the football pitch, the smell of grass strong in the air. Stray cats walk past us, and the boys stroke them.

By now I feel there is a bond, a warmth, a connection between the boys and me. The peace of the English countryside is all around us.

'It's so peaceful here, isn't it?' I ask, inhaling the fresh air.

'Really is!' agrees Waseem.

Kamal adds: 'Whenever I am away and don't want to come back, the moment I am here it feels peaceful again.'

'What do you mean, go away and not come back?' I say, laughing.

He explains that during school holidays or long weekends at home, he often doesn't wish to return to the school.

We walk from the football grounds back on to the pathway that runs by the school buildings. The boys open another window to sneak a view into a classroom. As in Dewsbury, it is floor-based: there are cushions and wall rests and armrests for the teacher. Under the small plastic tables there are socks and pots of Vaseline and Nivea cream. I can only guess that it gets so cold they need to wear socks, and their lips and faces must get so dry early in the cold mornings that they need moisturisers.

Walking past the Arabic and Islamic studies classrooms, I spot books in Arabic and dictionaries and grammar books. The boys then show me the English literature studies room. It has chairs, tables, desks and bookshelves. I spot Roald Dahl's *James and the Giant Peach* and Shakespeare's *Measure for Measure* on the shelves.

'How do the boys feel that for Islamic studies they are on the floor, but for English they sit on chairs?' I ask Waseem and Kamal.

They both shrug and look at each other. Did I betray too much cynicism?

'We're used to it now,' says Waseem.

We walk past octagonal flowerpots with daffodils, roses and tulips, some still blooming. All of the garden's features keep to the same uniform brown stone as the earlier buildings that Yusuf Motala gradually extended.

'Hazrat Jee loved flowers,' says Waseem as he sees me looking at them. We approach a fountain shaped like the flowerpots, but the water is not flowing. The boys explain that during autumn and winter the water stops, but in the summer months the fountain is switched on; and around all the buildings and the main entrance to the school office there are more flowerbeds.

Hazrat Jee's vast library and offices occupy an entire suite of three rooms with windows on the first floor of a nearby building. One of the rooms has a dome set into the ceiling. 'That's where we study Bukhari,' says Waseem. As in Dewsbury, the teaching of *hadith* is given pride of place.

A man walks out of the main office with his son, who looks to be around fourteen. The father looks much like Uncle Jee from the mosque. Both are dressed in the long, white, flowing *thawb*.

'Hazrat Jee didn't like modern buildings,' says Waseem. I can tell as much, as all of the buildings seem to have been there since the very beginning, when the site was a mental asylum. What Waseem doesn't say, but is apparent to someone who reads the Quran, is that Hazrat Jee was trying to build a paradise here. The Quran describes heaven as a natural place with much greenery, flowers and flowing water.

As we walk towards the main exit, another couple of boys join us. I ask them what they all plan to do next year when they finish at Darul Uloom.

Waseem plans to go for an apprenticeship.

Kamal will work in his father's carpet shop.

Another boy plans to go to university in Manchester.

And another is looking for an apprenticeship in Information Technology (IT).

None of them wants to continue their religious education or become imams.

Another boy comes over as he sees us standing around, and says he wants to go to Egypt to study Arabic language at al-Azhar. He emphasises that his uncle wants him to do so. Is this a coded way of saying it is not his own choice?

As we stand there talking, one boy says to another, 'I'm going to smash your head in!' as he walks out of the school down to Ramsbottom. At the end of the day, schoolchildren are the same everywhere.

'How are the locals with you?' I inquire of the boys.

'Hazrat Jee said in the beginning they were racist, they smashed the windows and destroyed teachers' cars. But now it's all normal. They love us.'

'How do you know they love you?' I ask.

'We clear the snow for the whole village, and help cars go up and down the hills in winter. There's a local committee for the townspeople, and they invited us to join them.'

'And will you?'

Apparently Mufti Amin is thinking about it.

I thank the boys and wish them every success in their future lives. I head down to Ramsbottom, a small market town with pale stone Victorian buildings. In the nineteenth century Ramsbottom was an industrial centre with numerous spinning and weaving mills. The people here seem like those in any English village, calmly going about their Saturday business. On the quiet high street I see women having their nails done, men ordering food from a pizza place and a number of antique shops. I pass Cohen's Chemist and head for a pub called the Duckworth Arms. A couple of men sitting with pints of lager smile as I enter.

'Do you know anything about the religious school at the top of the hill?' I ask the men.

They don't. They are not aware it exists. The barman interrupts. 'Oh, yeah, what about it?'

'What are the boys like?'

He stops, thinks and puts his hand on his waist as he says, 'Lovely kids. They come down every weekend and go to Morrisons. No trouble.'

But what do former students think, those who haven't turned out like Muhammad al-Kawthari or Riyadh ul Haq – what do they say about Britain's most powerful and fastest-growing religious movement?

* * *

'They wasted five years of my life,' says Fadil, clenching his fist in anger. 'I came out with no skills that prepared me for the real world. All their talk against the world, against the *dunyah*, was a lie, because they wanted to make money off our parents. Hazrat Jee had several homes and his youngest wife was only seventeen years old, but we were taught to hate the *dunyah* and look away from women.'

Fadil studied at several Darul Ulooms in Britain; he now owns a chain of pound stores in Keighley and refuses to be seen as a cleric. It's as if he's been saving up his wrath for years as he pours his story out to me.

'Did you know many of them even forbade me from joining Facebook? Because on Facebook there are women, they said it's "free mixing" of the sexes on Facebook and we should not join, to avoid that *fitna*.

'In my last Darul Uloom, the kids always messed around, but we had a boy at the door to tell us before the imam arrived, because the imam hated us if we weren't ready on time. So after the boy saw the imam coming we sat down in rows, ready to stand up when he entered. One day we had a new kid join the school, and he didn't realise what to do when we got the signal. He remained standing when the imam came in, and when he saw him standing, rather than sitting, the imam beat him with a mop stick until he was bleeding. The boy called the police and left the school. At least that stopped the imam from ever beating us again, but he was still kept on at the school. I guess the boy's father didn't want to press charges.'

'My friends and I from our school years meet,' he tells me, reminiscing about those lost years. Most of them are not imams but own small shops or work in restaurants, and they recall small incidents from the schools that now, with hindsight, hold more meaning.

'The Darul Uloom even changed my name! My father had called me Tipu, after a military general in Bengali history. But because it wasn't Arabic and had no meaning to the clerics, the Darul Uloom insisted that my name be Islamic and Arabic. My identity, my being as an individual, was wiped out by them.'

In the last year of his studies, Fadil tells me, the teachers tried to emulate the methods of Imam Abu Hanifa, whose students apparently sat in a circle around him in eighth-century Baghdad, engaging in education through dialogue and questioning. 'So they'd sit in a classroom and say "ask us questions", but all the students would look down at the floor, avoiding eye contact with the teacher out of respect.

'They were all broken young men,' Fadil goes on. 'They couldn't think on their own, disagree with their elders, or differ in their opinions for their entire education, so how could they challenge the teacher now?'

And another thing. 'My father gave me a shorter *salwar kameez*, more like Imran Khan's outfits than the *thawb*, and they sent me home and insisted I wear the longer *thawb* … since when was all that "Islamic"?' asks Fadil.

'And you know how in ancient Arabic books the main text is within a frame on the page, and commentary is handwritten around the outside of the frame? We were so respectful of the authors of these commentaries and books that we wouldn't turn the book to read the commentary, we would physically get up and move around the book. When you've been in that system since age eleven you can't change, you don't see anything critically. How does such a mind criticise anything? It's like the boiling frog effect,' he adds. If a frog is put suddenly into hot, boiling water, it will jump out. But of the frog is put in lukewarm water, which is then boiled slowly, the frog will not feel the danger and will be cooked to death. 'You can't tell what is happening until it is too late.'

'What can be done to change these places?' I ask.

'You can't change them in one go,' cautions Fadil. 'The government and authorities have to stop respecting them and not intervening, but begin to interfere and demand changes in the syllabus.'

'What if we insist on teaching critical thinking skills?' I ask.

'Then you are leaving the monster behind the wall. And that monster will always bite. That monster is their reliance on *hadith* texts.'

'There's the *hadith* in Bukhari,' Fadil elaborates, 'that discusses the beating of one's wife.[20] Another that calls for those who take part in homosexual acts to be stoned to death.[21]

'Then there's the story where Mohamed puts a freed slave back into slavery, sells him to someone, and gives that money to his former owner.[22]

'Ali rapes a slave girl in *Bukhari*.[23]

'Hell is said to be full of women, because they are supposedly "deficient in both intelligence and religion".[24]

'Mohamed dreams of a black woman and says it's a sign of a travelling plague.[25]

'These are fabricated texts about their own Prophet, and they believe these as true. There are many others.

'*Bukhari* says, "May God destroy the Jews",[26] and that Mohamed wanted to expel the Jews and Christians from the Arabian Peninsula:[27] "The Day of Judgement will not come about until the Muslims fight the Jews, when even the earth will give up the Jews to be killed."[28] "Kill those who do not become Muslim or pay your taxes."[29]

' "Women can be beaten, but not on the face." '[30]

I vow to put these problematic *hadiths*, alleged sayings of the Prophet, to the best of *hadith* scholars in Britain, a man I know of who is based in London. How can Ofsted not identify these teachings as problematic? How can these be taught to British children in the twenty-first century? Why do we suspect and suffocate our God-given intellects and rational faculties?

Yusuf Motala struggled financially until the Saudis invested and supported him, Fadil tells me. 'That's why they added "al-Arabiya" to the school's official name, and for decades many students went to Medina after completing their studies at Bury. Only when Shaikh Hudhaifi attacked the Deobandis and Hanafis as *kafirs* [non-believers] in Medina did they stop sending students there, but by then Yusuf Motala didn't need the Saudis' help. Now the Saudis are modernising and liberalising, but Darul Uloom is stuck in the past.

'But why should they change?' he asks me suddenly, rushing on before I can answer: 'They have special status as a priestly class, and they control so many lives. When I was a student with them and said a few words in mosques, I would get envelopes from the businessmen who attended, especially in Birmingham. The first time I had no idea what was going on, but I remember one of my teachers looked at me with a grin and said '*hamarey saath raho*', 'stay with us!' in a sarcastic way. I later discovered the envelope had £1,500 in cash as a gift for the small lecture I had given in the mosque. The imams get many such perks, so although their salaries are low they make money with weddings and speeches and more of these community events.'

* * *

The next morning, outside a mosque in Blackburn, I wait for my friend Zainab. We were students together in Damascus between 2003 and 2006. I returned to Syria multiple times to see friends until 2010 and she was still there, studying Arabic, sharia and Islamic history. As I wait outside the mosque I send her a text message.

'Sorry, I am outside the mosque,' she responds.

As I wait, I watch the men leaving the mosque and heading for their cars. Then I feel a tap on my shoulder. A woman is standing beside me, and I am not sure how to respond.

'You don't recognise me!' she says loudly, with a smile. 'It's me! Zainab!!'

'God, yes, of course!' I am dumbfounded. She looks taller than I recall, more youthful, and I have never seen her without a hijab, so seeing the free-flowing hair of a woman who studied Islam in Syria throws me completely.

We are smiling and laughing now, and I'm aware of stares from the men leaving the mosque.

'Give me a hug! It's been too long!' she says, embracing me.

I feel awkward, as I sense I am being judged by the men leaving the mosque, and I worry for Zainab's safety. She reads my mind and picks up on my unwilling standoffishness. 'Oh, relax! Don't mind the bigots! They know I'll sue their asses if they mess with me or my women.'

Zainab runs a women's shelter. I wrote to her a week earlier, saying I would be in Blackburn and wanted to meet the other half of the population, who have been largely missing from my travels: women, either inside or beyond the mosque.

'Why?' she asked me.

'Because I am writing a book on Britain and Muslims and the future of our country,' I sent back.

'Then you must meet my Najma. I say no more. Just meet her. Her story, her life, her family situation is the story of a million women in this country. And nobody cares.'

I am definitely keen to meet Najma to learn more about her experiences.

'So what happened to the hijab?' I ask Zainab.

'Does Mishal still wear it?' she asks politely. Mishal is a mutual friend in London from our days spent studying in Syria.

'No,' I say. 'She says she realised that it isn't clothes that project immodesty, but the male mind. She saw veiled women in the carvings of the ancient, pre-Islamic ruins of Palmyra. Mishal spoke with many clerics, and it dawned on her that the hijab was not something Islamic or new within Islam, but Queen Zenobia's women wore it, as did Christians and Jews. It was an ancient Arabian tradition.'

'That's so interesting,' says Zainab. 'But Mishal will still wear it out of respect for the past and other traditions too, right?'

'She can, although Mishal says that she met women in Syria and Jordan and Lebanon who were deeply pious but didn't think a piece of cloth on their heads was a flag they needed to tell the world about their identity.'

'So it is about identity?' says Zainab.

'Hey, I've come all the way from London to meet you and ask you and your friend questions! So please do tell me why *you* decided to remove something so central to your identity and appearance, appearing almost like a changed person!'

She laughs. We stop at a pedestrian crossing and wait for the sign to change to green. 'I stopped wearing it after a visit to Turkey, where I saw that it was a political symbol for those who supported the government. I stopped wearing it when they started saying in universities here that it was a sign of feminism, because it isn't. And finally, when I kept searching in the Quran for a single command for me to cover my hair I couldn't find it. I feel normal now, and, strangely enough, even more close to God.'

As we cross, I want to ask about the powerful comments she's just made, but instead she grabs my arm and gives me some words of warning about our upcoming meeting.

'Be gentle,' says Zainab. 'Najma is still very fragile. She's older than us, just over fifty, so drop your Englishman ways and engage with her as a younger brother, a concerned Muslim.'

'Yes, boss,' I reply, not sure how to go about changing who I am. We enter a house through a side entrance; the front is open to the public. The building is a women's shelter offering accommodation as well as legal aid and advice.

Zainab leads the way, and we go upstairs. In a small, clean, tiled kitchen with white and dark grey cupboards, basic utensils and a plastic tablecloth, there is Najma.

She is wearing a long dark blue skirt and a beige flowing blouse with a cardigan on top. She is just over five feet tall and has stooped shoulders, almost as if she is carrying an invisible load. She has bifocal spectacles and her skin is fair, with scars from teenage spots on her face.

'*Salam alaikum*,' I say, and bow my head a little in respect. 'Sister Najma, I am delighted you've made time to see me. Zainab and I went to university together in Damascus. I wish she had told me that you were so young!'

She laughs. '*Wa alaikum as-salam*. Zainab is my lifesaver,' says Najma. 'She says I can trust you to tell my story to the world so others can be saved.'

'Sister, I'm not a journalist, so please don't think ...'

'No,' she interrupts me. 'I don't want newspaper or television people. I have seen others mistreated. I just want future people to know that I stood up, I defended my family, my daughter and two sons. Can I get you a cup of tea?'

I look at Zainab. She nods.

'Yes, please. No sugar, and while the kettle boils I will dash out for five minutes.'

I leave my bag and jacket upstairs to reassure the two women I'll be back, and hurry downstairs and out of the building to find the nearest newsagent's. I buy Hobnobs, digestive biscuits and a box of Cadbury's chocolates. Najma has a very weighty presence, saint-like, almost, and I feel bare and empty-handed asking her to share her life story without at least offering something to go with the tea. The tradition of Muslim hospitality, based on Mohamed's ways, learned from Abraham's renowned hospitality, is my excuse when I return upstairs. Najma is smiling: she recognises something in this act of buying gifts.

'I taught my sons to do that, too,' she says as she pours the tea. 'But will they teach their children?' Her English is poor, and she speaks slowly, yet for a simple lady with big problems she is very focused on the future.

'Sister, use Urdu if you want,' I say. 'I understand it.'

'*Bahuth shukria bhai*,' she says, mixing Hindi and Urdu. 'Very many thanks, brother.'

'Were you born in Blackburn?' I ask her.

'Both my boys and girl were born here, too,' she replies.

'Yes,' Zainab adds, 'Najma was born here, too.'

In response to almost every question I ask her, Najma instinctively answers by referring to her children. Here is a woman who has lived her life for her children so deeply, so constantly, that she cannot think about herself, but only them. She tells me her sons are now in their thirties, both working in Blackburn between jobs as taxi drivers and car mechanics. Her daughter is in her twenties and is a classroom assistant in a primary school. She begins to tell me about her husband.

'When he hit me, it was always the boys who stopped him when they became older, and then one day my daughter called 999. She always hoped he would stop, but one day she did call the police. When they arrived I denied that I was beaten by him, until two years ago when he pulled a knife on me for a second time. After the first time, he always promised me and the boys that he wouldn't … it was the night before Eid, and my headscarf fell down as I was cooking, and he said the angels had left the house because my head was not covered. He got me by the throat and tried to suffocate me as I lay on the stairs trying to escape from him, and the knife was on the kitchen table and I was terrified.

'I think it was the call to prayer or a phone call that took him away, otherwise he might have killed me that night. I lived in fear for my whole marriage to him. He was away on Tableegh for months, so it was not every day I saw him. When he came back each time he was more strong, more religious, more demanding.

'He would immediately punch me in the head in the mornings,' Najma continues, showing me the knuckles of her small hands as an example of what he used to hurt her.

Najma's husband was a member of the Tableeghi Jamaat, with its Deobandi literalist reading of ninth-century *hadith*, recalling seventh-century events in Mecca and Medina.

'When my daughter reached nine years old, he ordered her to cover her hair at all times, too. We would only remove our headscarves when he was away, and even to sleep I would wear it, and if it fell off and he came home late or woke up earlier than me to pray, he would shout and wake me to tell me to put on the headscarf. My daughter and I learned to wear tight headscarves to sleep. He stopped her from going to swimming lessons, music classes, watching television, and the boys were moved to Islamic schools to study. You probably prayed with them just now at the mosque.

'All this was the *dunyah*, and we as Muslims must save our children from the *dunyah* and focus on the *akhirah*, the afterlife,' Najma explains, with conviction in the truth of that religious sentiment.

'Where is he now?' I ask, understanding that 'he' is the way she refers to her husband, whom she still hasn't named. In South Asian and many Muslim cultures a woman does not refer to her husband by name. In deference to the importance of male children, she calls him 'Abu' (meaning 'father of') plus the name of their firstborn son. So if their first son is named Ammar the father will be known as 'Abu Ammar' and, to conceal the name of the wife, she will be called 'Umm [mother of] Ammar'. This ancient Arab cultural tradition has crept into many Muslim households in Britain, minimising the status of women. And Najma conforms to this practice, referring to her husband only as 'him'.

Zainab says, 'He's wanted by the police for conspiring to murder his wife and daughter, so he ran away to Pakistan. He's probably in Afghanistan by now.'

'He will be in the villages and far places doing the *da'wa* work of the Jamaat,' adds Najma. 'For thirty years he was with them, and when my daughter criticised the Taliban, he hit her for the first time, too. That's when I came to Zainab: he threatened to kill me, then kill my daughter, and the boys were witnesses to that. My eldest son complained to the imam and the imam said my husband is the *amir* of the house, the leader, and we must comply with his instructions.

'So on Eid night, when he pulled the knife, he said just as Abraham killed his son, he will kill his wife and daughter, send us to paradise, and then Allah would be proud of his sacrifices for religion.

'Before coming to Zainab, my sons went to the imam, and we had private courts at home with the imam and others. They always sided with him. I was forced to speak from the other room, and said I was hit, I had bruises. I have grown children at home, and it is humiliating for them to see their mother like this. The imam refused to see my bruises. My husband reminded them of the verse of the Quran that allows for the woman to be rejected from the marital bed and then beaten.

'One imam said, "You must beat lightly." And the other said no, there are *hadiths* that support beating.

'My daughter and sons heard that, and believed it was his right to beat me. Will they now beat their own wives? Will my daughter be beaten, too?'

She doesn't break down as she tells her story; I am the one battling tears. Najma herself is composed, and her strength comes from the fact that she has been to hell and back. She was married at sixteen in Blackburn by her father, also from the Deobandi movement. He soon died, so she no longer had recourse to him; both her brothers were part of the Tableegh and would not believe her allegations of abuse.

'I didn't believe my own daughter,' she says, 'when she told me her uncle, his brother, who was teaching her the Quran, touched her breasts and put his hands in her underwear. I thought my daughter was lying, imagining things.'

She tells me that now, as her daughter works in a primary school, she is ultra-protective of the girls she cares for. Zainab informs me of the counselling session she's recommended the daughter go through.

I look at Zainab again. 'We're moving them to another city,' she says. 'The agencies have been really helpful, and the father and his people soon won't know where they are.'

I ask if she has visited a sharia court, of the type I saw in Manchester's Didsbury Mosque, to try to resolve the issue. However, Zainab brings our conversation to an end by saying she has to go to another meeting. I want to sit and listen to Najma, though. I leave my phone number with her as an open offer of help. Zainab appreciates that gesture.

I can't help but look at the loose black hijab covering Najma's hair, new coloured henna on her hands. They're a habit, a way of existence. She comes forward and offers to shake my hand. Her courage, her forthright manner, has touched me, and I kiss her hand out of respect for her fortitude. She smiles and her eyes swell a little, with pride rather than tears.

'Do you know what, Ed?' says Zainab on our way out. 'You touched her heart. She opened up in a way I didn't expect …'

'Oh, come on!' I interrupt her. 'She has three more decades of experiences we didn't even touch on.'

'Yes, but now she will feel there are more Muslims on her side. You don't understand what that means for a Muslim woman, to feel that Muslim men are on their side, too, and it's not just me and other women. That our faith is not against women, only a certain interpretation of our religion is. You know her marriage isn't recognised in law?'

'What do you mean?' I ask.

'She and her husband had a *nikah*, a religious ceremony, and didn't register it with the civil authorities. There was no town hall registration – staying away from the British and the *dunyah*. We will get family assets through the children, but so many of my clients are in this position. Islamic marriages on their own are not legal in Britain.'

This stays on my mind, as Zainab and I part ways for different meetings. How can these marriages in Britain be illegal?

My mind drifts to another woman stuck in an unhappy marriage. Is Faiza, in Manchester, I wonder, in a similar situation that I did not understand? I promise myself that I will check in with her in the coming weeks.

Blackburn's ethnic, religious and gender divisions seem hard to bear as I leave the town. But what of Bradford in nearby Yorkshire, also populated by large numbers of Muslims?

4

Bradford

On the train up to Bradford from London, I am reading *The Consolations of Philosophy* by Alain de Botton. The main lesson for free inquiry and free thinking, I read, is to be able to ask questions unrestricted by the control of community or country. In this spirit, Socrates is known to have stopped the people of Athens on the streets to ask them questions on issues that shaped their lives and the lives of those around them.

Outside, Yorkshire stone houses stand in green fields under a grey sky, village church spires breaking up the horizon every few miles. We pass through Wakefield and Halifax, civil war battlegrounds where history is still very much alive.

Over the past several years, Bradford has been in the news for a number of troubling reasons, not least of which being its 2014 title, based on YouGov polling, of 'Britain's most dangerous city'. The local council has been forced to slash over £30 million from its budget for 2019–21, cutting library services, street cleaning and sexual health services, among other things. A local councillor was reported as saying of the cuts: 'We're not just having to cut to the bone, we're amputating some of our limbs.' In February 2019 the trial took place of nine members of a grooming gang who had sexually abused and exploited young girls in the city. Bradford also has the highest number of Universal Credit claimants in the

Yorkshire and Humber region, is one of the country's top areas for youth unemployment and experiences elevated crime rates. Its social make-up can be partially blamed for these figures, with over 30 per cent of its population under the age of twenty, but there must be more to the story.

As the train approaches Bradford, I decide to put an end to my previous fears of offending communities and their clerics, and to ask the questions that come into my mind if the behaviour of an individual or group is of relevance to the wider society. In the spirit of Socrates, I will enter this historic city, mentioned in the Domesday Book as Broad Ford and later the birthplace of the Brontë sisters, and exercise my freedom of inquiry.

After Birmingham and London, Bradford has the third-largest Muslim population in Britain, largely as a result of mid-twentieth-century migration and settlement patterns. After the Second World War and throughout the 1950s, the industrial city of Bradford saw thousands of Asian migrant labourers from Pakistan, India and Bangladesh arrive to fill vacancies in factories, mills and other heavy industry. From the 1960s onwards, many of the predominantly male workers could afford to bring their families over and settle in the city.

This large-scale immigration was not without historical precedent; indeed, Bradford has a long history of hosting migrant communities from the early decades of the nineteenth century. Known as the 'Wool Capital' due to the hundreds of mills that sprang up here during the Industrial Revolution, Bradford was home to a number of German-Jewish businessmen and philanthropists from the 1820s and throughout the Victorian era. Figures such as Charles Semon and Jacob Moser developed the city's commercial and industrial reputation and were responsible for the construction of many of its public buildings as well as a number of synagogues. Mills dominated the city, with over 300 active by the close of the nineteenth century. The most famous were Salt's Mill and Lister's Mill, which was once the largest silk manufacturing site in the world.

As the textile industry grew, the city became a hotbed of the Industrial Revolution, with a high proportion of Irish migrant workers arriving in the city in the 1840s and 1850s. The Catholic Irish community was subjected by the largely Protestant local population to intense racism and religious bigotry, with reports of factionalism and societal differences rife. Divisions were so intense that a number of riots broke out between English and Irish workers in 1848.

Rioting was to break out over ethnic divisions in Bradford again roughly a century and a half later, this time between the Asian Muslim community and the white population of the city. The Manningham neighbourhood, where the Jewish population had once settled, witnessed an outbreak of violence in June 1995, and further race riots erupted throughout the first half of 2001 in various areas of the city after a number of Asian-owned businesses were attacked. The city clearly had not reconciled itself with its longstanding societal divisions.

In the train carriage, the Asian woman sitting across the aisle from me with her three young children, who have been well behaved for most of the journey, stands up. She is wearing a designer T-shirt, light blue jeans and sandals for the summer day, and has burgundy-coloured fingernails and turquoise toenails. She smiles at me as she reaches up to the luggage rack for her bag and walks up the carriage. I smile mildly back before burying my head in my book again.

Several minutes later I glance up. The Asian woman across the aisle is back and is now visibly Muslim. Her identity is proclaimed by her hijab and the long, loose white shirt she is wearing to cover her chest and arms.

'Wow!' I exclaim. 'What happened? Is it that much colder up here than in London?'

She laughs. 'A little more, yes!'

A silence falls. I can tell she has not voiced all her thoughts.

'My husband is meeting us, and he doesn't like me dressed the way I am in London. Bradford is small; everybody talks. If I am seen without hijab and in tight clothing, it will be shameful for him and the family,' she says in a London accent. There is a defiant glint in her eyes, a certain confidence.

'Where are you from?' she asks me.

'London,' I respond.

'What brings you to Bradford?'

'I'm meeting friends and doing research,' I say. Keen to turn the conversation away from myself and back to her (and not wanting to blow my cover if Bradford is indeed as small as she says), I ask: 'How old are the boys?'

They smile politely at me as she points them out. 'Hamza, nine. Khalid, seven. And Ammar, five,' she says. These are all the names of martyrs in the early battles of Islam, I notice.

'Gosh, you've been busy!' I say.

She laughs. It is easy to speak with her. She is willing to talk – wanting to, in fact. We have been silent the whole journey despite sitting in such close proximity, but since the moment she turned visibly Muslim she has suddenly become more engaging.

The train pulls into Bradford Interchange and she steps on to the platform with her sons. Her husband is in the distance, wearing jeans and a white T-shirt, with a trimmed beard and uncovered head. The boys run towards him, and she rushes off without a backward glance. His presence alters her behaviour and there are no goodbyes. He hugs the boys but doesn't hug or kiss his wife, who follows him to the car park. The rules have clearly changed.

The station is small, with a 1980s feel. There is a Greggs and a WHSmith, but nothing more. Fake merchandise, including Louis Vuitton bags, is on sale from a pop-up stall right outside the station.

At the taxi rank, just up a flight of stairs, the taxi drivers are all Asian except for two white drivers. My phone tells me that the Great Victoria Hotel is only a two-minute walk away. I head past the Queen, a pub with portraits of Queen Victoria hanging outside, and make my way towards the hotel. I pass the grand St George's Hall, which has a plaque on its neoclassical façade proudly commemorating the nineteenth-century Jewish philanthropists who financed it.

I look down Bridge Street, one of Bradford's main roads, towards the Great Victoria, and see decorations and lights strung between buildings and hanging over the road, reminding me of London's Regent Street at Christmas. But it isn't Christmas. It is August.

In the rain, the decorative lights stand out, forming a green dome and a minaret with two crescent moons and a star. In red below this, sparkling letters read 'Happy Eid'. Most of the people passing along the pavements here do not seem to be Muslims; most are white Yorkshire folk going about their business in the city centre. Who is this message for?

Inside the Great Victoria, high ceilings, wide corridors and rows of chandeliers welcome the entrant, but my room is small, tired, and true to the hotel's three-star standard. It's the best hotel I could find in the city. I notice when I head out for the evening that portraits of the royal family cover the walls of the lobby.

A man is sitting in a white taxi parked near the station. I knock on his window and he presses a button to unlock his door. Ehsan is an intensely dark-skinned man with a trimmed white beard but no moustache. His skin is perfect and without wrinkles, but judging by his frame he must be at least in his early seventies.

'Can you show me around Bradford, please?' I ask him. 'Give me a tour of the rest of the city – it's my first visit!'

The *adhaan* is coming through on his radio, and I can tell he's listening to Sunrise station. The call to prayer ends, and an announcement tells us it was sponsored by a firm of solicitors specialising in immigration and divorce law.

'Where are you from?' he asks, as I open the door and get in beside him in the front seat.

'London,' I say.

'That must be really busy,' he replies.

'Have you not been to London?!' I respond, struck by his tone of wonder.

'Never have. Never will, probably. No need to go,' he answers. 'I'm a Bradford lad, mate. Life is quiet here, but the city has changed.'

'How long have you been here?' I ask.

'My father came in 1962 to work at Lister's Mill, and I came over in 1967,' he tells me. 'After school, I started in the mills, too, and then I started cabbing in 1974. So what would you really like to see?'

'Show me the rest of Bradford: the city centre, the sights,' I say.

'Well, this is it, really,' he says. 'On your right is St George's Hall, built by Jewish people before we got here, and on your left is Centenary Square and City Hall.' He points as we drive past, and I see the Gothic City Hall with its prominent clocktower.

'Let me show you the Central Mosque,' he says. 'It was built by the *mureeds* [followers] of Pir Maruf. The *pirs* and imams run Bradford now. When I came in 1967 we were all equal, we were all Asians working with white people. Now, the *pirs* and imams are the bosses.' *Pirs* are Sufi mystics who lead bands of followers and can often be more like cult leaders.

'Even the politicians need their support and votes to win elections,' says Ehsan as we drive past the vast structure of the mosque, with its small golden domes and a large central dome in grey stone. It has a vast car park. Opposite, I can see a Muslim prayer hall, a funeral director's and a gift shop. The Gaza Restaurant is visible around the corner beside a travel agent's office quoting rates for trips to Mecca and Medina. Then we drive past a *zawiya*, an Islamic monastery.

'What does a *pir* mean in Bradford?' I ask.

'The *pir* is the head of a clan and religious order. They follow his religious instructions in every aspect of life; he is above even the imam. This Pir Maruf was in Saudi Arabia two years ago, and they arrested him because he was doing things that are against the Saudi Islam,' says Ehsan. He can't explain what happened in more detail, however.

'Pir Maruf has many mosques here in Bradford, and many followers. He and his followers burned that Rushdie book in the town centre a few years back, and organised the first *milad* procession in Bradford, in '84, in honour of the Prophet's birthday.'

The 1980s seem like the recent past in Ehsan's memory.

As we drive along, he tells me that all the houses in this area of the city are Asian. We drive past Sylhet Close and the AllahDin Sweet Centre restaurant. 'Lumb Lane is important,' he tells me.

'Those idiots did the riot against the white folks and the police here. You know the riots, yes?'

'I remember,' I say. 'Yes, in 2001. The summer.'

'We never recovered,' he says. 'The city changed. The white people left. The *pirs* and the imams with their politician friends have been running down the city. My Bradford from '67 is gone.

'That, there, is the Lister's Mill where I once worked. Now it's apartments for people, and not fully used.' Some men wave at us from the pavement, and he smiles back. 'My nephews.'

A police station we pass has a placard on the front with the words '*Khush aamdeed*', 'joy and welcome', written in Urdu.

'There used to be a working men's club here,' he says, pointing to a building that is now obviously closed. 'There was a pub there, and another here.' He indicates buildings on either side of the road. Both are now closed.

As it starts to get dark outside, and once the call to prayer has ended, men in Pakistani clothes can be seen leaving mosques to go home as we continue to tour the city. Over the remainder of our ride Ehsan points out more than ten pubs and three working men's clubs that are all boarded up.

He holds his thumb out and clenches his fist as he says, with eyes full of yearning, 'This was a famous pub. Lots of girls and boys had fun here.'

'You went there?'

'Yes, every Friday and Saturday night after work. We all went. But we all drink at home now. Booze is cheaper, but also the *pirs* and imams can't see us there,' he says mischievously.

We drive past Ahle Hadith, a Salafi mosque that advertises an attached nursery and school, and then another Salafi madrasa.

Ehsan points out Southfield Square, telling me it is where Pir Maruf set up the first mosque in Bradford in a house he purchased in 1962.

Several minutes later we pass the sandstone building of Sunni College Bradford, covered in banners offering all kinds of religious studies courses, which I promise myself I will return to later.

More signs and buildings flash by: Hanfia Mosque, Islamic Tarbiyah Preparatory School, Tabligh-ul-Islam, IslamBradford, Living Islam, Eden Thawb for Islamic Clothes, Masjid Noor, Tariq Gift Centre, Shahjalal Latifiah Jame Masjid and Madrassah.

On Oaks Lane Ehsan points out more building damage from the 2001 riots. He tells me that BMW used to have a showroom here, but it was attacked in 1991 as well as 2001. After that they vacated the city and 'no other luxury car company has based themselves in Bradford since'.

On almost every corner there is a mosque of some sort. And then there are houses that also serve as mosques and madrasas, banners affixed to their façades.

'Where are all the white English people of this city?' I ask as we drive away from the city centre.

'Gone with the wind,' Ehsan says, looking me in the eye via the rear-view mirror.

A road rage incident breaks out in front of us. Two Asian drivers hurl abuse at each other in Punjabi.

'There are basically no pubs left in Bradford,' he says. 'Only about two. Before, there were seven pubs just here on Duckswan.'

As we pass near the city centre again, he points to an empty building. 'Morrisons started here, you know. In this building, and then it went national.' Ehsan has a sense of pride in his eyes, of this Bradfordian achievement that was recognised across the country.

'Wow!' I exclaim.

On Godwin Street, back near Centenary Square, I see boarded-up buildings, vacant shop fronts and derelict areas. An empty darkness envelops these places.

'I want my old city back,' Ehsan says. 'I am a Bradfordian,' he adds possessively. 'Too many Muslims and Asians have chased away the other Bradfordians.'

'Do you know how many mosques there are here?' I ask.

'No, but a lot, as you can see.'

I later find out that there are officially 103 mosques in the city. Most have institutions of learning for children and adolescents attached to them, and many more are being planned to open in the near future. Ehsan remembers the history of the city, pointing out what has changed.

'This was a working men's club, and now it is Lala's wedding hall.

'This was the Melborn pub. Now it is an Asian furniture shop.

'This was a pub, now it's Shahjalal Latifiah mosque.

'This was a pub, now Al-Khidr Carpets.

'This used to be a working men's club, too. Now we see Naushahi Zawiya, a sort of *pir* monastery.

'This was the Dolls & Dine dancing club. Now it is another Asian wedding venue. And then there's Dhangri Sharif and other mosques on the other side. Do you want to go?'

'Tomorrow I'll explore some more,' I tell him.

'You're tired?' he asks.

'To be honest, yes.'

'I live on the next road over. You are my guest. Come and have dinner with us,' he orders. Before I can consent, he picks up the phone and calls his wife. They have a rapid conversation in Punjabi that I cannot totally understand, though I hear the words '*mehman*', '*aaj raath*' and '*khana*', which I know in Urdu and Persian mean 'guest', 'tonight' and 'food'.

I notice a corner shop just down the street.

'Can you please stop here?' I ask.

With his driver's instinctive speed of reaction, he immediately stops.

'Is everything OK?' he asks.

'Just give me two minutes,' I say.

Inside the shop, which is full of fish, frozen vegetables, cooking oil, chapati flour and assorted household items, I ask the shopkeeper for chocolate, fruit, crisps, drinks. He points to a corner and I grab as much as I can. The Prophet taught Muslims never to go empty-handed to their hosts, and I need something to take to Ehsan's family to thank them for their kindness.

Ehsan opens the door of house number 17 in a row of identical terraced houses that all have loft conversions. Through a very narrow corridor with steps leading upstairs along one wall, we take a right turn into a small living room that has a television and a sofa.

Photos of Mecca hang prominently on the walls, and family photos sit above a fireplace. In the corner sits a lone goldfish in a bowl. The house smells deliciously of curry.

'Please sit down, my friend,' Ehsan says. I hear murmurs from the room next door, the soft clinking of plates and glasses being moved.

He leaves the room briefly and returns wearing comfortable Asian clothing, the salwar kameez, with someone behind him.

'This is my wife Asiya,' says Ehsan. I stand up and greet her by drawing my hand to my chest and bowing gently, not wishing to offend. She is elderly, with teeth missing, but has kind eyes. She has a light scarf covering her head and says, 'You are welcome to our home.'

'Please, come through,' Ehsan invites me, indicating through a doorway next to me. This takes us into the small dining room. Two mature men are standing there, evidently Ehsan's sons, ready to greet me. It dawns on me that we are the same age.

'This is Amjad, and this is Iqbal,' says Ehsan. I shake hands warmly with both men before following their lead and sitting down at the table, which is covered with old newspapers in place of a tablecloth.

Two younger women and a couple of children emerge from the kitchen, carrying plates of steaming food to us, the men at the table. I ask Ehsan if we are waiting for anybody else to join us, concerned that we are eating without the rest of his family. But Ehsan's wife insists we begin. The two sons' wives continue to bring dishes from the kitchen, supplying us with naan, chapatis and rice to eat with the deliciously spicy meat curries. There is minimal conversation around the table as Ehsan and his sons eat their meal; the sons clearly respect their father. When they do speak, it is in quiet tones, and in Punjabi rather than English. I can hear their wives whispering, also in Punjabi, in the kitchen, and find it odd that neither has greeted me. Their eyes were downcast when they brought out the meal. The children can be heard through an open window, talking and running around in the backyard.

I learn that both Amjad and Iqbal are Uber drivers and live with their parents. Iqbal is newly married, while Amjad has been married for several years; the two young girls outside are his daughters. Aside from this, the meal is strangely quiet. I can tell that the family is unwilling to speak English within their home. I am reminded of former Home Secretary David Blunkett's exhortation in 2002 to British Asians to speak English in the home to avoid generational and societal divisions.

'So what is that place you mentioned in the taxi called Dhangri Sharif?' I ask Ehsan to break the silence.

'Oh, Dhangri Sharif. It's named after a village in Kashmir, in Mirpur, Pakistan.'

'But "*sharif*" means holy,' I say. 'What makes it holy?'

'There is another *pir* there who is the son of another, who was also the son of a *pir*. So his followers call them holy.'

So clerics can emerge not only from their Deobandi or Barelwi seminaries, but also by being born to clerics. The hereditary principle, something Mohamed opposed (according to mainstream Sunni understanding), is a talking point tonight at a dinner table in Bradford, a city reportedly controlled by clerics.

* * *

It's now Friday morning, and I'm standing on the pavement on a quiet Bradford street. Louise Denham gets out of her car with a colleague and shouts, 'Ed! Welcome to Bradford!'

Louise is the enthusiastic and bubbly director of a theatre company dedicated to helping disabled children and those with special educational needs. We embrace and head into a nearby building. She offers me a coffee, and as we drink she gives me a tour of the facilities: classrooms, art studios, small auditorium, stage with wings.

'This is very impressive!' I say.

'You should come when we run our next play!' Louise replies.

'I'd love to! Do the children take well to strangers being in the audience?'

'We usually have a fifty-fifty mix of their parents and friends and our own network of supporters,' she replies proudly.

We walk down a hallway past drums, guitars, other musical instruments, costumes and performance equipment of all sorts. 'This really is very inspiring! So this is all for the kids in Bradford?' I ask.

Louise's infectious enthusiasm dips somewhat as she answers me.

'Well, yes, but sadly we don't have any children from the Muslim community in Bradford join us. We've been trying for many years to break down the social boundaries but haven't succeeded yet. We have children from all around Yorkshire and even farther afield, but none from this large proportion of Bradford.'

'But why?!' I ask.

I know Louise views everyone as equal, and would be reluctant to describe herself as a white liberal woman and cast others as Asian or Muslim, but she cannot avoid using the descriptors of difference when talking about Bradford's divisions.

'There are three main reasons. Islam, as I am regularly told, prohibits figurative art and also bans dancing. So the children are not permitted to draw or dance, and their parents cannot allow them to come here. Secondly, our rate is £40 a day and many families think they cannot afford it, not realising that their disability allowances can be increased to cover the costs. Thirdly, most disabled children are dependent on their parents for transport. Most Muslim families in Bradford have only one car at home, which is used either to get to work or often as a taxi, so can't be used for the special needs child's transport.'

'That's all wrong,' I say spontaneously, slipping momentarily from observer to judge. 'I'm seeing one of the main imams in the city tonight who has a great deal of influence here and will connect you,' I promise Louise.

'That'd be lovely,' she says, brightening. 'Really helpful. The Pakistani community here has a huge problem with Down's syndrome and other special needs conditions as a result of the interfamilial and cousin marriage culture. We can really help those children express themselves through art and give them confidence, purpose and a real sense of belonging.'

Within the Pakistani community in particular, marriages within the extended family are common. In Bradford, nearly 75 per cent of British Pakistanis marry their first cousins, which has resulted in a 4 to 10 per cent rate of children being born with genetic abnormalities that are often degenerative, sometimes fatal, and affect vision, movement and brain function.[1]

'Unless we help these children,' Louise goes on, 'they're forced to live life staring at the four walls of their homes, often locked up away from the rest of the family.'

'But you're offering such a golden opportunity here. How terrible that parents and guardians aren't more engaged,' I say.

'Fear of the Other is a big factor here, on all sides,' she tells me. 'It's only natural. We gather around those we know and seem most like us. It really is nature. The white community here have moved into the outlying areas while the Asians, the Muslim community, are gathered closely around the city centre.'

'Does the local council not try to help bridge these divides?'

'No, they're distant and motivated by winning elections. Their budgets have been decimated in the recent spending cuts. They build more shopping centres in Bradford, and bring in European money, but most people shrug their shoulders and say, "This doesn't give me a job" or "My bins still aren't collected, and there's rubbish everywhere on the streets".'

She folds her arms in a confident and reflective pose.

'People matter here, not parties. It's always been a Labour area, so it's not really about this or that party. And we try to make our services relevant to the lives of local families, but most haven't even been to the Alhambra, the main theatre in town. It puts on West End shows and concerts, but it's always the white middle classes from neighbouring towns who come for the show and then leave. Local Bradfordians, especially from the Muslim community, never go there.'

'Even though it's named after a Muslim palace in Spain?' I say, struck by the irony.

'It was built before the First World War and, yes, it has a Spanish Muslim name, but the local Muslims don't connect to that heritage or location. But it's more about the fact that their religion bans acting and dancing, and especially women on stage. Or so I am told when I'm asking the community gatherings I attend to publicise the theatre.'

From where we are sitting, we can see the old Lister's Mill in the distance, its chimney dominating the city view.

'Let me ask you a very blunt question,' I say.

'Go on, then,' she says, smiling. The natural teacher and trainer in her likes a challenge.

'That mill out there, in the 1960s, was full of young Asian men who came here, drank at local pubs, dated local women. If we had said to any of the old bowler-hat-and-suit-wearing, church-attending locals back then that by 1989 Muslims here would be burning a novel and calling for the death of its author, Salman Rushdie, we'd have been laughed out of town. If in 1989 we had said that there would be mass riots in 2001 carried out by the children of those first Muslim arrivals, where the police would be attacked, businesses burned down and white people chased out, we'd be thought mad. If in 2001 we had said that immigrant-dominated Bradford, beneficiary of the European Union and suffering from racism, would then vote to leave the EU because there were too many immigrants in the country, again, most people would have thought that improbable. Based on that trajectory, how do you see the future in thirty years from now?' I ask.

Louise cups her hands behind her head and shifts in her chair. Her lips quiver. 'Sorry,' she says. 'That's a really good question, and I will have to be realistic.' She wipes away tears. I look away and take some notes.

Sobbing now, she says, 'I see us becoming an apartheid city. You will now find me at my most negative. This is really upsetting to ponder. There'll be more pushback against diversity. We'll have parties like Nazi Germany organising against the immigrant and Muslim populations. The disabled children will be a target, too.' She stops and wipes tears away, then clears her throat.

'Everything we are building risks being destroyed. This city, this place. The pace of change is too fast. People are being unsettled in every way. The BAME [black, Asian and minority ethnic] populations are growing fast. In time, England could be majority

Muslim; I wouldn't be surprised. We British are fucking hypocrites. We went around the world and changed it to suit ourselves in India, Australia, Africa. Now it's happening to us.'

She stops and takes stock.

'Look at what happened in Syria. People can change quickly, and conflict can emerge with little warning.'

'You are the most positive person I have met in Bradford,' I tell her, 'and if your assessment for the future is so sincerely worrying, we have to act now. We are different in England. If we put our minds to it, if we talk about these issues. Unlike in France and Germany, Muslims here can modernise and integrate.'

'Oh, yes,' she says. We go on to discuss politicians and business people who have succeeded in this regard, but we both agree the problem needs wider national attention.

I leave the theatre with a sense of determination and make my way to communal prayers.

* * *

I reach the Central Mosque at noon. It is enormous, built in light brown stone with a golden crescent moon standing atop its grey dome. Across the road, past the Beehive Inn (built in 1901) and the lavishly decorated neo-Gothic exterior of St Patrick's Church, I can see the Living Islam shop (advertising hijabs, clothing, books), a Muslim funeral service, an old stone church with Gothic windows that has been converted into a Muslim prayer hall, and two halal restaurants.

The only person at the mosque is delivering Urdu newspapers for free distribution. 'You're too early, come back in an hour,' he tells me. It is raining now, so I head inside anyway.

Inside the mosque, the spotlessly clean ablution area has only a single user. I ask him what time the prayers start, and he tells me they usually begin at 2 p.m. 'The shaikh here talks too much,' he adds. 'I go across the road and pray at the other mosque. Your prayers there will be better and purer.'

What does that mean? I wonder. It seems rather ungrateful of him to use the hot water and cleanliness of this mosque to prepare for prayers elsewhere. I go along with him, however, to this other mosque to see what prayers there are like.

A couple of minutes away, behind the Living Islam shop I saw earlier and just past the burned-out shell of an old pub, we enter a car park. A square, grey-brick building stands at the far end, with the words 'The IslamBradford Centre' across its façade. It is a local affiliate of the Muslim Council of Britain. I see women and men entering, a sight uncommon enough to give me pause. At the door, men in long beards and Saudi-style robes greet me. 'Welcome, please come in, brother,' they say.

The main hall is packed with seated worshippers for the week's main prayer service. A man at the front orders us to stand up and move forward, saying, in English, 'We cannot have prayers outside today because of the rain.' I am struck by the fact that in a city of over 100 mosques this one is filled to bursting while the one across the road was so empty, especially on a Friday. The sectarian differences within Islam can be seen clearly here.

As the *adhaan* is called, I observe my fellow congregants. In front of me is a uniformed UPS delivery driver and I see a maintenance man in overalls nearby. The majority of the worshippers have long beards and follow the Salafi, or literalist, style of prayer, arms crossed militantly over their chests.

The Centre itself is reflective of this literalism in every way: it is not named after a mystical order or in complicated Arabic, and the building itself is simple, lacking the marble, calligraphy, domes, ornate carpets and incense of many of the mosques I have visited on my journey so far. The only thing on the walls is a projector in the main hall to show the imam preaching on the floor above.

In a city full of Muslims from the Indian subcontinent, the imam is black and from Ghana. Neither British nor Indian, he is connected to this city and its mosques through his faith, and his sermon bears out that identity. He is wearing a plain white *thawb* and a small skullcap, not a Saudi headscarf or a turban as many clerics did in the mosques I have visited so far.

He begins his sermon with a warning, commanding us to avoid the innovations, *bid'ah*, of the modern world. All new matters, he says, are deviations, and all deviations belong in hellfire. He speaks from paper notes and delivers the entire sermon in English, again differing from many other mosques I have encountered where Arabic and Urdu sections are also delivered.

The central theme for the imam's sermon is why Muslims are 'The Best of Nations'. Why are Muslims a 'nation'? I wonder. They come from every country.

'Allah says in the Quran: You are the best of nations, the best of people ever raised from mankind,' the imam begins. 'Why? Allah says we are the best because of three things. We enjoin what is good, we encourage each other to do good. And we forbid evil. And we have faith in Allah. We have certainty in this.

'Brothers and sisters, these three things are general for all Muslims. If we see evil, we should be able to stop it. And we should be able to encourage each other to do good. And we should have certainty in Allah. And today, focusing on the family – wives, children and husbands – let's see how much we are able to apply this verse in our lives, these three standards. Allah mentions this.

He starts by talking about the responsibility of a father to encourage his children to pray at the mosque, rather than plying them with modern distractions. 'Simple. If we cannot instruct our children to pray, how can we forbid them from what is *haram*, forbidden?

He laments what he calls the 'incomplete Islam' being practised by a lot of Muslims. 'So, brothers and sisters, if we are not practising Islam in its totality … for example, in our businesses, who is the lawmaker? Do we follow Allah's rules in business? Do we follow Allah's rules when dealing with our families? If we don't do that, then we are going to be following our own desires.'

He says that Muslims should be following the rule of Allah at all times. 'And *Jannah*, paradise, is the reward for those who follow Allah in *everything* they do.'

He pauses, sits down briefly. He stands again for the final part of the sermon, which begins with shorter prayers and praise of the Prophet Mohamed before he returns to his theme.

'Brothers and sisters, today, the Muslim ummah, we are facing very, very difficult and challenging times. The reality is, the fact is, this is just the beginning. It is far from over. Because *halal* and *haram* are mixed up. *Halal* is now becoming *haram*, and *haram* is becoming *halal*.

He revisits the subject of children. 'On the Day of Judgement, Allah will question us about them. True love for our children is guiding them to Allah until the day when Allah will unite us all in paradise.'

In summing up, he calls upon his audience to return to the Quran and a more 'complete' Islam. 'Today, if we look at what is happening in the Muslim world, in Kashmir, in Palestine and other parts of the world, the Muslims are going through very difficult times. Today we are two billion Muslims in the world and look at our state. So therefore, until we go back to the Quran and *sunnah* it is going to be very difficult for us to regain our dignity. We need to go back to the Quran and practise.

'Islam is not only limited to rituals, Islam is a way of life. Allah says in the Quran that He will not change the condition of a people unless they change what is within themselves. So before we can go back to victory, to regain, to be victorious in this world, we need to go back to the Quran and *hadith*.'

I choose not to pray behind this imam, but exit the prayer hall past the security guards and walk along Rebecca Street to the Central Mosque, which I know was founded by Pir Maruf and his Jamiyat Tabligh-ul-Islam movement that Ehsan mentioned yesterday evening.

On my way, I stop in at a shop. Inside are hijabs, male robes, caps and Gulf Arab-style checkered headscarves. Everything relates to Asian Muslim culture: mugs with Arabic script, children's books, an alarm clock that plays the *adhaan*, a 'Quran pillow' that plays verses into the ears of sleeping children, CDs and more. Again, the caliphist subculture hiding in plain sight.

In the book section I find a number of titles that illustrate the grip of superstition on the modern Muslim mind: *How to Protect Yourself from Jinn and Shaytan, Dajjal the Anti-Christ* and

A Concise Encyclopaedia of Jinn and Shaytan. There are copies of Saudi author and cleric A'id al-Qarni's self-help book *Don't Be Sad.* I also recognise Ghulam Sarwar's 'religious textbook' *Islam: Beliefs and Teachings,* having embraced its caliphist undertones when I was still a student. There is also a set of Quranic commentaries entitled *In the Shade of the Quran* by Sayyid Qutb, the ideologist of violent jihadism and a leading figure in the Muslim Brotherhood (then a terrorist organisation, and some governments would say now, too) in the 1950s and 1960s. A lavishly decorated two-volume set of commentary on *Kitab at-Tawheed* (The Book of Monotheism) is also available for purchase. *Kitab at-Tawheed* was written by the Saudi founder of Salafi literalism, Muhammad ibn Abd al-Wahhab. The Saudi government is trying to remove these books from shops in their country, yet here they are for sale in Bradford.

I make my way out of the shop and head to the Central Mosque.

Standing near the recessed entrance, which is decorated with carved stonework and inlaid with golden accents, are a number of elders from Pakistan with trimmed grey beards, holding bedsheets and ghee pots, collecting cash. At the last mosque I was not asked for money. Inside the main hall, the floor is decorated with ornate red and green carpets, and stained-glass windows let in light. Quranic calligraphy in gold runs along the walls. The interior of the grand dome is stunningly decorated, with textured layers and more stained glass.

The imam here wears a turban and is speaking primarily in Urdu, with occasional English and Punjabi phrases thrown in. The second floor is mostly empty, which strikes me as odd when, less than 200 metres away, the other mosque was packed to the brim with young people listening to an English sermon. Here is a more spacious and luxuriously decorated mosque, with a strong sense of local history, all but devoid of worshippers.

The imam is now shouting phrases in Urdu praising the Prophet, and the worshippers are responding with '*Ma sha Allah*', 'God has willed it'. He praises the Prophet, and says things in a mixture of Punjabi and Urdu that I can't understand, but I catch an Arabic *hadith* that says when a believer sees evil he must change it with his hand; if he cannot, he must condemn it orally; and if he cannot do that, he must hate that evil in his heart.

'These are not only words,' the imam says, 'these are the words of our salvation, our master, our Prophet.'

In Urdu, and then in English, he asks if we want to be strong believers or weak believers. Abruptly, he turns to politics, asking where the human rights organisations and politicians are who will stop the killings in Kashmir. He makes no mention of local British issues.

* * *

There is one more mosque I want to visit while I am here in Bradford. Among the largest mosques in Europe, with capacity for 8,000 worshippers, this is the mosque of Pir Habib-ur-Rahman, another of Bradford's influential *pirs*.

Bradford Grand Mosque, also referred to as Suffa-Tul-Islam, is the Dhangri Sharif that Ehsan mentioned to me yesterday. I want to find out why it is named after a village in Pakistan. The building is so large it can be seen from miles away. Its redbrick minarets and multiple green domes dominate the skyline of south-west Bradford.

The Sahibzada, meaning 'son of the *pir*', is waiting for me inside. A much older man waits outside on full alert as though I am about to enter Buckingham Palace. He verifies my name and then lets me in through the heavy gate of the mosque. 'The Sahibzada is inside the *khanqah*,' he tells me.

A *khanqah* or *zawiya* in the Muslim world is historically where a Sufi aspirant or seeker would lodge and meditate in search of God, and is similar in concept to a medieval monastery. A Sufi master (or *pir*) and his other disciples would traditionally finance the spiritual seeker. The *zawiya* or *khanqah* was largely known as a mosque, as it also housed a mosque, a madrasa, a library, a kitchen, housing and legal advisory services from sharia experts on divorce, custody and inheritance issues.

The Sahibzada greets me warmly with a loving embrace. 'We are honoured to have you here,' he says. 'Please come this way.' Over the years, at Muslim conferences, we had met and occasionally kept in touch.

He leads me through intricately carved wooden doors engraved with golden lettering in Arabic and English that reads 'Al-Jamia Suffa-Tul-Islam Grand Mosque'. We sit in his vast office, with its marble floor and stone walls, on luxurious leather seats.

A number of elders knock on the door and gently enter to ask my host if all should proceed. The Sahibzada slowly bows his head in approval and the elders walk backwards out of the room. It is the height of good manners not to turn their backs on the son of their *pir*, their intercessor with God in this life and the next. The obedience, control and hierarchy of the villages of Pakistan appears to be thriving in the cities of England, too.

The Sahibzada gives me a tour of the *khanqah*, this opulent and ornate mosque. No expense has been spared. The walls are sumptuously decorated in beige and white marble; gold is inlaid along the ceiling and illuminated Quranic calligraphy runs along every side. Huge bouquets of flowers stand beside doorways. In a reception area, a grand glass tower at least two storeys high is carved with the names of donors who have contributed to the construction of the building. The richness of the space suggests an investment of some type, yet I see signs on the walls asking for further donations, and white-bearded, smiling elders greeted me when I arrived with open baskets.

Off one side of the main structure an extension is being built. 'This is for the women,' the Sahibzada explains. 'We have over a thousand active women, but they are in another section. My father wants them all here in the same complex.' He shows me the current women's prayer area, with room for more than 500. It is covered in soft carpet and is immaculate, but is empty at the moment.

'Sometimes a student from the nearby Bradford University campus wants to pray and we let her in, but we don't really have a culture here in Bradford where women want to come to the mosque,' he says.

There is also an elegant and spacious library for students when they return next month for the new academic year. The huge carpeted space with its imposing bookshelves is a far cry from the small and floor-based 'library' I saw in Dewsbury.

The various meeting areas and offices are open for the local community to visit the Sahibzada and his father with their problems. Their circle of clerics also serve as a sharia court. Where there is a mosque or a cleric, there is involvement in marriage, divorce and inheritance, too. Due to the unlicensed and unregistered nature of this parallel legal system, we don't know how many such places there are in operation in Britain.

The Sahibzada constantly refers to his father, showing me where he sits, where he teaches, where his students wait for him and what he teaches (*hadith*, mostly). The Sahibzada walks with me beside him, but the few local volunteers in the building bow slowly and lower their gaze as he walks past. How does a thirty-nine-year-old command such power over grown men in the name and ways of religion?

The *adhaan* for *'asr* (late afternoon) prayers is called. He and I pray with his attendants and elders in the main hall. There is a short Sufi meditation session afterwards. My own father was from the Naqshbandi order of Sufis, so I am familiar with the breathing exercises and join in with the elders. The silence, the space, the spiritual calmness stir something within me. Soon the imam says some Arabic prayers from the Quran and we leave the prayer hall.

In the mosque's kitchen, volunteers have warmed up some food from the earlier *langar*, the food distribution of the *khanqah*. We sit and eat naan with meat curry and masala tea. The Sahibzada and I talk about our families. When we finish eating, we leave the remains of our meals on the table. The Sahibzada has no need to wash the dishes. The volunteers consider it their religious privilege to clean up after the son of their master.

Once his father passes away, these rights and special entitlements will come to the Sahibzada and his brothers. The eldest is classified as *gaddhi nasheen*, Seat Inheritor. For countless generations the *pirs* of Pakistan and India have passed on their amassed wealth and privileges to their sons. This birthright, this hereditary system of prestige and prosperity at the expense of others, continues in Bradford today. The three *pirs* who run the city influence vast networks of wealth and power known as *biraderi* (literally 'brotherhood'), even influencing local and national elections, and their followers are ready to devote their lives to these men who give them access to God.

The *biraderi* is a system of patronage determined by the subcontinental caste system made up of an extended network of clans and tribes. At the top of the pyramid are other *sayyid* families, those claiming descent from the Prophet Mohamed. The *pirs*, with patriarchal generations of *pirs* before them, claim to be *sayyids*. In Pakistan, local lands, rents, money, votes, jobs and largesse all lie in the hands of the *pir*, and by extension the *biraderi*. The earlier deceased *pirs*, going back centuries, are recognised as saints whose tombs attain mythical status and evolve into shrines where the rural poor sacrifice their meagre wealth and possessions in exchange for miracles from these religious dynasties.

In Birmingham, Rochdale, Bradford, Keighley and wherever else the Punjabis or Kashmiris have settled, the *biraderi* patriarchy controls the votes, and thus politicians are forced to pay homage to and visit the *pirs* to get their followers to vote. This impenetrable power structure lies behind several of Britain's parliamentary seats.

In late October 2019, Bradford West MP Naz Shah revealed her experiences with this previously in the run-up to the 2017 General Election. Her rival, Salma Yaqoob, allegedly sided with and was supported by local Muslim leaders who called Naz's mother a prostitute, compared her to a dog being checked for pedigree and denounced her for not wearing the hijab; Yaqoob denies these allegations. Shah has called out this vitriolic type of politics that is occurring across the north of England.

I leave the mosque, as I have a meeting with Yorkshire's most significant young Muslim influencer. He is an imam at a major mosque here in Bradford, and a madrasa teacher with hundreds of students across Yorkshire and, through his organisation, in Pakistan, too. We have met before at Muslim gatherings in the UK and were taught by the same teachers in Syria, where we both learned Arabic years ago. We meet in a private room at a nearby restaurant so that he will not be disturbed by followers.

Imam Hasnain is in his late thirties, fully bearded and with an endearing smile that radiates sincerity. The charisma of the clerics must be one reason why they control the conduct of their communities so effectively, I surmise.

'So what brings you to Bradford?' he asks, beaming at me as we sit down at the table.

'I'm travelling to different cities across the UK trying to get a sense of where we are as a country and how Muslims are adjusting to modern Britain,' I say.

'Ah. Let me guess, you have another book on the way!'

'You're a clever man!' I reply, neither confirming nor denying his suspicions.

If there is a single spokesperson for the Muslims of Bradford, it is Imam Hasnain. His students run the mosques, and his family network influences and directs a number of local organisations. I remember my promise to Louise that morning.

'Imam, I met the most amazing woman this morning in Bradford …'

Before I can finish my sentence, he joins in my enthusiasm. 'Really? Tell me more, Ed!' It is easy to see why he is so popular. Evidently he genuinely cares for other people.

'She's the director of a theatre charity in the Manningham neighbourhood, and her work is entirely about helping disabled children. But she told me that Muslims in Bradford are not engaging with the charity, and I suggested she should meet you. She is afraid to visit a mosque on her own, so …'

'Brother Ed, she will be my guest. We have regular open days, and I will personally welcome her. Our problems are far deeper than not engaging with art and theatre, though. There's widespread abuse of disabled children in the community. They're hidden away. Many of the Muslim parents just don't care about these children, and take their social benefit money and use it to support their families, open shops, back in Kashmir. So the government benefits go to buy a new taxi or develop a shop in Kashmir. Most Pakistanis here have strong links to the Kashmir region. The money intended to help parents with their disabled children is used for the parents' benefit instead. We aren't even ready to think about art and theatre.'

'How did Bradford become like this?' I ask, shocked. 'It's painful to watch part of our country becoming so segregated. I mean, where are the white English people around here? I've hardly seen any! And these attitudes to the disabled seem so far from mainstream culture. Can you see the cultural distance?'

On this point, Imam Hasnain becomes defensive. 'They are all around us, Ed. The white people are still here, it's only a few pockets of Muslims. You'll find the Muslim areas in the BD1, 3, 5, 7, 8 and 9 postcodes. The rest are more mixed.'

'It doesn't feel like that to me,' I protest. 'Every taxi driver, every shop, every house I have seen seems to be Asian and Muslim. The odd Polish place, yes, but it's all Muslim shops for Hajj, money transfers, halal butchers and hijab shops.'

He clearly doesn't like the direction our conversation is taking. His warmth evaporates. 'The British do this everywhere they go,' he asserts. 'Remember India? They divided the country and left the Kashmir issue unresolved, and now they blame the Indians and Pakistanis and urge them not to fight. They go to war in Iraq and create terrorism, then they tell us to stop complaining about foreign policy and deal with Islamic extremism. Do you know, when Syrians refugees arrived in Britain they sent many of them to Bradford? We have thousands of Syrians.[2] The government said look, there is a city with mosques and Muslims, let's send them there. Now the British say to us, "You have mosques, refugees and too much religion in Bradford" – they create the problem, and then they blame us.'

His blaming of 'the British' and casting Brits as 'the Other' creates a frostiness between us. He detects it, too.

'I am a proud Bradfordian,' he says. 'We complain to the local councillors about racism and segregation. They blame the MPs. The MPs, who are Labour, blame the Tories and the Tory government cuts. And then the government blames Brussels. At my level, in the mosque and dealing with our youth, we can only see problems created from above and thrown at us.'

'So here in Bradford, and Yorkshire more generally, what are the top issues that appear in your inbox?' I ask, curious to see how his perceptions differ from Louise's.

'The police want to come into our mosques and speak to the congregants about not grooming white girls. It has been an issue in the past.'

'And?' I ask, probing his reticence.

'I can't let that happen.'

'Why not?' I ask, aghast. 'Surely you've heard the facts about what happened in Rotherham, how Muslim men targeted non-Muslim white girls over decades?'

'What have these men to do with Islam?' he asks, with a defensive shrug and the characteristic twist of the hand of Asian elders.

'There are two factors involved in those cases again and again: drugs and alcohol. Does Islam permit these two things? Of course not. Yes, they have Muslim names and Pakistani backgrounds, but our mosques are not responsible for their criminality. These issues will be with us for a long time in Leeds, Bradford, Halifax, Keighley and other cities. But unless the police can prove it is not down to drugs and alcohol, we will not open the mosque doors to them.'

After a pause, he continues with a question. 'They are doing it again. Can't you see?'

'What do you mean?' I ask, genuinely puzzled.

'In 2010, they brought in laws to end corporal punishment. We as teachers in the mosque have no power over the children. They become teenagers and have no respect for us. The British limited us to the four walls of the mosque and then stopped our ability to control children, and now they are asking us to fix the problem of the grooming of white girls for sex. If not, they will blame the mosques.'

Perplexed by his reasoning, I ask, 'So what else is on your radar of top issues?'

'After Brexit, Islamophobia will come to the fore again,' he says.

'Can you see how your blaming the British can cause the Islamophobia?' I ask. 'Rather than take responsibility and fix the problems, you're playing politics with real lives and real issues.'

He reacts to my thoughts physically, by moving away from the table.

'I voted Remain,' he says. 'Brexit will show that Muslims did not go, and so the white English will attack Muslims again.'

'Hold on, fifty-four per cent of Bradford voted to leave the European Union, by a margin of twenty thousand votes,' I say. 'How can you blame the government for this, too?'

'They called the referendum. I asked my Muslim neighbours why they voted the way they did, and they said that new migrants, especially the Polish, were taking jobs and abusing the system.'

'Can I take you back in time a little, please?' I ask. 'Salman Rushdie, 1989. Was it right for Muslims here in Bradford to call for his killing because he wrote *The Satanic Verses*, in which he insulted the Prophet Mohamed?'

The imam falls silent. 'I tried to read the book. It doesn't make sense. Pir Maruf's main student, Haji Liaquat, organised the protests.'

'You mean the book burnings?' I ask.

'Look, it's not like that. Yes, books were burned, but it was a matter of love. You have to understand that when you play with emotions anything can happen.'

I inadvertently frown. Imam Hasnain notices my growing unease and adds, 'Even in the West, in matters of love we see death. Look at Romeo and Juliet.'

'You mention the West, Imam,' I say, 'but the West is nothing if not a place of ideas and values. And an important idea that is fundamental to the West is freedom of expression. Moses, Jesus and others are fair game for any individual to criticise, even insult. Why not the Prophet Mohamed?'

'The answer lies in your question,' he says. 'We also have the freedom to respond as we wish. I am not saying "kill Rushdie", no, but others have and will continue to do so.'

'But doesn't that slippery equivocation create Islamophobia? As Douglas Murray and others will say to you at this point, Muslims should grow thicker skins.'

'To them, I say that they should grow a thicker skin. We have to be logical; Muslims are a rational people. If you provoke me, I cannot be responsible, the guilt falls on you. Rushdie provoked Muslims, he offended love and faced death. I can't explain it, and nor can anybody else: this is a matter of love. It is our freedom of expression to respond as we wish.'

He suddenly changes topic. 'I've heard that some Conservative Party members want to bring back capital punishment. But if I were to say that, they would call me a Muslim extremist.'

Exasperated by his sophistry, I sigh. 'This is not going to end well, is it? Can you see the direction of travel here, Imam? Where are we heading? There are only three possible outcomes.'

'What do you mean?' he asks me, his first question in response to my arguments.

'I was in Vienna last week on holiday with my wife and daughters,' I reply. 'The Hapsburgs gave us a marvellous civilisation, a cosmopolitan empire, kept the Ottomans at bay for centuries, and allowed Europe to tread the path of Enlightenment, free from superstition.'

'It is a beautiful city, yes,' he concurs.

'Mozart, the magnificent libraries, Beethoven, opera, the waltz, diplomacy, architecture and Freud, Wittgenstein, Popper. And yet, and yet, that great civilisation and people gave us Adolf Hitler, an Austrian, which led to the utter annihilation of the great Jewish people of Austria and most of Europe,' I say.

'So what are you saying?' the imam asks me.

'We can go three ways from here. We keep these ghettos, close the doors of the mosques and face a race war. A religious war. You're already seeing football fans and army veterans supporting Tommy Robinson. Secondly, we self-deport or get deported. You've heard Trump tell US-Somali Congresswomen to "go back". Or, thirdly, we modernise, integrate, and live in peace and harmony with all our neighbours and contribute to Western society.'[3]

'Whoever is instigating these conflicts with Muslims must take a step back,' he says. 'We have done no wrong. It's a free society, isn't it?'

'Yes, it is, but we all have a duty to keep it free,' I say. 'That means celebrating that freedom and protecting it. Look, in which other country can you point to a prime minister with a Turkish background, a foreign secretary with Jewish ancestry in Dominic Raab, and Sajid Javid and Priti Patel from Asian backgrounds? Here in Bradford one of your MPs is Naz Shah, a Muslim woman, and the mayor of London is Muslim, too. And...'

The imam interrupts me. 'It still doesn't feel comfortable, does it?'

'Why not?' I ask.

'Ask anybody in the streets out there if they feel comfortable in Britain, and they'll say no,' he asserts.

And then this mainstream British Muslim leader makes his main point.

'You know, these politicians and police people always call us for support and help. They say give us a structure, a single leader. Many of them deal with me because I can help them access a large section of the Muslim community. And our students ask us, when is the caliphate coming? I always say to them, do your part. Qualify, take to community service and the mosque, and the caliphate will come. When it comes, we will swear allegiance to it because we must, as the *fiqh* [Islamic jurisprudence] books command. Until we have that single Muslim leadership, and we give the oath of loyalty to the caliph, we won't feel fully comfortable, and the British won't have the singular structure they demand of us.'

A short silence follows.

Caliphism is present in yet another British city.

'Anyhow,' says the imam. 'All of these matters are in the hands of God, and we should pray to God.' He leans forward and I stand up. We shake hands and I agree to put him in contact with Louise, although I am now having second thoughts. In all the years I have known him, Imam Hasnain has been a pillar of the 'moderate' Muslim scene in Britain, leading protests along with his father against terrorism, and most people have assumed him to be a liberal of sorts. This conversation and our mutual probing has brought to the fore a different persona. We agree to stay in touch as we part ways.

* * *

Five years before Salman Rushdie's book was publicly burned on the streets of Bradford, the headmaster of a major school in the Manningham area had warned about where British society was heading. In his 1984 article 'Education and Race', Ray Honeyford wrote of his own frustrations with the multiculturalism agenda, as students at his school (over 90 per cent of whom were of Pakistani or Bangladeshi heritage) were still enmeshed in the 'values and attitudes of the Indian sub-continent', yet protected by 'a framework of British social and political privilege' that was allowing the creation of 'ghettos'.

For these comments, and his opposition to the damage caused by political correctness, he was lambasted. The mayor of Bradford at the time, Mohammed Ajeeb, had Honeyford suspended on grounds of racism, and he never taught again. I want to see his school and learn more about the controversy.

The following morning, Saturday, I go to investigate. Outside a shopping centre I spot a line of taxis and approach the drivers, who are laughing and joking among themselves in Punjabi. They politely cease their conversation as I ask, 'Can you please take me to Drummond Road School?'

One of them opens the door of the car at the front of the queue for me.

'It's "Iqra" now,' says another to me in English. I don't really understand what he means, but I smile at him as I get in the car.

We arrive at Drummond Road and I ask the driver to pull over by the pavement so I can have a look around. There is a derelict Kashmiri community hall and an Asian convenience store. Down the road is Masjid Bilal and its madrasa; I go inside the damp space where a small group of worshippers have gathered. Back on the street, I come across the Al Markaz ul Islami community hub and school, which looks closed. The doors are covered in laminated sheets of paper announcing the next due dates for fees and the rules of the school.

Then I see a sign for Iqra Academy and realise what the taxi driver was telling me. Honeyford's school has been rebranded. Honeyford underestimated the problem, even in 1984. He did not, could not, foresee his own school being shut down and turned into a Muslim-majority school named after the first Quranic injunction: 'Iqra!' meaning 'Read!'. His concerns appear to have been made manifest, and it seems to me that multiculturalism has now enabled monoculturalism in this area of Bradford.

* * *

I return to Bradford in late September to see what the pupils and teachers, parents and community say and feel about the changes that have occurred at the school since Ray Honeyford's era. At 3 p.m., a staff member in a miniskirt leaves the building, gets into her Honda and retracts the roof as she drives off. A class of Year 4s or 5s who have been out somewhere return, wearing conventional school uniform. Two white teachers are with the small group of children; a single white child in the class walks along laughing and smiling with the others.

Parents now start to arrive. A Porsche Cayenne pulls up. A BMW 6 Series with a 2017 number plate parks beside me, then a 2005 Volkswagen. A lady wearing a niqab, lacking the confidence of the younger women, slowly strolls past me, struggling to walk. An Asian Muslim couple are sitting in another nearby car, waiting, both staring intently at their phones.

At the school gates I am now the only man in the midst of about forty women who have gathered to collect their children. Most of them are wearing headscarves and face covers in black; only a handful are dressed in normal, non-Muslim clothes. All the parents are Asian; one is Sikh, judging by her thick bangle, the *kara*. Soon she walks out with a young boy who has a small bun on the top of his head, an early turban. Other parents follow, coming out with their children – some speaking English, some Punjabi, but most seeming happy and engaged. 'He wouldn't play with me,' I hear a chubby boy complain as he walks past me.

'Why not, darling?' asks his mum.

'Excuse me,' I say, unable to stop myself. A lady has just walked past who is not covered, but who has with her a child, looking no older than ten, wearing a headscarf.

'Sorry to stop you,' I say.

'That's all right, love,' she says, in a reassuring way.

'I can't help but ask why the little girl is wearing a hijab,' I ask.

'She's my niece, but my sister says it's about religion and being modest from a young age. D'you know what I mean? Being Muslim is important.'

'Thank you,' I say. I want to ask her more questions, but she is obviously sincere about following a culture and respecting her sister's point of view.

I think of Ray Honeyford walking along this road, warning of the consequences of not teaching British values, but the Ofsted report on the school rates it as 'outstanding', which I have viewed, and confirms:

In discussions with inspectors, key stage 1 and 2 pupils said, 'We are taught that, in Britain, we value everyone and we all have a responsibility to be kind.'

Behaviour is excellent and harmonious relationships exist between the different age and ethnic groups. Pupils demonstrate great respect for cultures and beliefs that are different from their own and show care and kindness towards each other.

Some men begin to appear now to pick up their children. All are dressed in salwar kameez, except for one who is dressed in an Arab *thawb*. A pickup truck drives past, with Quran recitation being played through its speakers. In Arabic, the word 'Palestine' is pasted on its windscreen. On the back window, 'Free Palestine' is written in capitals, white letters on a black background.

A school bus with an Asian driver pulls up. Some of the children board the bus accompanied by their parents. The driver audibly greets them in a variety of English, Urdu and Punjabi, exchanging greetings like '*Salam alaikum*' with some, saying a simple 'Hello' to others.

A father in a red turban, marking him out as a Barelwi, collects two boys, both in school uniform.

I enter the school building and locate the reception area, wanting to ask the single question that I have on my mind, but it's very busy inside. I worry that the Socratic spirit may bring me harm here, if I question so much surrounded by so many Muslims. So I note the down the school's phone number in order to call the next day.

'I have a question to ask, if I may?' I say to the woman who answers the phone.

'Of course,' says a friendly voice.

'Why is the school called "Iqra"? It's an Arabic command to Mohamed to read the Quran, I am aware, but why change the name of the school to "Iqra" if it already had one?'

A brief moment of reserve, and then an answer follows:

'Oh, years ago, when we changed all the middle schools to academies, the governors chose "Iqra" to stand for Improvement, Quality, Respect and Achievement.'

'Ah, so it's not an Islamic school, then, with "Iqra" as a command to read the Quran?'

'The majority of our pupils are Muslims, but this is not an Islamic school. But, yes, pupils see "Iqra" in the Arabic way that you said, too. It works both ways,' she explains.

'I appreciate that. Thank you for your time,' I say, and end the call.

* * *

On my first visit to the school, however, this Saturday morning, I decide to explore the immediate area a little further. At the end of Drummond Road is a Baptist church adjoining the school complex. There are three black men and a mixed-race lady there holding a jumble sale. They have no customers. I wave from a distance and they wave back. I walk over.

'Hi!' I say. 'Lovely day! How long have you been here?'

An older man, bespectacled and wearing a flat cap, speaks up. He's suspicious of my enthusiasm and speaks in a guarded tone. 'You mean me, or the church?'

'You,' I say.

'Since 1962,' he says.

'And the church?'

'Since 1901, but the Baptist Church in Yorkshire started in 1753. How can I help you?' he says, in an accent that brings to mind Bob Marley's songs. During that moment of distraction, it suddenly starts to rain.

'Call Sam from inside,' the man orders the others.

'Let me help you,' I say.

I help to pack up the jumble sale tables, putting clothes, pots and pans, and other items into boxes and following the others into a large room inside the church that has a piano in the corner. After three rounds of dashing between the rain and the church, we finish the job. Smiles are exchanged. They seem to have warmed to me, their suspicion dropping.

'So where are you from?' asks the woman.

'London,' I tell her. 'I am here researching for a book I'm writing.'

'What is the book about?' asks another man.

'This country, us,' I respond simply.

'You look like a writer,' says the lady. Now I am not sure who is charming who.

'So, ask me questions,' says the man in the cap, assuming leadership of the conversation. 'What do you want to know?'

'That school next to the church ... do you remember Ray Honeyford?'

'Yes,' he replies. 'The headteacher who was in the media all those years ago.'

'Now it's a Muslim school. He was right, wasn't he? Bradford has changed in the way that he predicted.'

'I came here in 1962 and worked as a bus driver,' he says. 'I lived in Manningham, but moved out a few years ago.' The Jamaican accent becomes more pronounced as he speaks at length. 'The Muslims, I don't blame them. They grow in large numbers and they take over Bradford. We opened new schools for them. Look over there, Miriam Lord School. And there are others, too. I blame the British government for legalising abortion and making contraception available everywhere. In ten years we killed ten million lives in England, in twenty years we killed twenty million, but the Muslims, they don't have abortions or use birth control so they have more babies. Baroness Paisley – the wife of Ian Paisley – she warned this country in the House of Lords that we will lose the country if we kill our babies. The Muslims don't have same-sex marriages or abortions. So they will grow and we will not. But I do blame the Muslims for one thing.'

'What's that?' I ask.

'They chase out the white English businesses. After the riots in 2001, all the white businesses left. Now Muslims control most of the businesses and the money here. But if a Muslim applies for a job with me or my friends, and we say "no", they accuse us of being racist. But look at the Muslim shops and businesses! They only employ Muslims. They don't employ black people. They don't marry black people. This is racism, reverse racism, against us who are black in Bradford. I don't say they throw stones at us like the white folk say. I say there is racism and reverse racism.'

I listen patiently.

'Tell me,' I say. 'Why did Muslims here in Bradford burn effigies of Salman Rushdie and his book, *The Satanic Verses*, in 1989? And can that happen again?'

'I have a book at home,' he replies. 'It's a book on Islam by a Kenyan author. I read that book often to understand my neighbours. Jesus said "love thy neighbour", so I read to understand the Muslims, their religion, their rituals and how we can live in harmony. In Jamaica, we have a saying: "From many, one." We are one people, so I want to live in harmony. That book mentions in many places that Islam is a religion of peace and tolerance. But I don't see that in Bradford.

'But we Christians started all this. Do you know Richard the Lionheart?' he asks.

'Yes ... son of Henry II?' I say, confused.

'No, the medieval crusader against the Muslim lands,' he says. 'We went to their countries killing and pillaging in the name of religion, and now they're doing the same to us in Christian countries.'

Taking my leave, I thank him for his time and smile at the others. 'God bless you,' I say as we shake hands. 'I hope the sun comes out soon and the jumble sale takes off!'

'I doubt it!' he responds, laughing.

I walk along Carlisle Road and then turn down a residential side street. A Muslim woman turns the corner and briefly catches my eye, then lowers her gaze. A man is sitting outside his house installing a speaker in his Volkswagen and smoking marijuana. A few houses down, a door opens and a woman emerges with two children. When she sees me, she retreats inside and closes the door. When I am well past her house she comes out again with the children. As I feared, she wanted me, a Muslim man, to pass before she felt comfortable emerging from her home.

On Lumb Lane, where some of the 2001 rioting occurred, I come across the Sweet Centre restaurant that has been there since 1964, next to the Darulshafa alternative medicine store that sells Asian herbal remedies. Across the street is Bradford Reform Synagogue, the only remaining synagogue in the city. Several years ago the city's Muslims, led by the owner of the Sweet Centre, championed a fundraising campaign to save it from falling into disrepair.

Heading back towards Carlisle Road to catch a taxi back into town, I pass the Sunni College and Academy that I saw from Ehsan's taxi. Having time to spare, I peruse the banners and posters attached to its façade. They advertise Quran classes, weekend madrasas, children's classes on the Quran and the beliefs and etiquette of Islam, and adult scholarship courses in Arabic, Urdu, *tajweed* and *fiqh*, among others. Many of the banners advertise the *Dars-e-Nizami*, the same religious curriculum from India that I found being taught in Darul Uloom Bury, with its focus on tradition and opposition to modernity.

I step inside. The place is filthy, with rubbish piled up against the walls. There is nobody at the leaflet-covered reception desk, but I can see a turbaned teacher in a room at the back, teaching some boys in white robes who look to be about nine or ten years old.

As the time gets closer to 5 p.m., there is an outpouring of children on to Bradford's streets. The many mosques on the numerous street corners of Bradford are open to the children and their parents for Saturday Arabic classes. The children are now in uniform – not the conventional British school uniform of Iqra, Miriam Lord or other schools: varied, assorted, different. This uniform really is uniform: all the girls, from children to teenagers, in black robes and headscarves, and all the boys in white Arab *thawbs* and skullcaps. In streams across Bradford their mothers, mostly, sometimes fathers, take them to mosque doors and let them in to mosque halls to study and memorise parts of the Quran in Arabic.

How do the children feel about this switching from modern schools to traditional mosques, from English to Arabic? Nobody is asking that question.

As I leave Bradford that evening, I ask myself, 'Where were the Union Jacks? Where were the Muslim-white or other mixed-race couples or friendship groups? Where were the pets?'

I wonder how my next destination, Birmingham, will compare.

Birmingham

It is 5 p.m. Birmingham Grand Central offers a better welcome than Bradford or Manchester's main railway stations. The platforms are cleaner and more spacious, and a vast array of shops and restaurants are fully visible within a structure designed like a spaceship. The circular, dome-like glass ceiling welcomes in natural light, and provides cover for the familiar retail outlets of modern Britain: John Lewis, Nespresso, Moleskine, Jo Malone, Boots, Pret a Manger, The Body Shop and a slew of others. Shoppers are busy and the station, with its wide corridors, cream-white walls and dark-grey slate floor, is full of activity.

I see the rainbow colours of Gay Pride flags strung prominently across the station by Network Rail on makeshift barriers between platforms and shops. There are more rainbow flags flying in and around the station, in shop windows and from the ceilings. This is Gay Pride Month in Britain. I wonder if I'll see similar symbols of LGBT pride in the areas of Birmingham I plan to visit.

Immediately outside the station the city centre looks part derelict, part building site. Concrete car parks and office blocks from the 1960s and 1970s stand empty. The taxi drivers, again all Asian men, are lined up at the different exits from the station. A black cab to the Hyatt Regency hotel costs me less than £5. Two empty plots near the hotel seem ready for tractors and diggers to move in, with 'No Entry' signs affixed to the metal barriers that surround them.

Birmingham, the country's second largest city, was nearly a quarter Muslim in the last census, in 2011. A high proportion of British Islamists have come from the city, including its first al-Qaeda-linked terrorist, Moinul Abedin, and many who went to Syria to join ISIS. In 2014 Birmingham was the site of the 'Trojan Horse' scandal, where Islamists were alleged to have had plans to infiltrate certain schools in the area. The original letter purporting to outline the plot was later proved to be a hoax, but not before several years of sensationalised media coverage divided opinion over Muslim schools in the area.

Right across from the hotel, a brand new central library building covered in filigree-like metal designs that envelop its glass exterior stands juxtaposed with the Victorian neoclassical architecture of central Birmingham, which houses the city council several blocks away in Victoria Square. In the library's shade, homeless women and men in sleeping bags sit among cardboard boxes.

Nearby, a group of Jehovah's Witnesses, three women and a man in their fifties, stand beside a vertical stall with their magazines, smiling at passers-by and strangely oblivious to the begging and rough sleeping right beside them.

Strangely, the receptionist at the hotel is also called Viktorija, just like in Manchester but spelled differently. The old monarch of England, Victoria, left an imprint on many lives.

'Why does the city centre feel like a building site?' I ask.

'We are hosting the Commonwealth Games in a few years,' she says, beaming with the pride of someone who feels a sense of ownership of her city.

'Is Alum Rock far from here?' I ask, with a view to my evening dinner plans.

'It's only a few miles east of the city centre, in the Saltley area,' she replies.

I thank her and go to my room to leave my bags before heading to Alum Rock.

My Uber driver, Mohamed, is waiting outside the hotel. Less than ten minutes later, he indicates a busy high street. 'Alum Rock is a very long road,' he says. 'Where would you like me to drop you off?'

'Please drop us off here,' I instruct. 'Right after the roundabout.'

Atlanta Neudorf, my research assistant at a London think-tank, is with me. She is a Cambridge graduate, Canadian, white, and in her twenties. Perhaps she will see things that I miss, both as a man and as someone who has memories of this place. It isn't long before she does.

I remember the neighbourhood from my childhood days. During my time in secondary school, I spent a week in Birmingham with family and friends each summer for a few years. We stayed in nearby Adderley Gardens, just behind the high street. Alum Rock Road was the bustling, buzzing centre of the local community back then. There was a big Woolworths and the Midland Bank where I used to withdraw and deposit cash. There was the fish and chip shop, and the newsagent's where I bought the *Independent* because I liked reading Andrew Marr, Robert Fisk and Yasmin Alibhai-Brown. What felt normal, noisy and cheerful then feels different now; the change is immediately noticeable as I get out of the taxi.

This long road, packed with cars and shoppers, doesn't have any of the British brands we saw at Grand Central or in the city centre. Shop after shop is a halal butchers, a hijab shop, or selling 'Islamic' gifts or books. In countless shop windows there are mannequins of women, and young girls as well, in full hijab, with covered faces.

We see the Bangladesh Welfare Association & Community Centre, Oriental Trading shop, Lahore Pizza Restaurant, Pak Pharmacy and Pak Supermarket. There is not a Boots, Tesco, Sainsbury's or Aldi to be seen. A panel on the side of a brick building has clearly been painted over at some point in the past and now reads 'Bismillah Building'. The shop housed here is called Perfect Hijab. Nearby, I notice the Junaid Jamshed Clothing Store. Junaid Jamshed was a popular Pakistani singer and preacher linked to the Tableeghi Jamaat who epitomises Pakistan's political and cultural shift towards hard-line Islam. Jamshed went from being a rock star and playing the guitar to abandoning music because it was *haram*. Influenced by Deobandi clerics, he refused to shave, wear Western clothes or meet women unless they were immediate family members whom he could not marry. He launched a clothing brand that was 'Islamic' – long robes and loose sindbads – grew a long beard, and sang only religious songs with no accompaniment. Near Jamshed's stores, there are other Islamic shops.

There are several shops called 'Madina Gift Store' selling books and CDs. I make a mental note to visit one while I'm in Birmingham. The movement responsible for these stores is the Barelwis. But that visit will have to wait.

Atlanta is the only woman around with her hair uncovered. I suddenly realise that she is also the only white person. And I notice that she and I are the only male and female walking side by side on the street. As we proceed down the pavement, we are stared at. For a reprieve, and for interest, we duck into a bookshop that also sells hijabs for little girls. Atlanta picks up *Gift for a Muslim Bride*, curious to see what advice the book will give to married women in an area where wives, with their hair covered, demurely walk several paces behind their husbands.

I take a look as well. As I flip through the book, these are some of the lines that catch my eye:

- 'A wife is to please her husband "by fulfilling all his permissible desires"', p. xxii
- 'It is the responsibility of the wife to make her husband lead a pious life', p. 61
- 'The wife should immediately ask for forgiveness as soon as she notices her husband lose his temper even though she is not at fault', p. 89
- 'Women cannot be equal to men'; 'Women should purge their minds of the misconception that they are superior or equal to men', p. 123
- 'The emergence of the woman from her home is like the emergence of *Shaitaan* [Satan] himself ... women should not

roam about and should make every effort to stay away from mixed gatherings', p. 224
- 'A woman will be guilty of extreme laziness and insolence when she responds coldly to her husband's warmth ... as he makes advances towards her', p. 229
- The wife is commanded to 'not eat before' her husband, not to 'discuss matters that do not appeal to him', and to 'beautify yourself as he prefers', p. 247
- 'Because mothers are too busy in offices and businesses, they are depriving their children of breast milk and ... misappropriating a valuable trust that Allah has placed in their custody. Whereas Allah has granted breasts to women for the purpose of suckling their children, today's women have corrupted its role by using them as showpieces in night-clubs and on the streets', p. 411
- A woman must keep her body hidden or she will 'become a cause of attracting Allah's wrath her way', p. 418

As we exit the shop and make our way to the restaurant, we still see no other white people.

'Where is the 'multi' in Britain's multiculturalism here?' I wonder aloud.

We walk on silently.

'Would you come here alone if I was not with you?' I ask Atlanta, curious.

'No way!' she says without hesitation.

How have we sealed off parts of Britain like this in the name of multiculturalism and multiracialism? Where is the plurality here? Where are the pubs? The shops?

The Khyber Pass is a tiny restaurant. Its name reminds me of that encounter in Blackburn where it was used in a negative way, to indicate the segregation occurring in the city. Dark purple cloths cover the narrow tables. They have clearly not been replaced since the smoking ban came in, as they are covered in small burn marks from cigarettes. The cheap varnished balsa wood that panels the walls looks equally tired, and customers at the few occupied tables look up at us as we walk in.

All the restaurant patrons, aside from one table, are white: a family with two young boys engrossed in their iPad games; two middle-aged women talking quietly over a plate of poppadums; and, at the back of the restaurant, a pair of men with shaved heads, tattoos and black T-shirts drinking bottles of beer that they have brought themselves. These people have clearly come from the other side of Alum Rock Road, stopped here to eat, and will then leave. What else is there for them here? What could the shops selling halal food, hijabs and religious books, or the money transfer offices and foreign travel agents, possibly offer them? Only one table of customers appears to be local: a husband eats his biryani with relish as his much younger wife looks on. They do not speak to one another.

As we sit down, I realise ours is to be the only multiracial table.

Our hosts arrive. Shaikh Paul Salahuddin Armstrong is a white English convert to Islam and lives in Birmingham. He is a co-director of the oldest Muslim organisation in the country, the Association of British Muslims (AoBM). It dates back to 1889, when small communities of English Muslims living both in Woking in Surrey and in Liverpool came together and set up Britain's first mosques. Shaikh Paul wears a pointed black hat and a dark yellow shirt with flowers on it. 'These were gifts to me from Muslims in Indonesia,' he says, removing the hat. He shakes Atlanta's hand without hesitation and sits down beside her.

Mohammed Abbasi, his co-director, joins us a few minutes later and shakes our hands warmly and naturally. He is a leadership coach who focuses on the methods of ancient Chinese strategist Sun Tzu. He brings a gift for me: *Ripley's Believe It or Not!*, from a shop he passed on Alum Rock Road on his way here.

We order an array of Indian dishes to share, mostly grilled meat. Mohammed orders chicken and chips.

'I am becoming more Asian,' says Shaikh Paul, 'while Mohammed is becoming more English.' We all laugh.

As we eat, Shaikh Paul talks us through his conversion to Islam nearly two decades ago. He was and continues to be drawn to the mystical Sufis, remaining active in interfaith work in Britain as well as consulting with Islamic *ulama* – theologians and scholars – across the world, but particularly in Pakistan and Indonesia.

I probe him on his reliance on these experts, but he remains committed to them, particularly praising the theological work of the Indonesian *ulama*. I wonder silently why he is so dedicated to learning from foreign thinkers when there is such a large community of Muslims in our own country.

'So what brings you to Birmingham?' asks Mohammed.

'You guys are always in the news!' I retort. 'This stuff about Muslim parents protesting outside schools to stop children being taught about homosexuality – it's a real problem. There are tens of thousands of schools across the country. Why are these protests only happening at those two schools? We're here to understand life in Birmingham a bit better. After Brexit is over, the government will surely want to turn to strengthening civil society, starting with understanding the challenges we face in our major cities.'

'Shakeel Afsar, who's leading the protests at one of the schools, is a student of mine,' says Mohammed. 'He's not a radical. The problem started much earlier, when Hizb ut-Tahrir held events here against the pro-LGBT curriculum and the new laws that are going to make it compulsory to teach about different types of families.' He shows me the poster for a community *iftar* dinner event held by Hizb ut-Tahrir a month earlier. It has the strapline 'Hope, Vision, Victory' and promises instruction on 'the Quranic vision for ruling, economics and social affairs'. 'This is where the controversy actually originated,' Mohammed tells me.

I have seen Afsar's videos on Facebook. He sits at a desk in front of a map of Kashmir accusing local Birmingham schools, councillors and politicians of failing to represent the interests of those they serve. He has threatened these people, opined against the government and argued in the most explicit manner that children must not be taught anything that goes against the religious and moral values of their parents, citing the Equality Act and the upholding of human rights.[1] How has this message been legitimised and supported here in Britain, the birthplace of the liberal tradition?

'You know the community that organised the first school protests earlier this year is from Alum Rock, don't you?' asks Mohammed. 'That school is just around the corner.' We are sitting in their territory.

'I wanted to learn more about what actually happened,' says Shaikh Paul. 'I visited the school and met its head teacher, Mr Andrew Moffat. I tweeted and wrote about my visit, too,' he enthuses, scrolling through his Twitter feed to show me his retweets in solidarity with the LGBT community in Birmingham over the past few months.

Then he shows me the article he had published on the AoBM website after visiting the school and discussing the curriculum. Shaikh Paul had written that the controversial curriculum being taught there (called 'No Outsiders') focuses primarily on 'being respectful and inclusive towards everyone, which, far from being something un-Islamic that Muslims should be avoiding, is in fact at the heart of Islam's teachings'.[2] He could find no examples of the allegedly sexually explicit messages that Muslim activists had been protesting against. The books associated with the curriculum merely mentioned the possibility of someone having two mummies or two daddies.

'What's wrong with two mothers?' asks Shaikh Paul, as I hand back his phone. 'There are plenty of kids here who have two or three mothers,' he adds sarcastically, hinting at the hidden practice of polygamy in many Muslim communities.

'You see? This is where our friends in Indonesia and other parts of the Muslim world fall behind where we are as progressive British Muslims,' I say, wanting to remind him why it may not be productive to engage with Muslim communities in the global South with a view to imitation.

We enjoy the rest of our dinner in pleasant company before parting ways.

Afterwards, Atlanta and I wander around the nearly identical backstreets of Alum Rock. Each one has rows of small, two-bedroom terraced homes whose front doors open right on to the pavement. Many of the houses are engraved with names and the dates of their construction; most are from the late nineteenth and early twentieth centuries. With names like The Laurels, Clovelly Villas, May Villas, they evoke another age.

Nearly every single one now has religious writing, in Arabic or English, displayed on the front door or in its windows.

'*Ya Rasul Allah*, O Prophet of God,' says one.

'*Ma sha Allah*,' says another.

'*Bismillah*,' reads a banner above a doorframe.

Many houses have opulently framed photos of the Kaaba in Mecca displayed prominently in their front windows.

* * *

It is now almost 8 p.m., and piously bearded men dressed in white are gathering on street corners, some heading towards the mosque. The drivers of the cars that pass us are all Asian men. There are no women.

I stop a couple of teenage boys coming out of a house and ask where they are going.

'We're heading to play cricket,' says one.

'Have you always lived here?' I ask.

'Yes, we were born here.'

'We're from London,' I say, 'but I have to ask you something.'

'Sure,' the boy says. He is bearded and wearing glasses. He exudes a striking confidence and warmth.

'Where are all the white people?' I ask.

'They are here,' he says, slightly defensively. 'You'll see them, we have people from Romania, Jamaica, all over the world living here.'

Just like the hotel receptionist, he displays a strong attachment to the city and a desire to defend it.

As we walk, we see that on every street corner there is a pile of black bin bags. Is there really so much fly-tipping on a weekly basis in Birmingham?

The diverse Alum Rock I knew as a child is no more. I see a large photo of a begging child under the words 'Reach out to the Ummah', calling for donations to the Ummah Welfare Trust.[3] This is a clear appeal to a sense of global Muslim nationalism. What of the poverty in this country? Should that not be a priority?

We walk towards Adderley Gardens, where I used to stay. Seeing us on the pavement, a young man inside a house pulls the blinds down. Soon afterwards, though, he comes out. He is Asian and speaks fluent English with a Birmingham accent. I recognise him as a friend from the old days when I used to visit, and we embrace.

'What are you doing these days?' I ask. 'Alum Rock has completely transformed!'

'I look after mainly Syrian refugees and help them find housing when they're brought to the UK,' he says. 'This area has changed, it's not what it used to be. Now we have Kurds, Afghans, Syrians, Romanians, Somalis and so many others. Before, everyone lived here.'

'What's it like, working with the Syrians?' I ask.

'They are wonderful people,' he says. 'They are professionals, doctors and lawyers, and want to enter our society and earn an income. I meet them at the airport and they are so grateful for the opportunities this country and this city offers them. It's the Kurds and the Afghans who pose a risk,' he says.

'What about them?' I ask.

'They both resist authority. They come from war-torn countries, and the kids walk around with military masks, always looking for a fight. They're traumatised from their pasts,' he says.

Again a familiar theme emerges: these are similar concerns to those expressed by my friends in Manchester, and their trepidation about some of the new Muslim migrants.

After reminiscing about our teenage years, we say our goodbyes.

As Atlanta and I walk back towards Alum Rock Road, we both notice a hand-painted sign in Urdu with an arrow pointing down a gated alleyway between the backs of some stores and a row of houses. I translate the words: 'Salman Shah Hujrah – Room of the Pilgrim Salman Shah'. Normally found in the villages of India, Pakistan and Afghanistan, such signs point the way to male clairvoyants or dream interpreters. Unfortunately, the gate is closed this evening.

The Uber driver back to the hotel is named Mohammed, a Muslim again. I recall that we have seen no Gay Pride flags all evening, just a few miles from the flag-festooned city centre. Will we see any tomorrow?

* * *

In the morning, before heading to Friday prayers at the mosque, we meet a senior local Muslim councillor near the hotel. I want to know his thoughts on the Birmingham education controversy.

'We have three hundred and thirty thousand children in Birmingham's schools,' he says in response to my question. 'Almost a hundred and forty thousand are Muslims, so why are there protests outside only two schools?

'There are other forces at work here, though,' the councillor goes on. 'Moffat and other aggrieved teachers became embroiled in a debate with the Department for Education earlier this year, when legislation was passed in the House of Lords requiring primary schools to teach inclusivity, including of LGBT people and families. He and others felt this didn't go far enough, so he developed his own curriculum of inclusivity, to be implemented in his school, called "No Outsiders".

'We have nothing against LGBT-positive education, but not at age five,' he continues. 'The concept of gender identity and sexuality should be taught later, around puberty. Why are our children being used as a political football between the central government and activist LGBT teachers?'

I am also curious to learn about the extent of Islamist extremism here in Birmingham, especially among young people. The councillor informs me that the local Prevent team has only received a handful of serious referrals this year. 'The real threat these days,' he tells me, 'is the rise of far-right extremism and the resulting hate crime.'

In November 2019, several months after my discussion with the local councillor, Birmingham City Council succeeded in having the protests outside one of the schools in question, Anderton Park, banned by the High Court in Birmingham.[4] How can this be a long-term solution to such a divisive issue?

* * *

Our Uber driver to the mosque is Abdul Ghani, another Muslim.

Birmingham's Central Mosque was the first purposely designed mosque in Birmingham and opened in the early 1970s. Not far from the city centre, it is easily visible from the shops and cafés on the upper level of New Street station. Built of red brick, it has a white dome and minarets. We pass a church just before turning into the mosque car park, but that looks as though its best days are behind it. The mosque car park is organised, with bays for disabled parking and emergency vehicles, and guidance for the women's areas of the complex.

Near the main entrance there are several charity boxes for donations of clothes and household items, and there is a food bank in several Portacabins. A sign says it is open every Tuesday and invites donations of sugar, tinned fruit, UHT milk, tinned tomatoes, squash, cereal, rice, tinned soup, tinned beans, pasta, noodles, sweet treats and other items for the needy. The entrance to the mosque is surrounded by large flowerpots filled with bright blue and purple petunias.

I enter the mosque's ground floor main entrance with Atlanta, slightly nervous as to whether or not she will be welcomed, as a non-Muslim white woman with her hair uncovered. Even in mosques in Turkey they demand that a woman wear an all-enveloping cloak, or an *abaya*. Atlanta is dressed in jeans and a T-shirt.

The first thing I notice in the entrance hall is a large banner prominently placed in the foyer. It reads:

Her Majesty's Government
HOME OFFICE
Community Engagement

The controversy generated by the government's 'Prevent' counter-radicalisation agenda has led many mosques to rethink their strategies for engagement with non-Muslims.

A man dressed all in white suddenly appears from an office. He has rimless glasses and a long beard with no moustache, and before he can say anything I greet him with *salams*.

'My friend and colleague wishes to observe the prayers. May she?' I ask.

'Of course. Please bring your sandals in and go upstairs through here,' he says, opening a door and pointing. 'You can use the bathrooms there and there if you wish.'

He doesn't look away from her but makes eye contact, and makes her feel welcome. I thank him and head into the main prayer hall as Atlanta makes her way upstairs to the women's section.

I see a smiling Sufi in an olive-coloured turban shaking hands with all the men in the front row. Olive is understood to be a colour that was loved by the Prophet Mohamed. The mosque is vast, with capacity to hold about 3,000 worshippers.

There are signs on the walls forbidding the use of telephones. There are also large posters advertising a new extension to the mosque building. An extra prayer area is planned, and funds are currently being raised for the new unit, which will have a golden dome. There are security cameras in every corner; I feel watched.

Other congregants slowly arrive for communal prayers. The gathering is genuinely mixed. Muslims, white, black and brown, of all cultural backgrounds are here. There is clearly no fixed dress code. It isn't obvious to me that this is either a Deobandi or a Barelwi mosque, as was the case with mosques I encountered in Dewsbury and Manchester.

I sit with my back to a pillar. In front of me, a man stands praying with his legs wide apart. He is following the *hadith* that forbids standing with your ankles touching, so the devil cannot enter between the rows of the believers. A man who looks Chinese or Central Asian now goes to the front row and greets some of those there that he knows. He also acknowledges me from afar by touching his chest, and I reciprocate. In the quietness, much as in Dewsbury, I hear prayer beads clicking as the Quran is silently recited by worshippers. The occasional conversation can be heard, too, and then the call to prayer, the *adhaan*. The wording is exactly the same as in Dewsbury, Manchester and every other mosque in the world.

The imam appears. It's the same man who showed Atlanta the way to the women's section. Now wearing a *ghutra*, the traditional headdress worn in Saudi Arabia, and a black, gold-threaded *bisht* (robe) of the kind worn by tribal leaders, the kind man who welcomed us to the mosque is leading the congregation in prayer. His earlier warm welcome and respect now means even more to me.

He begins by giving a fifteen-minute sermon in Urdu, delivered from an iPad, then switches into English, and finally delivers the same message in Arabic, citing verses from the Quran on kindness and gentleness and *hadith* on being compassionate to one's family. In all three languages he is consistent in conveying the facts, dates, meanings, verses of the Quran and narrative.

His message focuses on the upcoming summer holidays and parents' obligations to protect, educate and care for their children. He highlights the length of the summer holidays, saying that for some parents they can be a 'dreadful thing'; many people living in poverty rely on school lunches to feed their children and wonder how they can afford to put food on the table during this long break. He implores the worshippers: 'If Allah has blessed us, we should help these people by donating to the food bank if we are able. It's not just in the cold winter months that deprivation hits.'

He speaks of the parental responsibility to safeguard our children, making sure they are looked after and not neglected over the long holidays when we may be at work during the day. He highlights the possibility of online abuse and our children coming to harm if they are not properly cared for. 'They need to relate to us and be able to talk to us. Addiction and harm start from neglect.'

The imam speaks about the high numbers of marriages that take place in the summer months, and asks for mindfulness in this respect. 'Arranged marriages are completely fine, as long as everyone is happy. Forced marriages are not OK.'

After prayers, he reads out the names of many, many women from the local community who need help and prayers in their hour of need or illness, or ahead of travels. This is the first time I have heard the names of women being called out so freely in a mosque.

In more literalist mosques, such as in Saudi Arabia, this would be considered immodest.

The mosque is now packed. In front of me is a young man wearing an Armani Exchange top and Adidas jogging bottoms. Another beside him is wearing a black kippa-like cap over long hair that reaches down to his shoulders and has a fistful of beard. Many Muslim men grow their beards to at least this length because it is believed that Aaron once grabbed Moses's beard, so there must be enough to be able to be held in this way. The second caliph, Omar, taught that the head should be shaved and the beard trimmed once a year, at the Hajj. Today, more literalist Muslims let their beards grow in accordance with this ruling.

Two rows in front of me is an African man with his two daughters on either side of him. They are no older than about eight, but they are standing in the men's section, praying with their father.

A young man on my right, a complete stranger, smiles at me and says, '*Salam alaikum*, Ed.' He is in his late thirties, wearing a T-shirt and blue jeans, with a set of keys from a BMW and his wallet on the floor beside him so he can kneel and prostrate himself in comfort.

'How are you?' he asks.

'I'm very well, thank you. How are you?' I ask.

'I'm fine, thank you,' he says, maintaining his smile. He's not wearing a headdress, nor traditional Eastern clothes. 'I moved here recently from Luton.'

'Oh, great!' I say.

I notice during the prayers that he doesn't join his hands over his navel as many of the others do, but leaves them resting at his sides, as the Maliki school of Islamic jurisprudence teaches. He leaves straight after the ordinary prayers end.

I remain to perform additional prayers, and when I exit the mosque there are men outside distributing leaflets. A young student with a beard hands me a pamphlet entitled *Islamic Wedding*, written by a Shaykh Muhammad Saleem Dhorat. It sets out religious principles that should be followed in religious weddings. My eye is drawn to a list of customs that have apparently been added to modern Muslim weddings; one line reads: 'The intermingling of the sexes is an act of sin and totally against *sharia*.' Its author is the founder of Leicester's Islamic Dawah Academy as well as another school in Ilford, London. Is this the kind of thing they teach there?

We are also given a postcard about a 'sisters only' Summer Fayre at a nearby girls' school. 'No boys over the age of 10 allowed,' it warns. Krispy Kreme doughnuts are on offer, along with henna painting of the hands, bouncy castles, a barbecue, soft drinks and candyfloss. Again a caliphist community and subculture seem to be operating, with entirely separate arrangements for Muslim women and girls apart from the rest of society.

'Read al-Quran, the Last Testament,' says a billboard outside the mosque that faces the A4540, where thousands of cars must pass daily. That sign has been there since the days when I attended this mosque on my childhood visits to Birmingham. Despite all the claims of British Islamophobia, and amidst the hatred stirred up here by the English Defence League, the sign still stands.

Remembering the Madina bookshops I saw on Alum Rock Road yesterday evening, I decide that now is the time to check out what they have for sale. As we enter one the shopkeeper, an older Asian man with a long grey beard, dressed in a white salwar kameez, glances up from the till. The shop sells clothing, Qurans, religious textbooks and more. Atlanta notices a slim red pamphlet entitled *Western Science Defeated by Islam*. It is written by Imam Ahmad Raza, the founder of the Barelwi movement.

I flip through the pamphlet, which is a denunciation of an American astronomer's 1919 doomsday prediction, based on Raza's 'Islamic' science that accords with the Quran. In the preface, Raza is praised for his criticism of Newton and Einstein. The fact that the astronomer's prediction failed to occur is hailed as a 'victory for Islam and a defeat of Western science' and the heliocentric theory. Raza warns that 'it is a clear denial and rejection of the Commandments of the Holy Quran to accept the Sun as a static centre and the Earth as revolving around it'.

I have some questions to ask of the Barelwis to judge their tolerance and openness as citizens of the UK, but the shopkeeper and his assistant deny any affiliation to Dawat-e-Islami, the global movement run by the Barelwis. The presence of multiple branches of their shop on Alum Rock Road, right here in the neighbourhood linked to the school protests, must indicate something, however. Frustrated, I check online to see if there are any explicitly Dawat-e-Islami institutions in the area that might be willing to talk to me. I find one several streets away. We grab an Uber and head there.

Surrounded by warehouses, car mechanics and a row of small terraced houses, we enter the bookshop. There are *milad* lights on display in the window. Much like Christmas lights, these are used to light up homes to celebrate the *milad* or birthday of the Prophet. Only the Barelwis and other Sufi-influenced Muslims celebrate Mohamed's birthday with such panache.

A door at the back of the shop connects to a large hall where dozens of young boys are sitting on the floor wearing white salwar kameez and bright green turbans. The bearded shop assistant is also wearing a green turban, has dyed his beard red with henna (as some believe the Prophet did), and has a special breast pocket for the traditional twig with which to clean his teeth before prayers.

I greet him. 'I sometimes watch your television channel on Sky 828,' I say.

'Thank you,' he replies.

'Can I ask you a few questions, please? Your organisation is very prominent in Pakistan and South Asia and is now on the rise across England,' I remark. 'In 2011, the elected governor of the Punjab, the most populated part of Pakistan, was killed – no, assassinated – by a member of your organisation, the policeman Mumtaz Qadri. He shot Governor Salman Taseer dead for supporting a Christian woman who allegedly insulted the Prophet Mohamed.'

His expression changes to one of concern. I continue.

'The issue is this: your movement and large numbers of its supporters believe that Asia Bibi, the Christian woman who was given asylum in Canada this year, is a heretic, a *gustakh-e-Rasul*, an insulter of Mohamed. By supporting the heretic Asia Bibi, Governor Salman Taseer was himself indirectly insulting the Prophet. Therefore, they say, any Muslim who is a lover of the

Prophet, an *ashiq-e-Rasul*, had to kill the *gustakh*. In this way Pakistan's harsh blasphemy laws were being upheld, and the killer became a martyr when he was sentenced to death by the secular courts and later executed. His tomb is a shrine today. Do you personally support this?'

The shop owner looks uncomfortable, and says, 'Some say that happened, others deny it. We can't believe the media.'

'But do you condemn Mumtaz Qadri as a killer, a terrorist?' I ask.

'Some think he was,' says the shop owner.

'But what do you and your movement say?' I press.

He remains silent.

'Can you see how Salman Rushdie was declared a *gustakh-e-Rasul* and Iran's Ayatollah Khomeini was called *ashiq-e-Rasul*?' I ask.

'That happened a long time ago,' he says. 'Our children don't even remember it.'

Each question I put to him, he deflects.

He looks away and says, 'We do not believe the media. Besides, the incident you were talking about is an isolated example.'

This denial of this aspect of caliphism, the argument that laws can be flouted to suit a specific and literalist interpretation of Islam, is not limited to the Barelwis. There is another group with a strong presence here in Birmingham that supports a similar approach.

We take an Uber to the Small Heath neighbourhood. Here, too, rubbish heaps are present on street corners and black bin bags are piled on the pavements. Our driver is a friendly Somali gentleman fluent in Arabic. As we drive, he tells us he used to live in Leicester, but life in Birmingham is much cheaper so he moved here. He points out the different 'areas' – the Yemeni area, the Somali area, the Pakistani area – as we head towards Coventry Road, Small Heath's high street.

The shop I am looking for is large and modern in appearance, with a glass-panelled front and shiny wooden floors. Coventry Road's Salafi Bookstore is staffed mainly by Afro-Caribbean converts with large beards who refuse to acknowledge or make eye contact with Atlanta. The shop sells glossy English translations of works on Islamic jurisprudence and aspects of the faith, mainly by

Saudi Arabian theologians. It also stocks beard oil, honey, olive oil and the black seed oil purportedly used by the Prophet. The focus of this particular interpretation of the faith is the eponymous *salaf*, the first three generations of Muslims who followed the Prophet Mohamed's teachings, and who arguably established and practised the purest form of Islam. Salafis strongly oppose any 'innovations', or *bid'ah*, in Islamic law and theology from this period in history onwards. Not all of them, however, are violent jihadis who oppose the West, and many are apolitical literalists.

Much as I found in Dewsbury, Manchester, Blackburn and Bradford, however, the underworld of caliphism is on show here. French converts to Islam frequent this shop and area. The French government's niqab ban and its unwelcoming attitude towards hijab wearers has led these converts to settle here in Birmingham. The fact that they feel free to set up home and practise their literalism here in the UK rather than in Saudi Arabia is telling. None of the men browsing in the shop makes eye contact with Atlanta, either.

We peruse the bookshelves and choose some volumes that are telling of the Salafi worldview. Among them are criticisms of Sufism and the Tableeghi Jamaat, a purported exposé of Barelwism, a book of advice to Western Salafis, and a book called *The Evils of Music: The Devil's Voice & Instrument*. I take them to the till, intending to look through them on the train back to London.

'What brings you to Birmingham?' asks the shop assistant as he scans them through. 'Are you here for the conference?'

'Which conference?'

'It starts tonight and runs all weekend,' he says, handing me a leaflet.

The topic of the conference is 'Muslim Unity, Splitting of the Ummah and the Methodology of the Scholars of Hadith'. One of its main speakers, the director of Birmingham's Salafi Mosque, Abu Khadeejah Abdul-Wahid, has in the past called polygamy a 'good family practice'[5] and endorsed the right of a husband to divorce a woman by simply pronouncing '*talaq*', while a wife can only obtain a divorce by applying to a sharia council.[6] He has also written a Quranically justified treatise on the custody of children

after divorce, stating that a woman loses custody over young
children in the event of her remarrying as 'her main concern now
is her new husband. She cannot busy herself with her baby to the
disadvantage of her husband ...'[7]

Abu Khadeejah has also written a guide to (his interpretation
of) Islam's stance on homosexuality, in which he cites the story
of the Prophet Lūt (Lot), who criticised the 'transgressions' of
homosexual lust; and he denies transsexuality. He acknowledges
that 'Muslim doctrine does not remove from the fold of Islam
the one who practices the major sin of homosexuality', but calls
homosexuality 'a corruption of the natural state' of being that
God has given humans, as well as a major sin. His solution is as
follows: 'Muslims who find they are afflicted with temptations or
unnatural desires must learn to resist, turn to Allah, supplicate to
Him for strength and guidance (and get married).'[8]

* * *

We are now down to our last twenty-four hours in Birmingham. On
the way to the mosque this morning we drove past the Birmingham
LGBT Centre, located on a busy roundabout not far from New
Street station. In all the time we have spent in the neighbourhoods
surrounding central Birmingham, this was the first place outside
the railway station where the Gay Pride flag was visible. Atlanta and
I decide to pay a visit to find out more about how LGBT people
in Birmingham are treated, and the major challenges they face in
the city.

We walk in. There is no security, no buzzer. Inside, there are
posters and fliers on a notice board, including information about
a local group called 'Finding a Voice' for LGBT Asians in the city.
The contact details provided are for an active gay Muslim man,
Khakan Qureshi.

The reception area is inside another door and seems more secure.
We press the intercom and are buzzed through. A young Muslim
woman in her twenties wearing a grey hijab, and with a striking
wedding ring on her finger, smiles at us.

'Hi,' she says, beaming and confident. 'How can I help you?'

'We're here to try and understand more about homophobia and the life of gay people in Birmingham,' I say. 'I detect a London accent in your voice!'

'Yes!' she says proudly. 'My husband's from Birmingham and he insisted we should live here in his bigger house, so I moved up here to be with him.'

'You seem to be Muslim,' I say. 'We especially want to know more about how the Muslim communities here in Birmingham respond to LGBT issues, especially after all the press coverage of the school protests earlier this year.'

'I'm not from the LGBTQ+ community myself, but I support their cause,' she says.

'Do you feel a contradiction between Islam and homosexuality?' I ask.

'Not at all!' she says. 'On the contrary, my religion doesn't teach that we should hurt people or support injustice. There's a lot of injustice against gay and trans people here, and I want to help. I'm trained to be a domestic violence specialist worker, and I want to help this community.'

As she speaks, I glance at the sign-in sheet on the desk in front of me. Of the twenty-five people who have signed in today, six have Muslim names.

'Do your family and friends know what you do?' I ask.

'Absolutely they do,' she responds confidently. 'I couldn't hold down such a public role here otherwise. Nobody has opposed me helping gay people and the domestically abused among them.'

'What do you mean?' I ask.

'People in homosexual relationships are more likely to suffer domestic violence; in fact nearly one in four same-sex relationships will see domestic abuse occur. Trans people are even more likely to suffer abuse. The rate is nearly fifty per cent. My job is to support them.'

I notice a massive bucket of condoms. I blush.

'What is all that about?' I ask.

'This is also a sexual health clinic,' she explains. 'Please feel free to take some. Those are for all our visitors, so they can practise safe sex.'

She gives me a selection of leaflets from a display on the front desk. They advertise support for gay and bisexual men and women as well as for trans people. There are specific support groups for Afro-Caribbeans, for Middle Eastern and Asian men, and for people of colour more generally.

'How do you come to terms with the chapter on Lot in the Quran, and its condemnation of homosexuality?' I ask, curious to know how this liberal young woman reconciles her religious and social beliefs.

'I have my own personal interpretation of Islam, and I don't agree with anybody who opposes gay and trans rights,' she says.

It's been an exhausting day, but we leave the meeting feeling energised by this young woman's enthusiasm. I thank her for her time, and she invites us to phone her or come back should we wish to learn more.

Birmingham may have its caliphist Salafis and intolerant Barelwis, but it also has its luminary progressives and liberal conservatives who think for themselves and are not controlled by clerics. They retain their faith in God, and not in mere dogma and doctrine, as they move ahead with the modern world. This woman is a beacon of hope for a modern, Western Islam.

* * *

The imam has been waiting for me since afternoon prayers. His is a Barelwi mosque: more Pakistani, more colourful, more decorated and more modern than some. Imam Ajal is young, in his thirties, and speaks English fluently. He is from Nottingham.

'Tell me what is on your mind. Over the next ten years, what do you see as the biggest challenge for your mosque and the wider Barelwi movement?'

'First, are you aware that Pakistani politics is influencing our community more and more every year, even every month now?'

'Well, yes,' I reply innocently. 'Imran Khan is prime minister, and a cricket-loving British Muslim population with a majority of Pakistani heritage will naturally be drawn towards Imran, right?'

'It is deeper than that, my friend,' he says.

Imam Ajal explains that for almost ten years, since the killing of Salman Taseer in 2011, attitudes have been hardening here in Britain. Khadim Hussain Rizvi has accumulated a vast following in Pakistan with his Tehreek-e-Labbaik party, which Pakistan's information minister has described as 'a continuous threat to the life and properties of the citizens', accusing it of 'doing politics under the guise of religion'.[9] The word 'labbaik' in the party's name comes from a prayer, '*Labbaik, ya Rasul Allah* (we are here for you, O Messenger of God)'. The group has not only harangued and silenced politicians, liberals and secularists but also maligned Taseer and celebrated his assassin Mumtaz Qadri.

Rizvi is widely respected across Pakistan and is considered a *pir* within the Barelwi movement. He is also vehemently opposed to any loosening of Pakistan's blasphemy laws and was briefly arrested in October 2018 for his incendiary speeches in favour of mass protests.

'I have met with the Dawat-e-Islami in Birmingham and have encountered only silence and sophistry when asking about these things,' I say.

'It is a far wider problem than Dawat-e-Islami,' he says. 'That is a growing organisation, but the broader movement of Khadim Hussain Rizvi and his Tehreek-e-Labbaik are spreading here. So that is my first concern, to tell you about this.'

He, like others, has seen me comment on Muslim and national security concerns on television and is aware of my writings and affiliations in Westminster. For people in the northern towns, any link to Westminster seems to suggest a connection to some higher sort of power. Imams talking in private to me express fears that they won't voice in public. Much like politicians, they have no sure sense of the direction of travel in their communities. As with politicians, all too often it is a matter of self-preservation. Imam Ajal can see something else in the making, too, in this newfound fear of extremism in the Barelwi movement, and this is the second concern he lays out for me.

'In Birmingham, Nottingham and elsewhere, there are younger clerics who are fully in support of Rizvi in Pakistan, and want to impose control on all of us here. You know Dr Musharraf Hussain al-Azhari, right?'

'Yes, he's one of the best imams we have in Britain,' I say without hesitation. 'He invited members of Her Majesty's Armed Forces to pray at his mosque in Nottingham, and I recently met him in Abu Dhabi for a peace conference – but we also travelled to Israel and Palestine together to help build bridges between the Abrahamic faiths.'

'That's the problem,' says Imam Ajal. 'These visits abroad, outside the control of the younger British clerics. And Dr Musharraf's new translation of the Quran, which he wrote without their permission, angered them.'

'Who is "them"?' I ask.

He is silent.

I try to imagine who in Birmingham has a large following and is close to Pakistan's religious hardliners.

'Saqib Iqbal?' I venture.

Imam Ajal nods.

'Saqib and some other young clerics summoned people in a makeshift court to put Dr Musharraf on trial for this Quran. They found many differences in it from their own interpretation of *aqeedah* [accepted creed].'

'But this is like a Papal Index of forbidden books!'

'Exactly!' says Imam Ajal.

I then find out that the quibbles were over Dr Musharraf's translation of certain phrases. Was God 'the Unique' or 'the One'? Did God 'allow' jihad or 'ordain' jihad? Was Mohamed 'the seal of the prophets' or 'the final prophet'? Dr Musharraf's opponents questioned why the patriarch Jacob was called 'an old fool' rather than the more traditional translation, 'senile'. These new Barelwi clerics seem to want to impose Pakistan's blasphemy laws on our free society.

Imam Ajal uses the phrase 'controlling of our thoughts' multiple times in reference to these actions. He emphasises once again that the Barelwis are facing a real problem in Birmingham, and that these young clerics' rigidity is likely to create more problems in future.

'But I was at the main mosque in Birmingham, and it was very civilised! I didn't come across any issues that worried me,' I say.

'These mosques have been under public scrutiny by *Panorama* from the BBC and Channel 4's *Dispatches*, so they've changed to adapt to Britain. But the younger clerics, like Saqib and his group of *mureeds* [followers], will rise up and impose more controls on us, and our thinking and behaviour.

'They don't understand that the law takes precedence over the honour of the Prophet. That same man, the Prophet Mohamed, who taught us this religion, also put the law above his own personal honour. We are a people of the rule of law, not the mob of Pakistan.' He looks deeply worried.

Imam Ajal has reason to be concerned: Saqib Iqbal Shaami has around five million followers and likes on Facebook; his rabble-rousing video lectures in Urdu mix messages of Sufi love with praise for the movement that endorses killers – in one, he praises Khadim Hussain Rizvi.[10]

* * *

For dinner we are meeting Ala, who owns local businesses in Birmingham and spearheaded the 'Muslims for Britain' movement. The group spent hundreds of hours campaigning across the Midlands and the south of England, in the lead-up to the 2016 Brexit referendum, for an independent Britain. I want to hear his side of things as a prominent local Muslim figure.

We meet him at the Tipu Sultan restaurant in Balsall Heath, south of the city centre. Ala is tall and thin and has a long black beard. As we greet each other he embraces me and shakes Atlanta's hand; his warmth is immediately apparent. Given an MBE for his contributions to his local community in Birmingham, he is down-to-earth and good-natured.

The venue is a world away from last night's Khyber Pass. Huge doors flanked by full-sized cannons and marble statues of lions, and a marble foyer panelled in mirrors, are my first impressions. The seating area is massive and takes up four different rooms; there must be at least two dozen tables in the section we are seated in. Scores of waiters bustle between them, carrying trays heaped with delicious-smelling food. The first page of the menu briefly tells the history of the restaurant's eighteenth-century namesake: Tipu Sultan, a prince of northern India descended from the great Mughals, is remembered for killing a tiger with just a dagger when his gun failed to fire.

After we have ordered a number of dishes to share, I ask Ala about his involvement in the Brexit campaign. 'As a businessman I'd go to Indonesia, Malaysia and other countries, and the political leaders would want to strike free trade agreements with us,' he explains. 'We'd come back and relay that to our government, and then we'd be told that these decisions are made in Brussels. How is that possible? We are Brits, and our government can't deal with other countries freely, individually? That was my first indication that something was not right and needed to change.

'Secondly, for our weddings and Asian gatherings, we couldn't bring over grandparents and other relatives from back home to join us and attend. They were subjected to humiliating questioning and then rejected for entry by the Home Office. That generation, two and a half million of them, fought for Britain in the two world wars. And now we see Germans and others coming and going freely in our country with no visas required, but our relatives cannot. How is that right?' asks Ala.

'Channel 4 did a documentary about Alum Rock,' he goes on, 'where many Asians voted to leave the EU in the referendum due to the thefts, and pressures on doctors, schools and hospitals, that came with the influx of Polish and Romanian migrants.'

In the referendum, twenty-two of Greater Birmingham's forty wards voted to leave the EU. The city's vote was far from unanimous, however, with 50.4 per cent choosing to leave.

After parting ways with Ala outside the restaurant at around 9 p.m., Atlanta and I decide to walk back to the city centre. Noticing a striking nineteenth-century brick building with its windows boarded up, we stop to look around, wondering what such a grand building could have been. Directly behind it is another building. There's a man leaving it with his bicycle, so we stop him and ask if he knows what it might have been.

'It was a tram depot!' he tells us. 'But now it's a skatepark and climbing centre. Come on, let me show you around.'

He leads us inside and we marvel at the cavernous interior, its walls covered in brightly coloured hand- and footholds. Pairs of men and women are busy rock-climbing. The other half of the building is a skateboarding park with ramps and jumps. A group of teenage boys are skating and performing tricks on a twenty-foot-high ramp. As we thank our willing guide for showing us this unexpected locale, I notice two teenage girls of Somali heritage skateboarding in another section of the park. They are wearing canvas trainers, sweatpants, hoodies and headscarves. I am struck by the different Birmingham this reveals: in Alum Rock I haven't seen a single woman out on her own, let alone skateboarding in a predominantly male setting at 9.30 on a Friday night. How has integration occurred so easily in some communities, while in others it is impossible to defy the village norms enforced by clerics from Pakistan or Afghanistan?

A few blocks away is Birmingham's famous 'Balti Triangle', where curry restaurants have vied for customers for decades. One side of the triangle, Ladypool Road, is reminiscent of Alum Rock and Coventry Road: all the shop names evoke the Middle East or South Asia, and the advertising is for hijabs, curries and Arab foods. At ten o'clock on a Friday night, the only people on the pavements and driving down the road in their flash cars are Asian men, most of them young. Each one we pass avoids eye contact with Atlanta, their eyes sliding past her as if she is not there. Several of the restaurants advertise 'family seating', meaning that they provide a separate section for women and children. How have so many neighbourhoods in Britain's second largest city become like this?

* * *

The next morning, before returning to London, I go to Glovers Road, home of the local African Muslim community, who are mostly new arrivals to the UK. A Somali friend of mine has recently moved here from Saudi Arabia. He and his brother Ahmed studied in Britain during the Tony Blair years and gained British citizenship, but went on to live in Saudi Arabia. Today we discuss Middle East politics, and his three children, all under the age of eight, speak to me in Arabic. They seem confused when we switch to English.

'What would you do if your children were taught about gay rights at primary school?' I ask. He seems surprised that such a question could be asked between Muslims.

'We have lost shame. We would leave this country,' he says, without pausing to think. His brother agrees.

'Let children be children,' he says. 'They can learn about these things when we can explain what is right and wrong. *Haya* [shame] is an important part of our faith. A man to man relationship is *haram*, forbidden.'

'We can't change our religion to suit Britain,' says Ahmed. 'They want us to change because they see us as a strong people. Now they want to weaken us. Salafi Publications now talk to the government. They are entering our community.' As Salafi Muslims, they feel betrayed that their main publisher is in communication with Her Majesty's Government.

'But the government provides you with security, health, housing, education. Why is it a problem if your institutions are in touch with your government?' I ask.

Ahmed frowns. 'I have no government. We are waiting for our government of the sharia to return again, headed by a caliph.'

The rest of our conversation constantly returns to issues in Somalia, Ethiopia, Eritrea, Saudi Arabia, Yemen and Afro-Arab politics. This new generation is more focused on matters there than here. They feel lost, in a no man's land. Earlier generations of immigrants who arrived here in the post-war decades were more willing to integrate and accept the values of British society. What has changed since then?

Qasim, my Uber driver, pulls up, and we head towards New Street station for my 2.30 p.m. train to the sound of the car radio.

'Do you speak Hindi?' he says.

'Why do you ask?'

'I can stop the music if you don't like or understand it.'

'Keep it on,' I respond. 'I will try to understand it.'

Back home in London, I speak only in English. A few days in Birmingham, though, and my Arabic, Urdu, Hindi and Bengali skills are constantly called to the fore.

'The music keeps me awake and alive,' he says, with a sigh of remorse and melancholy.

'How long have you been working today?' I ask.

'You are my first customer.'

'And why are you so tired?'

'Life, my brother, life. This city, this country, this continent, it tires me … Listen,' he says, as the music plays. A forlorn, lamenting melody fills the car. He starts to translate for me with passion, his hands moving, his head slightly swaying from side to side:

Eh Daulat Bhi Le Lo,
Yeh Shohrat Bhi Le Lo,
Bhale Chheen Lo Mujhse Se Meri Jawani,
Magar Mujhko Lauta Do Bachpan Ka Sawan …
Wo Kagaz Ki Kashti, Wo Baarish Ka Paani …

Take this money,
take this fame as well,
snatch my youth from me if you so wish,
but return to me those rains of childhood,
that paper boat, that rainwater …

'I was a teacher in a secondary school in Murree in Pakistan, on the outskirts of Islamabad. It's a beautiful, hillside part of the world. Google it. Why am I here?

'In my village, I was king. I taught the children from 8.30 in the morning until 2 p.m. Then all day I visited and enjoyed time with my cousins, many cousins. I had fifty-seven first cousins in Murree …'

'Who do you have here?' I ask, interrupting his misty-eyed nostalgia for his home.

He sighs. 'I married my cousin,' he says. 'My parents insisted I marry my cousin here, so the wealth could stay in the family. For six years I stayed in my school in Murree and then we had a son, so my parents said I must be in England. I arrived in 2000.'

His son is now twenty-two, and his daughters are eighteen. They are all at university.

'But here I am, lonely and alone, my friend.'

He translates another verse of the song:

Muhalle Ki Sabse Purani Nishani,
Wo Budhia Jise Bachche Kehte The Naani,
Wo Naani Ki Baaton Me Parion Ka Dera,
Wo Chehre Ki Jhurrion Me Sadiyon Ka Pehra,
Bhulaye Nahin Bhul Sakta Hai Koi,
Bhulaye Nahin Bhul Sakta Hai Koi,
Wo Chhoti Si Raaten, Wo Lambi Kahani …

The oldest remnant of the area,
that old lady we children used to call naani [maternal grandma]
that camp of fairies in the granny's talks,
that guard of ages in the wrinkles of face,
no one can forget, even on trying,
those small nights, that long story …

'These songs of childhood and love keep me company, my friend. They remind me of Murree.'

Qasim is only in his late forties, yet the man's sadness is palpable. He gives me his phone number and asks me to call him if I ever have time to go to Murree, and he will show me his country and village.

That Hindi song about the paper boat and the rainwater plays under the grey skies of Birmingham. I tip him generously to help lift his mood.

With half an hour to fill before I leave Birmingham, I look for a café in the Bullring, the shopping centre attached to the station. The centre is packed. The adjacent streets are full, too. I have coffee and a scone in John Lewis and look out over the city. I can see the Central Mosque from here, its dome showing up clearly beyond the brick and concrete of the city centre. This quiet café reflects a different Birmingham from the one I have seen in the suburbs. All the customers here are white and speak in quiet tones. Only two members of staff are from coloured ethnic minority backgrounds.

Back on the train, I look through the books we purchased from the Salafi Bookstore. Several are highly critical of the Barelwis and the Sufis, whom the Salafis view as heretical, describing as sinful their 'innovations' that 'pollute' the pure faith. The authors of these books are Islamic scholars based at universities in Saudi Arabia. One claims that the Sufis' veneration of the dead and praise of saints is sinful, as is their mystical understanding of Allah's presence in the world, which deviates from the Salafi focus on the oneness of God. It argues that all good Muslims should 'strive hard in waging war against all those who are in opposition to the *Sharee'ah of Islaam*, whether they are communists, atheists, grave-worshippers or Sufis'.[11] It also criticises 'the greed and avarice of the Jews'.[12]

The second book is critical of the Barelwi movement, calling their faith 'a mish-mash of superstitions, fairy tales, grave worship, saint worship, distortion of Quranic verses and negligence of the authentic *Sunnah*'.[13] It denounces the founder of the sect, Imam Ahmad Raza, and analyses writings by the movement's scholars in light of literalist readings of the Quran, accusing them of perpetuating false beliefs 'cloaked in the garb of religion'.[14] Its author accuses the Barelwis of having 'fabricated many innovations in order to trap the common masses and generate a profitable livelihood' and failing to meet 'the challenge of secularism' in today's society: another hint at caliphism.[15] The book ends by focusing on the writings of the Salaf (the early generations of Muslims in

Arabia), quoting the eighth-century scholar Sufyan ath-Thawri as saying 'innovations are more beloved to Satan than sin'.[16] How can there be such division within the faith?

Another publication, equally typical of the Salafi reliance on literalism, expresses opposition to music and singing. It quotes and endorses the opinions of early Islamic scholars that 'whoever listens to a songstress ... will have molten metal poured into his ears on the Day of Judgement';[17] 'singing is the utterance of illicit sexual relations [*ruqyah az-zina*]';[18] and it 'destroys an individual's manliness [*muru'a*]'.[19] Singing and music apparently intoxicate and distract a person away from their rightful focus on God; indeed 'the Quran and singing can never coexist in a single heart'.[20]

I wonder if I will encounter similar literalism on my next stop – Cardiff.

6

Cardiff

Cardiff Central railway station feels old, but it is spacious, full of people and has an assortment of shops and cafés: Spar, WHSmith, Pumpkin Café, Upper Crust, Gourmet coffee bar and a Marks & Spencer. The Gay Pride flag flies above the station's basic neoclassical exterior beside the Union Jack and a Welsh flag. Pret a Manger, Cardiff University, the BBC and an open square in the city centre welcome visitors. The taxi rank is more diverse than I have seen on my other trips so far: there are white drivers, black drivers, Asian drivers and female drivers.

I walk for about twenty minutes, passing law firms, roundabouts, large office complexes, housing estates, newsagents and the Romanesque St Mary's Church. A sign on its exterior tells me the church has been in existence since 1107. I see signs for legal aid on numerous buildings, but no signage for the mosque I'm looking for. Youths in white robes and Yemeni caps gather outside the Bab al-Yemen restaurant. I am heading to Butetown and the Bay area of Cardiff, formerly known as Tiger Bay.

This has been a site of Muslim settlement since the mid-nineteenth century, when Yemeni and Somali sailors worked here on ships and in the Merchant Navy. Today, there are just under 25,000 Muslims in Cardiff, many of them the descendants of those early migrant labourers.

Almost exactly a century before my visit, in June 1919, Cardiff witnessed three days of violent race riots that led to the deaths of three people and hundreds of injuries. There is no memorial or plaque in Cardiff to remember this early flare-up in British race relations. Here, in these streets of Butetown, white servicemen returning from the First World War clashed with Arab and West African Muslims. Families across Cardiff were caught up in the violence, and the riots spread to other parts of the city. Many stayed indoors for days. Houses were ransacked and shops looted, according to local press reports. Twenty-one-year-old Mohammed Abdullah, a fireman on a ship, died in hospital from a fractured skull after being attacked inside a boarding house in Bute Street. John Donovan, thirty-three, was a former soldier who had also worked on the railways. He was shot through the heart and lung at a house in Millicent Street. Frederick Henry Longman, a former soldier, also died, after being stabbed.

In the century since the riots, Cardiff's ethnic minorities have tended to settle around the Bay area and Butetown, presumably feeling stronger and safer in numbers, with the added benefit of police protection in the immediate aftermath of the riots, which saw the army called in to restore order. If Cardiff, 100 years after a riot, still lives in its shadow, and minorities continue to congregate within their own communities, what hope for Bradford's future?

The area still appears to be predominantly Muslim, as I pass a number of men wearing *thawbs* on their way to Friday prayers, but there are also black, white and Asian people doing their shopping and waiting at bus stops. A little boy heads towards me on the pavement wearing a Yemeni belt, dagger, *thawb* and shawl. I smile; he smiles back. There are white kids playing football with Arab and African children down the street. The area feels mixed, and relaxed, with none of the suspicion I encountered on the streets of Birmingham's more ethnically uniform neighbourhoods. What appear to be council houses border the main roads, many with white taxis parked outside.

Eventually I manage to locate the South Wales Islamic Centre on Alice Street, where a white man is sitting outside drinking tea and reading a newspaper. The Centre is a central gathering point for the Yemeni community that has been in Butetown for more than a century, many of them followers of the spiritual, mystical form of Islam known as Sufism.

The small redbrick mosque is striking, but nowhere near as domineering of the skyline or as excessively decorated as the ones I saw recently in Bradford, and it has a separate but well-marked entrance for women. It is strange how, although more people have jobs here, in a much older community, the mosque does not compare with the wealth of Bradford's mosques.

The smell of incense burning inside wafts past me as I enter. It reminds me of the mosque in Manchester. The corridors in the mosque are quite cramped, but I can see that the communal prayer area is relatively large, with several adjoining rooms, and can probably hold around 500 worshippers. Plain white walls are offset by brilliantly coloured stained-glass windows set into the recess of the dome. I head to the ablution area and quickly wash up; the smell of mothballs is strong to the point of suffocation, though I suppose that is better than the stuffy air of other human beings and toilets. At least the towels provided are fresh. As I emerge, I notice a young man sitting outside playing Candy Crush on his phone.

I enter the prayer hall and see about twenty Yemeni and Somali elders, some sitting on chairs, others on the floor, many holding rosary beads or copies of the Quran. They all have trimmed beards, and some are wearing Arab-style white *thawbs* while others are in street clothes. The room is filled with the loud, clear, melodious recitation of the Quran by popular Egyptian reciter Shaikh Qari Abdul Basit. I grew up listening to Abdul Basit. He was a legend before the fast-paced, rap-like Saudi style of Quran recitation became popular with many Muslims, thanks to Saudi satellite television channels and the rise of Salafism. In Cardiff, among these older Muslims, it is still the clean-shaven, modern Egyptian Abdul Basit with his opera-like high notes that remains standard.

I sit on the floor after greeting the group of elders with a '*salam alaikum*'.

'Do not walk upon the earth as haughty …' intones the recorded voice of Abdul Basit.

On the other side of the prayer hall I notice a chubby man in his fifties sitting on the floor in a suit and tie, clearly his Friday best. Among those gathered for Friday prayers, some are talking and others are laughing, reciting the Quran, or listening to Abdul Basit's voice coming through the speakers. Nobody is suspicious of me sitting there taking notes and observing the space.

'*Ya akhi*,' I hear a voice behind me say. 'Hey, brother!'

I look round, prepared to speak in Arabic.

'*Na'm, habibi?*' I reply, with the warmth that is appreciated across the Arab world. 'Yes, my dear?'

'Watch out,' the man says, indicating that my bank card is in danger of falling out of my pocket. I thank him and firmly put it back. The feeling of being looked out for strengthens my sense of safety in this space. A Saudi or Gulf Arab man enters the hall. I suspect he is a Saudi religious student, judging by his commitment to wearing Arab clothing: a shiny collared *thawb*, with a *ghutra* (a traditional Arabian cloth headdress) and *iqal* (a black cord worn doubled on the head to keep the *ghutrah* in place) on his head. He prays in different parts of the mosque, moving around the hall, performing units of prayer in each spot and moving round again. The rationale for this behaviour comes from a *hadith* that says the earth or piece of land on which we pray today will testify for us on the Day of Judgement. He appears to believe that the more places he prays in, the more worthy he will be of testimony in the next life.

The mosque slowly fills up for the communal prayers. A man sits down on a chair in front of me. Elderly, a little frail, he is wearing tracksuit bottoms with a white *thawb* on top. Beside him to the right are several young boys and two toddlers. They are all looking at him and giggling. Unable to make out what is so funny, I peer around and see that the elderly man is pretending to be asleep but holding a lollipop in his hand in view of the boys. Which child will dare to come and take it? One by one, they each get a lollipop as he pretends to wake up, smiles at them, and produces another lollipop from inside his *thawb*. Their laughter fills the mosque, as the Quran continues to be recited and the mosque gets busier.

Looking before me, I notice something that has not been present in any other mosque that I have visited: a perfume stand. Several bottles of perfume are placed there for worshippers to use freely. Muslims believe that the Prophet Mohamed praised perfume and generally encouraged his companions to use it. Muslims commonly use oud and rose musk, but I don't remember ever seeing an allocation for use inside the prayer hall of a mosque.

Many of the congregants wear smart, professional clothing. Several walk in on crutches, and I sense that they were perhaps injured in the wars raging in Yemen and Somalia. A man sitting next to me bears seven scars from slashes on his forearm. He wears white socks and an agate *aqeeq* ring on one of his fingers. Such rings, set with semi-precious stones, are worn in emulation of the Prophet, who is thought to have worn one in commemoration of the removal of idols from a mosque in Mecca.

It is now 1.30 p.m. The *adhaan* is called by a layman from the front of the mosque; his *tajweed*, or Arabic pronunciation, is weak. The normal praise of God, the witnessing of Mohamed as the messenger of God, and the call to prayer and felicity takes place.

Then a tall man, Tunisian in appearance, I think, with his trimmed beard, fair olive skin and curled hair, ascends the *minbar*. He wears a red fez, its tassel firmly covered and held down on the sides by a very small white cover, a turban of sorts. This tassel was traditionally used by Muslim scholars in the Egyptian theological centre of Al-Azhar as a reminder that knowledge comes from God and God can also take it away from our heads. It is a way of remembering that Muslim scholars should be humble before God.

The imam steps up and starts his sermon by praising God and the Prophet. Judging from his Arabic, and occasional slips into the Egyptian dialect, he is Egyptian: he says '*masgid*' for 'mosque' rather than '*masjid*', for example, the typical Egyptian substitution of the hard 'g' as in gold for 'j' as in jam.

The first part of his sermon is in classical Arabic. The imam emphasises the importance of continuing the lessons of Hajj, the annual period of pilgrimage to Mecca that finished only recently.

'He is God, the One; the eyes and senses do not perceive Him, but He perceives us. He is gentle, loving and informed.

'Today's lesson from the Hajj is on reflection and learning lessons,' he says.

And so he explains why reflections on God, and applying the lessons learned at Hajj, even for those who did not participate in it, are important for the life of the Muslim. He cites verses of the Quran to remind us that Abraham was commanded to sacrifice his son, Ishmael in the Quranic narrative. Abraham called out to God that he was leaving behind his offspring in this 'wadi [valley] with no food' and committing his family to God through prayer. The devil tried to distract Abraham and Ishmael, as are we distracted today, the imam reminds us.

'Addressing Mohamed, God says "worship your Lord until certainty arrives", and so it is for us, to worship when doubt overcomes us. And to stay on the oath of obedience to God.'

And so he continues. Then he translates his speech into English, with a heavy Egyptian accent, for the second part of the sermon. At no point, however, does he attack theological innovations and modern practices. After the imams in Bradford, this stands out for me as significant.

Immediately after the prayer a young man in a white *thawb*, with a Yemeni scarf wrapped around his head as a turban, jumps up to the microphone and announces that he represents the charity Al-Safah and is collecting for Yemen today so that children can go to school in the months ahead. 'We are a registered charity,' he emphasises, and then repeats the words in Arabic.

On my way out after the service I find a tall Somali man selling prayer beads, perfumes, shawls. Tens of empty taxis are parked outside, their drivers still inside the mosque. A white woman driving by smiles as she stops to allow a group of worshippers to cross the road.

The youths head away from the mosque towards the shops and restaurants of Butetown. Unlike in Bradford, I note, there is no security or command and control at the mosque. Worshippers are free to enter and exit as they please.

* * *

Down the road, there is a mural of Fidel Castro on the wall. Again, unlike the areas of Bradford and Birmingham I have seen, this is a street full of all kinds people from different ethnic backgrounds. The Sherman Theatre and Cardiff University Students' Union building overshadow the al-Manar Centre. This Salafi mosque and Islamic centre is located in a row of terraced brick houses just to the north of the Butetown area. It seems much smaller than the South Wales Islamic Centre, but immediately upon entering it I'm struck by the activism.

'*Salam alaikum*, brother, welcome to the mosque. Where are you from?' asks a young man with a long beard.

'London,' I say. 'I will go and pray.' I make my excuses so as not to engage in a long conversation during which, I am almost sure, he will try to preach and evangelise. This is what Salafi mosques and their activists do: preach and convert, to guide Muslims back to the 'straight path' of the earliest generations.

Much like IslamBradford, al-Manar mosque is a very functional building with no ornate decorations and no dome. Inside the mosque hall a young blonde girl in a dress is running from end to end with a boy I think must be her brother and two of his friends. One of the friends is Asian and the other black, but all are talking fluently in English as they play. These are British children.

I pray inside this mosque, too, but I can't stop myself thinking about its past and present connections and the future of these children. In June 2014, two twenty-year-old boys from Cardiff – Reyaad Khan and Nasser Muthana – appeared in an ISIS propaganda video from Syria. Both were known to have worshipped at al-Manar. Journalist Andrew Gilligan has suggested that at least six British members of ISIS, including Nasser's younger brother Assel, had prayed at al-Manar. The mosque has vehemently denied any role in their radicalisation and insists they were influenced online. Indeed, in the past decade al-Manar has hosted a number of problematic clerics including Saudi-trained Haitham al-Haddad, who has previously endorsed anti-Semitic views; Saleem Chagtai, who has spoken about the superiority of Muslims over all other people; and Muhammad Mustafa al-Muqri, a former leader of Egyptian Islamic Jihad, a group that has been linked to al-Qaeda. The father of the Muthana brothers, who worships at the mosque I visited earlier, has said that the boys were radicalised neither at al-Manar nor online but by organised networks of Muslim extremists in Cardiff who leafleted its Muslim communities and organised support for the Islamic State.

Struck by the mosque's constant denial of its links to extremism, I take a look at the main bookshelf inside the prayer hall, where there is a wide array of books. In English there are several books by Sayyid Qutb, a major influence on the thinking of Osama bin Laden and al-Qaeda. Qutb, an Egyptian religious theorist, wrote many of his works in prison and was hanged in 1966 for plotting to overthrow Nasser's reformist government. His seminal work, *Milestones*, sets out a radical Islamist worldview and advocates for violent jihad against anyone he deems un-Islamic. The literalist, multi-volume *In the Shade of the Quran* sets out his ideal of a scripturally based society and system of government.

I also spot *The Fundamentals of Tawheed* by Bilal Philips. I was given this book when I was studying for my A levels. Many of my fellow students were influenced by its message; for a while I was, too. A Caribbean convert shaped by the writings of Mohammed Qutb (Sayyid Qutb's radical brother and another inspiration to Osama bin Laden), Philips was a student at the University of Wales in the early 1990s. He has written on the role of women in Muslim marriages, stating that a woman is scripturally 'obliged' to have relations with her husband whenever he desires it, thus denying the possibility of marital rape. He has also justified suicide bombing and homophobic attitudes within Islam. Today he is banned from entering the United Kingdom and a host of other Western countries because of his Salafi, anti-West extremism. What is his book doing here?

In *The Fundamentals*, Philips calls for the implementation of sharia law in predominantly Muslim countries, arguing against 'imported' Western law systems and claiming that Muslims who accept secular law are undertaking acts of *kufr* (unbelief). He also denounces Sufi mysticism (and by extension the Barelwis) as a heretical and polytheistic practice of satanic rather than divine inspiration. Later chapters of the book focus on the worship of graves and saints and represent a direct attack on almost every Muslim who visits shrines or mosques that have tombs within them. This is why Salafis cannot pray at mainstream mosques with Sufis and others: they gather separately, within their own sect, to avoid the perceived heresies and innovations of mainstream Islam – another way in which caliphism raises its head in our communities.

The presence of these books suggests an explanation for the links between the ISIS bombers and this mosque and others like it across the country. They would not have felt able to pray with the *pirs* of Bradford or the Sufis from Yemen, because the majority of mainstream Muslims venerate saints. It is only in literalist, Salafi mosques that such extremists would have found comfort and solace in being accepted as fellow Salafis.

By the shoe shelves in the entrance area, where I put my shoes back on to leave the mosque, there is a television screen advertising classes and events. As I tie my shoelaces, I see the following:

Ladies Study Circle – Every Wednesday, 1.30 p.m.

Girls Halaqa/Study in English (10 years and older) – Every Friday, 7.00–9.00 p.m.

Youth Camp 2019 – 28, 29 August 2019 with Imam Ahmed Ali and Naveed al-Rahman

Share Islam: Invite them to a one-to-one session at al-Manar

Classes for New Muslim Sisters, every Tuesday 6 p.m.

Nearby, there are advertisements on noticeboards for learning Arabic and studying the Quran.

Outside, a woman in niqab wearing all-black loose robes and Nike trainers is undoing the padlock for her bike. She wears glasses, which somehow stand out and look rather strange over her niqab; I guess that she is a student.

'*Salam alaikum*, sister,' I say, remembering the spirit of Socrates.

'*Alaikum as-salam*, brother,' she replies. She's squinting slightly – is she smiling beneath her veil?

'May I ask you a question, please? I'm from London, and you're the first person in Wales I have seen wearing a niqab. And …'

'Oh, no, brother,' she says, before I can even complete my question. 'There are lots of us. I'm from Malaysia. Here in Wales, I discovered true Islam and I started to practise.

'The Prophet's wives covered their faces and it's the highest form of Islam to cover everything,' she explains in a warm, punctuated Malaysian accent. 'Except in front of my family, of course.'

'What are you studying?' I ask.

'Architecture,' she tells me.

I want to ask her: what of beauty, aesthetics and art? How can she contemplate such ideas when she is invisible, hidden beneath her niqab?

'That's interesting,' I say instead as she gets on her bicycle.

'We have a gathering for the brothers every Thursday,' she tells me. 'Will you be in Cardiff again soon?'

Once again, the activism and *da'wa*, proselytising, begin almost immediately.

'I'm not sure,' I say. 'But I'll keep it in mind.'

We exchange smiles before she rides away; at least I think she may have smiled under her niqab.

Crossing over to the nearby high street, Salisbury Road, I see a representative of the al-Manar mosque conducting *da'wa*, proselytising, on the pavement. He's distributing leaflets to passers-by, conversing with those who stop, being ignored by others. As I approach, he asks me if am a believer in God.

'Yes,' I tell him.

'That's great,' he says. 'That is ninety-nine per cent of religion, of everything. You are a believer. Where are you from?'

'London,' I say. 'And you?'

'Libya,' he says, but he clearly wants to go back to discussing Islam. 'They say we're terrorists, but here is material you should read about Islam as a religion of peace.' He holds up some brochures.

'What's that?' I ask. I've noticed something – a small device – on his lapel.

'It's a camera,' he explains. 'Sometimes I get insulted here.'

'That's terrible,' I say. 'So why do you stand here and preach?'

'Because I get rewarded by God.'

'So you think God is an accountant who tracks your deeds?'

'No, God isn't an accountant, but he wants me to do this,' he says. 'They say we are bad neighbours.' He hands me one of his leaflets called *What Prophet Muhammad said about Neighbours*. I tell him that won't be necessary, but he insists I take it.

Throughout our conversation, he starts almost every sentence with 'they say we are …'. There's an obsession with how the media perceive activist Muslims and their form of Islam, and a desire to correct their negative image.

The brochure he forces on me is published by the Muslim Council of Britain. This group has previously refused to attend Holocaust remembrance ceremonies, on the grounds of Israeli human rights abuses against Palestinians, and successive British governments have refused to engage with the group due to its ideological leanings. The first page of the booklet quotes the Quran and claims that 'it is obligatory for all believers to obey the Prophet's commands and rules', while the text describes how true believers should not harm but support their neighbours, whether they are Christian, Jewish or Hindu. It is full of cartoon illustrations. Where women are depicted, they are wearing headscarves and full body coverings.

* * *

Imam Zain has read my book *The House of Islam* and asked to meet me via a mutual friend in London. In his youth he was the shaikh's star pupil at a large seminary, one of the Darul Ulooms in the north of England. He later became an imam at a mosque in Newport. We meet at an Indian café not far from Salisbury Road. We make small talk at first, and I mention the Qutb and Philips books that I've just seen at the al-Manar mosque. He tells me it is 'shameful and intolerable' that such ideas are on display.

'We should ban these books,' he says. 'Our youth only read these fascists on politics and *aqeedah* [creed], but forget we have others on politics and doctrine from the first centuries of Islam. Why is the mosque not stocking al-Farabi on politics? He was a translator of Plato. Did you know that?' he asks me.

'Yes,' I say, 'his book *On the Perfect State* was an early Muslim translation and commentary on Greek writings.' It's exciting to meet someone interested in the philosophy of the medieval Muslim thinkers who were influenced by the ancient Greeks. I want to ask him why today's Muslims cut out that connection to Greek philosophy.

As tea and samosas arrive, he strokes his grey beard. He is in his late forties but looks much older; the frown deeply engraved on his face gives him a permanent look of concerned misery.

'The clerics and community leaders always defend and make excuses for these ideas being so common, while the rest of Britain looks on in silence. But for how much longer will it be like that?' he asks.

'Freedom of speech?' I suggest.

'You're missing the point,' he tells me.

'What do you mean?'

He remains cryptic.

After parting ways with the imam, I walk along Miskin Street. I take a turn on to a narrow side street, Ruthin Gardens, for some quiet, wondering what I can do to help him. There's a black Audi parked under a tree, with blacked-out windows. It's a hot day, so the front windows are slightly open, and I hear Indian music coming through the car's speakers. As I pass, I notice there's a couple in the back. I see an Asian woman in a knee-length skirt, but her face isn't visible – she's pulled a blanket or chador over it in reaction to my passing by. There's a man beside her, but he's brought his body forward into the brace position in order to hide his face. Clearly they came here to be alone. My presence has again triggered that common Asian and Muslim emotion from the East: shame.

The city centre has Gay Pride flags flying everywhere, and young white couples kiss and embrace openly in this area that has so many university students, yet here is an Asian couple feeling shame at being seen together, seen by a fellow Asian. The car, the dark windows, the alleyway, the covering of faces, all point back to shame.

On my Uber ride back to the station, Alan is the first white British driver I have had in all my travels. He tells me he has been in Cardiff since 1981 and came down from Manchester. He's very friendly and laughs as two Gulf tourists shout loudly at each other across the road just outside Cardiff Castle.

'Does that offend you?' I ask. 'The shouting, the noise pollution?'

'Not really,' he says cheerfully. 'We're used to it in the city centre. They're tourists, and we need them! We're the third fastest growing city in Europe, and the tourists help us.'

'This is a very mixed city,' I remark.

'Oh, yes,' he says. 'I definitely couldn't do this job if I was a racist. I have all sorts in the car. The Chinese seem to be here in large numbers these days. We all rub along just fine.'

So if the Welsh capital, Cardiff, is expanding, and people here coexist – or think they do – I wonder if the same is true of Belfast, another British national capital? Has that city, with its centuries of religious and social division, got any closer to healing itself and finding peace? And how does it treat its Muslims?

7

Belfast

The short walk from the tarmac to the grey carpet of George Best City Airport is the first of many walks in Belfast. The grey metal ceiling, and beyond it the grey sky, come as a shock only an hour and twenty minutes from London, where the weather was warmer and sunnier. In less than a minute I have reached the airport's main entrance. On my right are the only two shops in the entire central concourse: Costa Coffee and WHSmith; to my left, a sign beside a door indicates a 'multi-faith quiet room'; in front of me, there is a plethora of budget car hire kiosks.

I enter the 'quiet room'. A blond, spotty young man in chinos and a woolly jumper is sitting on a chair, head down, hands clasping his Bible, clearly in prayer.

He looks up to see me and I apologise for the interruption. It is a tiny room. A small cabinet holds prayer mats for Muslims, a Quran, several Bibles and some copies of the Bhagavad Gita.

Heading outside again, I see the taxi rank here is all white, all male. My Uber driver Aiden Richards arrives, a Northern Irishman with a thick accent. During our drive to Belfast Islamic Centre, the city's main mosque, I have to ask him to repeat everything so I can understand what he's saying.

Countless billboards and signs advertise Tayto, 'Northern Ireland's No. 1 crisp brand'.

We drive past an IKEA neighbouring the airport compound. Within moments of being on the main road, I notice three flags flying everywhere. In Cardiff it was the Union Jack, the Welsh flag and the rainbow Gay Pride flag. In this part of Belfast, at least, it is the Union Jack, the Scottish Saltire and a strange flag I have never seen before. But why the Scottish flag? I will come to understand this later.

'What's the purple flag?' I ask Aiden.

He grins, then looks at me in the rear-view mirror.

'The UVF,' he says.

'I don't understand,' I say, thinking I heard him say 'IVF', for 'in vitro fertilisation'.

'The Ulster Volunteer Force,' he says, pronouncing his 'r's heavily.

'God, yes, of course,' I say. 'But they're an outlawed organisation, terrorists, aren't they? How can they be flying their flag so prominently, so openly, on the main road right by the airport?'

'Welcome to Northern Ireland.'

I continue to see the three flags displayed for more than a mile along the road.

'What would happen if there were al-Qaeda or ISIS or Hezbollah flags flying here?' I ask, probably unwisely.

'The UVF would kill them,' Aiden says, with complete certainty. 'Don't get me wrong,' he goes on. 'The UVF started as a volunteer force for the First World War. That was great. They were a different breed of men.' He stops for a moment, reflecting.

'They were real men,' he asserts. 'Today the UVF is full of criminal thugs. They're trying to start the conflict again and take us back to the Troubles.'

The UVF represented one side in Northern Ireland's 'Troubles', a period of conflict that lasted from the 1960s until the Good Friday Agreement of 1998. Alongside other loyalist paramilitary groups, the UVF was involved in the events of that period in opposition to Irish republicanism and in favour of Northern Ireland staying with the British. The loyalist movement proved equally as violent as its opponents, the IRA and other Irish nationalist and republican groups.

Belfast feels quiet, yet the air is charged with history. I feel much more of a stranger in Belfast than in any other part of the UK. Historical sensitivities and allegiances are still alive here, and Protestant–Catholic sectarianism is more than academic. The grey skies, the brown brick buildings and the many, many churches conceal communities and feelings that remain as deep and dangerous as in times past.

The ethno-religious tensions in Northern Ireland have a history spanning nearly four centuries. The original Ulster settlements of the seventeenth century were largely made up of Protestants and Presbyterians from England and Scotland. The Ulster Presbyterian Scots had been the victims of a massacre by Irish Catholics as far back as 1641 and were known for their religious fundamentalism, influenced by John Knox (d. 1572), the Scottish fire-and-brimstone preacher. Hostility between the Ulster Scots and both Irish Catholics and Anglicans representing the English government remained for centuries. For Knox and his later followers, the congregation of believers was a central focus of life: dispensing legal judgements, setting harsh and violent punishments for dissent, organising charity work and festivals.[1] Knox's literalism forbade dancing, music, acting, gambling, and sex on the Sabbath. The parallels with today's hard-line Islamism are hard to avoid.

As we keep driving, Aiden points out the redbrick St George's Market and informs me that it is the oldest market in Belfast, dating back to the 1890s. Then we drive past the neo-Gothic brick main buildings of Queen's University, formally opened in 1849, whose central tower mirrors that of Magdalen College, Oxford. It is noticeable that here, unlike in Bradford or in Dewsbury, there are no minarets or domes dominating my view of the city.

Belfast is surrounded by green hills. Yet despite its natural beauty, and the fact that its neighbours Ireland and Britain are free democracies with full marriage and abortion rights, Northern Ireland retains some ugly attitudes, the legacy of deep historical divisions. Despite the peace agreement reached in 1998, old hatreds are still very much alive, and although the violence is largely over, divisions in Belfast must still be clearly felt if the UVF flag is flying high on a main thoroughfare.

Fear of Muslims in Belfast, as manifested in the 300-plus hate crimes against them reported in the past five years, is thus part of an established and much wider narrative. If religious extremists here are still holding on to their theological and historical differences, what, I wonder, can I expect of Belfast's Muslims, let alone those in places like Bradford where there has been societal prejudice and rioting?

* * *

I am now walking along Wellington Park, a leafy, largely residential street in South Belfast. I am looking for a mosque at number 38, but I walk past it until a red flag outside a more traditional-looking brick office building catches my eye. The Northern Ireland Public Service Alliance (NIPSA) building is just next to the mosque and flies a communist flag outside it, yet the mosque has no signage at all. The NIPSA building's boardroom at the front is full; I can see a group of white men gathered around a table just inside.

Turning back, I find the mosque, a double-fronted, two-storey townhouse painted a light grey. I knock on the door to its office.

'*Salam alaikum,*' Grace says. 'Great to see you again!' I have met Grace before at book-signing events in Scotland.

'This is Mumina, she basically runs the mosque,' she tells me, as another woman steps out from behind a desk. Both women come over without hesitation to shake my hand in turn.

Grace is a white convert to Islam, and Mumina's family came to Belfast from Pakistan. They sit opposite me at a table in the office, offer me chocolate, and engage in conversation without embarrassment, not lowering their gaze as they speak with me. With these two, there's no need for partitions on account of our different genders. They are both wearing colourful clothes and headscarves, and are fully confident, speaking with booming voices.

'Can I just say that this is the first mosque I've seen anywhere in Britain where women are out there in front?' I say exuberantly.

'No way!' they say together.

'You'll see,' says Grace, 'Mumina really does run the mosque.'

Mumina, in her thirties, laughs loudly and freely in response.

'This space is too small for us,' says Mumina. 'We have people praying in the kitchen and on the steps and down the corridors. We have two Friday prayer gatherings here, and we hope to be moving soon to a new mosque building that we're hoping to purchase.'

'How's the fundraising going?' I ask.

'We're struggling, but coping. Our congregation is very generous!'

'You should go to Bradford,' I say. 'The mosques there are luxurious, full of marble and huge chandeliers.'

We laugh. 'But in all seriousness, we have tried to raise funds over in England, but the Muslims there always ask us if we are Barelwi, Deobandi, Salafi or from the Islamic movement [polite reference to Islamists].'

Again, Mumina laughs freely at the recollection.

'We're a mixed bunch here, and we try to hold everyone together rather than fight on sectarian grounds. And so because we can't answer their questions, we can't tap into the wealth of Muslims in England.'

Curious, I ask, 'And by the way, what made you become a Muslim?'

'I'm not the only one. There are several of us. I converted because I was studying Arabic and theology, and Islam made sense to me,' she explains. We then discuss hostility to Islam in Northern Ireland. She mentions a Pastor McConnell.

I have heard of the Christian fundamentalist James McConnell before. In 2014 he caused uproar by preaching that Islam was a 'satanic' religion spawned in hell. The Unionist First Minister of Northern Ireland, Peter Robinson, originally defended McConnell's views but later came to the Islamic Centre to apologise and smooth relations with the Muslim community.

'McConnell often said that Muslims can't be trusted, and that feeling's quite widespread here,' Mumina continues.

'That must be related to the Shi'a concept of *taqiyya*, denying your faith in response to persecution, right? But you're Sunni Muslims?' I verify.

'Yes, but they don't know that we don't believe in *taqiyya*. Somehow the trust between us is broken and there's always doubt.'

'Why do Christians feel so threatened and horrified by Islam? There's such a small Muslim community here, something like half of one per cent of the population, right?' I ask.

'Yes, but these are very sheltered communities that have been Baptist for four or five generations. But luckily I didn't face any threats to my life. Others have been targeted and threatened for converting to Islam. It's also a class issue here. Loyalists and paramilitaries can often be working class, so the violence is a reflection of that. My father was an engineer and we had an educated, middle-class home.'

'But what does that working-class paramilitary culture mean for Muslims?'

'Well, we've had people who've been forced at gunpoint to leave their homes, held up on the streets, where a paramilitary has thought the person no longer belonged in the community. We've had people whose cars have been shot at. We've had people whose homes have been firebombed.'

'Just for converting to Islam?'

'For converting or being married to a Muslim. For a lot of people, it's almost like the American South here – being in an interracial relationship, or mixed race, is seen as being a race traitor. "Islam is against us white Christians." As a convert, you're against your own people.'

'But in Northern Ireland why is Islam against anyone?' I ask. 'In Bradford, where there's so much social and religious division, I get it, but why here?'

'One hundred per cent of our terrorism problem originates with white Irish people. Just this year a couple in Ballymena were arrested for possessing an arsenal of weapons. Bombs. Guns. All this because they were inspired by a sermon about the end times.'

'The end times!' I am aghast. 'How is that any different from ISIS taking the town of Dabiq because of seventh-century references to the end times and Armageddon?'

'They genuinely believe that one world religion is coming. Interfaith work is the work of the devil. Muslims worship Satan. In Ballymena, there's a church building a whole village on the premises of the Wrightbus company, that makes the London red buses. Very wealthy, outwardly modern, but their view of the UK is stuck in Victorian England,' Grace explains.

'So what about LGBT rights?'

'Oh no, no, no,' she says firmly. 'You know gay marriage is still illegal here? At least until next year.'

Mumina interrupts to say happily, 'This year Belfast had its largest Pride festival,' but then her face falls as she remembers: 'There were protests, too.'

'They keep emailing us, the Christians, to ask if we can join their protests against the "normalisation" of homosexuality. We've had about seven emails. And the same with abortion, if we can join their protests against legal abortions. But as you know, Islam's view of abortion is much more liberal and oriented towards individual choice. I did write back and explain this to them,' she recalls.

'People were literally being forced to travel to England to have abortions. They couldn't legally terminate their pregnancies in Northern Ireland. There was a case of a woman conceiving because of rape, and a policeman had to accompany the victim. It was a thirteen-year-old child, actually. The police had to take the child to England for legal reasons.'

'Where are you here in the mosque on LGBT rights?' I ask.

'We don't have a particular position, do we?' Grace says, looking at Mumina.

'So what if someone gay walks into the mosque?' I ask, keen to test the tolerance of this apparently moderate institution.

'I know we have gay Muslims here. We've had transgender people come on open days, too, and we treat them just like everyone else. We have sisters who are lesbian coming during Ramadan. Islam has a don't-ask, don't-tell attitude, and so do we.'

'So don't men here complain that you women run the mosque? This is very novel!' I say.

'No,' beams Mumina. 'They like it, and they're used to it now.'

'If anyone complains, it's usually the convert women,' says Grace. 'They sometimes convert abroad and come back with a more hard-line Salafi approach.'

'Why would a convert woman complain about you running the mosque?!'

'Because we might steal their husbands!' Both women roar with laughter again. The mosque door is open, and men are slowly gathering for prayers, but this doesn't stop these women having the freedom to think and form their own judgements. Throughout our entire conversation, no cleric or male community leader has interrupted to give me the official community line.

Now a man in a suit enters the room. He is clean-shaven and probably in his fifties. The women cheerfully say '*salam alaikum*' to him and offer him a chair. Mumina introduces him to me as the treasurer of the mosque.

'How are things on the mainland?' he asks.

I explain that this is the first mosque in the many I have been to where I've been met and welcomed by women.

'This is normal for us,' he says, as another man comes in and asks Grace and Mumina for the keys to a particular room. 'They are the bosses here!'

Grace offers me a tour of the building. She takes me first to the women's room, opening the door and leading me inside. I have never been in the women's section of a mosque when prayers are being said. Several women are praying; some are reading the Quran. One looks up and smiles politely. Then Grace walks into the other two rooms, where there are men seated on the floor praying or reciting. No one seems in the least bit troubled as we walk around freely.

She leads me up the stairs to the imam's office.

Shaikh Mustaqbil is young, or at least looks younger than his years, because he has been here for almost fifteen years. Previously he was the imam of the central mosque in England, Regent's Park. It turns out we have friends in common and much to talk about.

The shaikh is wearing trousers and a shirt, not Arab or other ethnic clothing, not even a skullcap. He tells me about the English classes on offer at the mosque for congregants who are new to Northern Ireland.

'No other mosque I have visited has these facilities,' I tell him.

Someone overhearing us says, 'In England you don't need English, you need Urdu! But we want to be part of society, not separate from it.'

'We've had eight of our youth get their Duke of Edinburgh awards through the mosque,' Grace adds proudly.

'Tell me something,' I say. 'In England, most Muslims will have two marriage ceremonies. One at the mosque for religious blessings and another …'

'No,' interrupts the shaikh, before I can complete my sentence. 'I am a marriage registrar, too. I'm registered with the local authorities here so that when I conduct a *nikah* [Islamic marriage ceremony], it's a legally documented marriage.'

This is an important issue within Muslim communities in the UK. Many mosques that conduct the *nikah* ceremony under the auspices of sharia experts don't submit such marriages for registration under British law. This places women at risk in a number of ways: their husbands can divorce them unilaterally, leaving them without recourse to legal protection in terms of financial support and custody of their children. It is a mark of a progressive, socially integrated mosque to understand this issue and make provision for British law to be accommodated within the mosque ceremonies. In contrast with the sharia courts and conversations I had in Blackburn and Bradford, here in Belfast I'm finding greater awareness of the benefits of not operating a separate legal jurisdiction in which social separatism can breed.

'We have forty-two different nationalities represented here,' says another worshipper passing by the office and overhearing the conversation. 'We can't accommodate so many different cultures, so instead we unite around the country and the culture here in Belfast. Please stay – we'll be talking about racism after the prayers.'

I learn that after the usual Friday gathering today there is going to be a meeting to discuss the rise of Britain First and racism against

Muslim communities in Northern Ireland. I ask Grace if I can join
in. She readily agrees.

As we mill about in the mosque corridors, women and men
together, the call to prayer goes off and we make our way into the
prayer rooms. Shaikh Mustaqbil won't lead the prayers today, as he
likes to encourage others who are qualified to come forward. There
seems to be a strategy here to stick together, while opening up
challenges and debates within the mosque, rather than following
the Bradford model of having several mosques on the same road to
cater for a spectrum of sectarian positions.

Shaikh Ahmed is the imam today, another imam with no head
cover, no ethnic clothing, but wearing chinos and a white shirt,
which is untucked. He stands up, puts on a light cotton *thawb*
and starts his sermon in Arabic. I wonder why more imams cannot
dress like this. Imams in Syria, Egypt and Turkey all adapt to the
modern world in this way.

Still, I can tell he is a Salafi from the very start of his preaching
by the aggression in his voice and his continual citations of *hadith*
literature. He is clearly the mellowest of Salafis, though, as I saw
him interacting without rancour with the women in the corridor
earlier. I was told by Mumina earlier that he spent five years
studying in Saudi Arabia, and I have yet to meet anybody who
has studied there as a foreigner and not been influenced by the
Salafi literalist approach, applying quotes from *hadith* and history
without understanding the context of the age in which we live.

He follows the same formula as the preacher at the IslamBradford
mosque I visited, warning the congregation against innovations
(*bid'ah*) within Islam, and arguing that all 'new matters' that are
included in the religion by other sects belong in hellfire. This
literalism reflects a Salafi belief that in AD 622, when the Prophet
Mohamed started preaching, he began with the statement,
preserved in a *hadith*, that 'every innovated matter is a deviation,
and every deviation leads to hell'.

Shaikh Ahmed starts with quoting this *hadith*, too, and then
tells us that he will address the importance of dreams in Islam.

'What is the importance of dreams from an Islamic perspective?' he begins in his own words. 'Dreams are important in Islam. Allah talks in the Quran about the Prophet Yusuf [Joseph], saying "and thus the Lord will choose you and teach you the interpretations of dreams and complete his favour upon you and the family of Jacob as completed upon your fathers before, Abraham and Isaac. Indeed, your Lord is knowing and wise." '

True to his Salafi leanings, the imam goes on and on citing one *hadith* after another on the topic of dreams:

'The dream of a Muslim is one of the forty-six portions of prophecy,' he cites.

'The Prophet never had a dream that did not come true as bright as day,' he quotes.

'Those who are the most truthful when they speak are more likely to have dreams that are also truthful,' he references.

'It was narrated by the Persian scholar Al-Tirmidhi, in his ninth-century collection of *hadith*, that the Prophet said dreams are of three types: the righteous dream that is good news from Allah; dreams in which Satan frightens someone; and dreams about something that will happen to the dreamer himself,' he recalls.

Then he comments on the interpretation of that alleged saying of the Prophet.

'This *hadith* is evidence that not all that is seen in a dream is good or right. For example, if someone sees in a dream something that scares or shocks them, what we these days commonly refer to as nightmares, these are from Satan in an attempt to bring sadness and despair to the believer.

'The other types of dream are mundane dreams, which people see as a reflection of their day-to-day routines.

'It was narrated by al-Bukhari on the authority of Jabir[2] that the Prophet said: "If anyone sees a dream that he does not like, he should spit on his left side three times."

'Now, when I say "spit", I mean very, very slowly,' he comments. 'Don't go and spit by your wife so she wakes up and asks, "why did you spit on me?" and you say, "Shaikh Ahmed told me to do so". Don't get me into trouble.

'Don't tell your dreams to everybody, because their interpretations can be wrong and then your actions will be misguided,' he advises.

As the imam continues to speak about dreams, a child beside me plays with a pound coin and waves to other children near the staircase. The congregation here is a mixed one, with many nationalities represented. With the exception of two men in Arab attire, every one of the 500 or so Muslims present in the mosque is dressed in Western clothing. The covered soles of the man praying prostrate in front of me have the words 'Tommy Hilfiger' emblazoned on them, prompting me to look around to see how he compares with other worshippers. Almost all of them are wearing socks, I notice. This suggests they wear closed, Western shoes rather than the sandals of the Arab world and Muslim East, thus telling me something about their cultural attitudes.

The imam then brings the sermon to a close as he prepares us to pray.

'O Allah, dignify Islam and Muslims, humiliate polytheism and the polytheists,' he repeats three times.

As the prayers end and people make their final prostrations and bows, Shaikh Mustaqbil takes the microphone and reminds everybody, first in English and then in Arabic, about the English classes being held at the mosque. He also reminds people to stay behind for the event at 2.30 p.m. on combating racism and anti-Muslim hatred.

The second prayer commences, and the same sermon is delivered again. This time the imam records himself with a video camera that he sets up in the hall. The mosque is too small for the Muslims of Belfast, and rather than build more mosques they are praying twice in the same mosque.

After the second ceremony ends at 2.30 p.m., several of the women enter the main hall on the upstairs level. The men set up a table and bring chairs into the hall. Mosque committee members and congregants are joined by a handful of non-Muslim men and women from the local council, police force and local human rights organisations. Food, including cakes, is being sold, and those joining the meeting from elsewhere come in eating the food they have purchased outside. All have removed their shoes, and the women's hair is uncovered. Nobody from the mosque insists that non-Muslim visitors must cover their hair, which is rare among British mosques. The women from the mosque sit at the front. Again, this is an unheard-of occurrence in most mosques. In total there are about a hundred in attendance, and men and women mingle freely, sitting beside one another.

There is a widespread sense that Muslims are under siege in Northern Ireland. Grace is joined by Fatima, another woman in the mosque, and they present the facts: Muslims have been in Ireland since the 1950s, through immigration. Three hundred and twenty hate crime attacks against Muslims have been reported in Belfast in the past five years, but this is a gross under-representation because many victims do not go to the police (for various reasons, not least that many do not speak English). Unlike in England, Grace had explained earlier, there is no official hate crime offence in Northern Ireland. Britain First have demanded that no more mosques be built in Northern Ireland. Recently, graffiti has appeared outside Muslim homes and centres saying, 'Muslims Out'.

Under the British government's Vulnerable Persons Resettlement Scheme, around 1,500 Syrian asylum seekers have been resettled in Northern Ireland since December 2015, but no new mosques have been built to accommodate this addition to the local Muslim community of four or five thousand, a 40 per cent increase.

Grace talks of her personal experiences of being hounded by men in a supermarket for wearing a headscarf, where nobody came to her rescue; the fear of fleeing to her car, jeered at by men calling her 'bandage head' and other names.

Fatima then stands up and reminds the audience that Northern Ireland is 99 per cent white. She has very dark skin and wears a headscarf, making her trebly different from the white men at her university or on the bus: she's female, dark-skinned and visibly Muslim, all of which makes her life difficult. During her undergraduate course at Queen's University Belfast she was insulted by her lecturers. In classes unrelated to Islam, while she sat in their classes, her psychology lecturers disparaged Muslim women who wore headscarves.

In front of local councillors and representatives from the PSNI, the Police Service of Northern Ireland, Grace and Fatima ask if other members of the audience have had similar experiences, and if they were reported. Everybody has a story, it seems, but very few went to the police. Grace asks if making the mosque a place for reporting hate crimes would make it easier or less shameful.

One woman, a white convert, tells us about her 'mixed-race' son having been attacked so often by groups of other boys that he now wants to carry a weapon to defend himself. He is alone and scared at home, and the trauma risks making him turn violent.

Another man asks for that to be translated into Arabic so that he is sure everyone understands. He then talks about being spat at on the bus, but says other people came to his defence, so there are good people out there, and we just need to win others over by creating awareness campaigns.

A secondary school pupil talks, when prompted, about having fun poked at him, but says his bullies changed their behaviour when he engaged with the other boys.

The imam comes in at one point and asks the women who are running the session if he can do anything to help. They ask him to arrange for tea and see if the projector can be fixed. The imam makes calls for a handyman to come and help; the women are still firmly in control.

Another man asks the PSNI representative, 'If someone is going to attack me, can I take shelter in a café or shop? Is that allowed?' The PSNI spokesperson reassures him that, yes, he can ask for help from people or shops nearby.

Fatima asserts firmly that 'we should always stand with the victim, Muslim or not'.

A range of media headlines and news images are shown to the group on the projector:

Eight men wearing the white robes and conical hats of the Ku Klux Klan and holding wooden crosses protest outside a mosque in County Down at Halloween in 2018.

A severed pig's head is left outside the same mosque a year earlier.

Pastor McConnell is found not guilty by the courts of 'grossly offensive' remarks against Muslims.

Protestant and loyalist politician Ian Paisley retweets a post against Muslims originally written by the journalist Katie Hopkins.

Hatred and hostility is shown towards Syrians and Somalis across Belfast with home attacks and insults.

A city centre statue is covered with a headscarf in 'Ban the Burqa' campaign by far-right group Generation Identity in 2018.

Britain First is targeting Northern Ireland and has opened offices, circa 2017.

Syrian and Somali asylum seekers who have not been granted settled status now depend on charity and food banks for survival.

Syrian refugees appear in the media conversations again and again, but none are in the room today.

Three things strikingly absent from the Northern Irish media are any mention of Muslim terrorism; the Irish backstop conversation that is currently swirling around Westminster; and the presence of politicians from the DUP (Democratic Unionist Party) or Sinn Fein.

* * *

The Northern Irish identity crisis is best encapsulated by the 'peace walls' of Belfast and other Northern Irish towns. Covering dozens of miles, they were originally constructed during the Troubles as barriers between nationalist and unionist neighbourhoods. Even today, the gates that perforate the walls are only opened during the day, with most shutting at 5.30 or 6 p.m. They are decorated with political murals on both sides, reflecting divisions that even now reflect loyalist and republican themes.

I ask a taxi driver, Oliver, to show me one of the peace walls, which has now become a tourist attraction.

Every Muslim I have met here seems to be inclined towards identifying with Great Britain: none has expressed a desire to be united with the Republic of Ireland. This might lead one to assume, therefore, that Northern Irish Muslims would be allies of the unionists and loyalists, the supporters of the British. But it is paradoxically among the loyalist paramilitaries and evangelical Protestants that Muslims feel most threatened, as I realised in my discussions with Grace and Mumina at the mosque earlier.

As we approach the wall I say to Oliver, perhaps unwisely, 'So we protest the war between Palestinians and Israel, and oppose Donald Trump's wall with Mexico, but here, in our own country, we have a wall between communities.'

He is silent for a moment. Then he says, 'This wall keeps us alive and safe. I'm sure Trump wants Americans to be safe from the Mexicans.'

On my right is a mural with the Palestinian flag on one side and the Irish flag on the other that reads 'Free All Political Prisoners. End Internment. End Administrative Detention'.

Another mural says 'Palestine, 1917–Today', with smaller writing underneath proclaiming, 'It's time the Irish government show some humanity and act for the Palestinian people!'

Oliver doesn't look at the wall, or at me, but keeps his eyes firmly on the road.

'They would kill me if I was here after 9 p.m.,' he tells me. 'This is not my side.'

Next is a mural of a man in a blanket with his fist raised, a reference to the republican prisoners' 1976 blanket protest and subsequent hunger strike.

Oliver takes me to some black marble monuments further down the wall next to an Irish flag. Beside them has been daubed praise for the Irish Republican Army (IRA), those who died fighting 'on behalf of the residents of the Falls Road', and the second battalion of the IRA 'who made the supreme sacrifice in their quest for Irish freedom'. In one of the most infamous events of the Troubles, the British Army blockaded thousands of homes in the Falls Road area, then a bastion of IRA nationalism. IRA reprisals against the British led to the deployment of tear gas and the deaths of four civilians, with nearly eighty wounded. The 'Falls Curfew', as it is now known, ended after three days when women and children marched in with supplies for those within the blockade.

There is Gaelic writing, too, and fresh flowers laid beside the monument.

I spot a Sinn Fein office nearby, with words in Gaelic across its walls: *Tech Mich Giolla Bhuidhe*.

Above a small terraced house, I notice a black commemorative plaque that reads:

IN MEMORY OF I.R.A. VOLUNTEERS

GERARD CROSSAN   TOM McCANN

TONY LEWIS   JOHN JOHNSTON

WHO DIED WHILE ON ACTIVE SERVICE

ON THE 9th MARCH 1972 AT 32 CLONARD ST.

ERECTED BY THE GREATER CLONARD EX-PRISONERS ASSOCIATION

The men died in a premature bomb explosion, a result of IRA weapons stockpiling during the Troubles.

A few moments later I spot a Kashmir Road, presumably named in solidarity with Kashmir. In a cul-de-sac, Oliver shows me a vast mural that reads 'BOMBAY STREET NEVER AGAIN!'. It is dedicated to the memory of Gerald McAuley.

I learn that in 1969 a loyalist mob had caused over 1,000 people to lose their homes when a massive fire was started in the Bombay Street area, which was largely settled by republicans. McAuley, a fifteen-year-old member of a youth nationalist group, was shot dead defending the area from the loyalists during the clashes.

Above another house, there is a plaque that reads: 'In loving memory of Volunteer TOM WILLIAMS C Company 2nd Battalion Belfast Brigade IRA who lived here and was executed in Belfast Gaol 2nd Sept 1942 aged 19 years'. Williams, also a resident of Bombay Street, was hanged for causing the death of a Royal Ulster Constabulary officer during the pre-Troubles clashes of the 1940s.

As if Belfast's commemoration of the Troubles, tying its hands to history, is not enough, there are further murals dedicated to events in Kashmir and Palestine. One depicts Palestinian and Catholic Irish prisoners shaking hands. I also see a mural that reads 'Freedom for Öcalan'. This Kurdish leader, a founding member of the Kurdistan Workers' Party, the PKK, is currently in jail in Turkey for his involvement with the group. Its armed conflict with the Turkish state has led to the deaths of over 40,000 people.

Then Oliver takes me to the other, 'Protestant', side of the wall, and suddenly he is talkative, keen to explain every mural and memorial.

One mural reads: 'The Battle of Britain – Band of Brothers – Winston Churchill – Love Demands Sacrifice – The Legend of 303 Polish Squadron. The Polish Nation – Part of Us Then – Part of Us Now'.

'So you love the Poles in Northern Ireland?' I ask.

'Yes, definitely. They're like us,' says Oliver.

'But they're mostly Catholic, right?'

'They're white,' he says by way of explanation.

If the Irish republicans who decorated the other side of the wall supported Palestine, the unionists are clearly with Israel. I spot Hebrew on various murals, with one saying 'We salute you' next to a quote from Prime Minister Netanyahu and a depiction of an Israeli Defence Forces soldier.

'Are you one of Kitchener's Own?' asks another mural, plastered with Union Jacks. Oliver's comment about the Irish affinity with the 'white' Poles still troubles me. The next murals are dedicated to the sacrifices made by India, Australia and South Africa.

'Look over there, Oliver. India and South Africa. Men in turbans.'

'Yes, and we were the empire, the rulers.'

And then it comes back to me that all this division is not just about events in the last decades of the twentieth century, but goes back long before.

A mural on a street corner depicts King William of Orange riding a horse on water, with the date 1690. This is a reference to the Battle of the Boyne, fought in the modern-day Republic, where England's

King James II was defeated by the Protestant forces of William of Orange, enabling William to secure the crown of England and Scotland and permitting the continuation of Protestant rule over Ireland. 'Orangemen' still march in Belfast each year to celebrate that history, that battle, that colour, that king, representing the Protestant-backed anti-republicanism promoted by the Ulster Volunteer Force.

As we head for the airport, I ask Oliver if he has been to London recently.

'Years ago, probably not since 1980.'

'How do you feel about this government in London now?' I ask.

'Theresa May and Boris Johnson are only there because of our support from the DUP. Northern Ireland is the power behind the throne.'

'Right,' I say. 'And what about the new chancellor, Sajid Javid? Or the home secretary, who's responsible for security around here, Priti Patel? Neither of them is white. Even Boris Johnson has Turkish ancestry. How do people around here feel about that?'

He doesn't answer. There's something deeply stubborn about Oliver, almost verging on denial of reality.

'We are loyal to Her Majesty the Queen,' he says, finally.

The atmosphere in the car is very tense. I want to ask him about Meghan Markle, and the possibility of a non-white monarch on the throne one day, but I don't want to cause any more antagonism.

'What do you do?' he asks me. 'Are you a journalist?'

'What makes you think I am a journalist?'

'Only journalists and American tourists ask so many questions,' he grumps.

I don't answer his question, or ask any more of my own. Now it is my turn to be silent.

The departure lounge at George Best City Airport has more food, drink and shopping options than the arrivals hall. Its vibrant cosmopolitanism and capitalism make me feel as if I'm back in the twenty-first century again. And the friendliness of the Scotsman who serves me at Starbucks sets me thinking ahead to my trip to Scotland next week.

8

Edinburgh and Glasgow

EDINBURGH

He comes up to me as I approach King's Cross station for my train north.

'Are you Muslim, brother?' he says, with a hint of a Scottish accent.

'Yes,' I reply, looking up at a man taller than me, with a rough beard and wearing sports clothes. He's Asian, a teenager or in his early twenties at most.

'Can you help me, please?' he asks, and stops, making firm eye contact for a moment. But he can't hold my gaze, which makes me suspicious.

'I'm a *hafiz* of the Quran,' he resumes. 'You can name me any *surah*, any chapter, and I can recite it for you if you don't believe me. I studied at Glasgow Central Mosque, brother. But I'm stuck in London and need to get back up to Scotland. Can you lend me £30?'

I walk on; he walks beside me. Being just yards away from the station, with its surrounding vagabonds and homeless beggars, makes me wonder if he's telling the truth or not. I'm about to ask him to recite a chapter when he says something that makes me change my mind.

'We Muslims have to help each other, brother. The *goras* will never help us.'

He keeps walking beside me as I pick up my pace. '*Gora*' is a pejorative word for a white person, and it irritates me when Asians are racist while complaining about racism incessantly themselves.

'Being racist won't get you far,' I tell him. 'Anyone here in London will help you if you're not racist and genuinely need help.' His words remind me of earlier conversations in Blackburn, Birmingham and Bradford about racism not being a one-way street.

'I'm not racist!' he protests, apparently sincere.

We reach the entrance to the station.

'You called people "*goras*" – that's racist,' I say, and head for the train departure boards.

My point is clearly lost on him. I feel a little guilty for not helping him, but I manage to lose him as I make my way across the station. I'm not sure what has annoyed me most about this young Scot: the begging, the abuse of religion or the racism.

* * *

'Oh, cows! There, look – sheep!' exclaim the elderly women sitting opposite me as we leave Berwick-upon-Tweed station and enter Scotland. The sea is a beautiful blue along the coast, with clear skies and the sun shining. On the other side of the aisle a man is reading a biography of Leonardo da Vinci. A frail man nearby takes a call from his health carer, Ayesha – a Muslim name. He's upbeat and reassures her that he will be home by the evening in time for their appointment.

Edinburgh's vast Waverley station, one of the largest in the country, has multiple exits to navigate. I'm aiming to find Old Calton Burial Ground, not far from the station, to pay my respects to David Hume (1711–76), the great Scottish philosopher who boldly questioned organised religion and the validity of miracles, and sought to think critically about the role of reason in our lives. I can't locate the cemetery in the end, so I take a taxi from the station to my hotel instead.

The station has several taxi stands at its numerous entrances. The drivers appear to come from a diverse range of ethnic backgrounds, not just Asian as in Bradford. An elderly French couple don't notice there's a queue and walk up to the first taxi; I'm happy to let them go, but the Scots behind me intervene and ensure that the unspoken rules of the queue are upheld.

Once in the taxi, I share my frustration at not finding the cemetery. 'David Hume!' exclaims my exuberant, elderly white Scottish driver. 'Great man! Great Scot! He fought for our independence from you people,' he jokes. I don't have the heart to argue that Hume was a direct product of the union between England and Scotland in 1707, and known for his conservative, monarchist politics. Hume thrived because the English tradition and institutions protected him from Calvinist zealots in Scotland.

'Aye, those were the days ...' my driver reminisces, as though he were still living in the past centuries that he recalls. 'Mary, Queen of Scots; Robert the Bruce; David Hume; all together before the English invasion ...' I can't concentrate on the rest of his recollections, as he has confused the historical timeline and forgotten that the Scots invaded England, too. In his version of history there's no mention of the strengths of the present arrangement.

The 1707 Acts of Union saw the kingdoms of Scotland and England united into one under the name of Great Britain. This followed the Union of the Crowns of the two countries under James I (of England) and VI (of Scotland) in 1603, after 300 years of intermittent warfare over Scottish independence.

'I guess you're an SNP man,' I say, not wishing to dispute his history or facts.

'Aye, through and through,' he says, rolling his 'r's strongly.

This hilly city centre, overlooked by Edinburgh Castle on its history-soaked mound, has been the setting for a thousand years of Scottish monarchy and its later fusion with the English crown. The main shopping thoroughfare, Princes Street, is lined with statues of great Scottish contributors to civilisation, at which I gaze with interest as we drive towards the Bonham Hotel. I spot Sir Walter Scott and a number of Scottish MPs from the Victorian era.

On my right are some of Britain's top retailers: Fraser Hart, Peter Jones, M&S, Waterstones and many more. We pass stone houses from the Georgian era. The medieval castle, Renaissance houses, and the neoclassical architecture of Edinburgh's New Town all contribute to the deep sense of civilisation with which the city seems imbued.

There has been a Muslim presence in Scotland since at least the early nineteenth century, when lascars – Arab and Indian seamen – worked the ports of the great industrial towns. Glasgow had become a major industrial centre and was referred to for a time as the 'Second City of the Empire' after London. The change in immigration laws post-1945 permitted settlement in Scotland as well as England, bringing as many as 4,000 Muslims to Scotland by the 1960s. Many of their descendants live in Scotland to this day, primarily in Edinburgh and Glasgow, where there has been a mosque since 1944. The first Scottish Muslim Justice of the Peace, Bashir Maan, was instated in Glasgow in 1968, and 1970 saw him elected as Britain's first Muslim councillor.

No major race riots have broken out here as in Cardiff or Bradford, but isolated hate crime incidents are known to occur, such as the stabbing of local British-Asian youth Imran Khan in Edinburgh in 1988. However, Omar Afzal, the head of the Muslim Council of Scotland, has challenged the idea of Scottish 'exceptionalism' with regard to integration, and has highlighted the under-reporting of Islamophobic attacks and discrimination.

Last week, in Belfast, I learned that politicians from the DUP and Sinn Fein were distant from the small Muslim community in Northern Ireland. Muslims there, despite being more educated and better integrated, were not represented in high office. They didn't appear to aspire to being part of a local government divided between pro-British and pro-Irish sentiment, which at its core is still a religious divide, albeit expressed in nationalist terms. Here in Scotland, however, Britain's first Muslim MP, Mohammad Sarwar, represented Glasgow Govan (later, after boundary changes, Glasgow Central) for Labour from 1997 until 2010. His son, Anas

Sarwar, also became a leading Scottish politician and was a Glasgow MP from 2010 to 2015.

A few months ago I was having dinner with a friend at the Landmark Hotel in London, and Anas was kind enough to come over and say hello to us. Upon my arrival in Scotland, my Facebook account alerts me to a campaign sponsored by Anas, a 'Public Inquiry into Islamophobia in Scotland'. The campaign page explains that a Cross-Party Group in the Scottish parliament was set up in 2018 under Anas Sarwar to explore 'the nature and extent of Islamophobia in Scotland and how it can be challenged and overcome'. A similar inquiry by Westminster MPs into Islamophobia in the UK, begun in spring 2019, became mired in controversy over the group's proposed definition of Islamophobia.

* * *

As my Uber driver Gordon, a white Scot, drives me later to Edinburgh's Central Mosque, I see numerous Gulf Arab tourists on the main shopping streets of the city centre. They always seem so well behaved, busy shopping, minding their own business. Hijab-wearing beggars, most likely from the Balkans or Romania, sit cross-legged in doorways and on the pavement. The thoroughfares are full of young people visiting the city centre; I spot many young couples of mixed-race backgrounds as well as older white Scottish shoppers.

The old stone buildings house gift shops selling tartan and Harry Potter paraphernalia, but I notice there are no skyscrapers in Edinburgh. The largest buildings I can see are the castle on its hill and a huge neoclassical structure, the Scottish National Gallery. The winding streets seem unplanned; a sense of mystery hangs in the air. But where does mystery end and fiction begin, as with that taxi driver's version of Scottish history?

The architectural design of the Central Mosque is a reflection of the sandstone Georgian buildings that define Edinburgh with their straight, symmetrical lines. Corinthian columns, Georgian windows and chimney stacks proliferate across the low skyline of the New Town. The mosque doesn't dominate the city. In fact, it's compact and far from imposing, standing on a street corner not far from Edinburgh University's George Square. Its largely unadorned exterior exudes a Moorish flair, with recessed pointed arches above the entrance. Minarets to each side of the door, one tall and the other much shorter, contain bricks of a darker shade built into the exterior that spell out 'Allah' in Arabic.

A golden plaque on the wall commemorates the patronage of the mosque by King Fahd bin Abdulaziz Al Saud, and its inaugural opening hosted by HRH Prince Abdulaziz bin Fahd bin Abdulaziz Al Saud in 1998.

I wonder, if this is a Saudi-supported mosque, will the sermon and congregation be Salafi, like IslamBradford and the Salafi bookstore crowd I encountered in Birmingham? I enter hesitantly, walking past several security guards in high-vis jackets. The mosque has been the subject of several arson attacks in recent years, most notably by a neo-Nazi youth in September 2017.

In the mosque's small lobby area, women part from their male companions and head towards the female prayer room.

'See you back here at 1.45,' says a woman in English to her partner in a loud and confident voice – everyone can hear her. The green carpet on the floor leads to a vast open space with white walls and a prominent brown pulpit. It feels Mediterranean and welcoming. The prayers will start at 1.15 p.m., and the mosque is already packed out.

There must be over 2,000 men crammed in on the ground floor, and the glass gallery for women looking down from the first floor also looks full. Two elaborate glass-and-metal chandeliers stand out amid the relative simplicity of the hall.

There are more men wearing baseball caps in this mosque than there are wearing Muslim skullcaps. No more than ten men wear Islamic headdresses; all the others are bareheaded. Much as at Belfast Islamic Centre, almost everybody is dressed in Western clothes: jeans, tracksuits, three-piece suits, chinos, shirts. It feels as if regular Scots from the streets of Edinburgh have stepped inside. There's a comfort and confidence about the place. There's not a turban or a Saudi checkered scarf to be seen in the entire congregation, nor any of the large beards of IslamBradford. I spot many people wearing lanyards from universities and the city council, who presumably work in the area.

The imam ascends the *minbar*. Pale-skinned, in his late fifties, with a trimmed beard, he wears a white skullcap and smiles as he sits down and the call to prayer, the *adhaan*, is called. He doesn't appear Salafi in his dress.

He delivers his sermon in classical Arabic followed by a short summary in English.[1] The bulk of the Arabic address goes as follows:

'All praises are due to God, from whom we seek all help and assistance. From God we seek protection from the evil of our egos and worst of our deeds. Prayers and salutations to our beloved Prophet, the Messenger of God, Mohamed, beloved and dear to God.

'Whomsoever God has guided, none can misguide. And those whom God has misguided, none can guide.

The imam talks at length and in detail about the dawn prayer, the first of the five daily prayers. 'God ordained the dawn prayer, this special prayer, to have great significance. He ordained it with remembrance of it in His Book: "Establish prayers at the setting of the sun, and at its rise the Quran of the dawn is witnessed."

'The recital of the Quran in dawn prayers is witnessed. Who witnesses it? The angels of the Most Compassionate God.'

The imam smiles at us, in his eyes a glint of warmth. 'Give praise to our Prophet for showing us the ways to God.' The congregation recites prayers of blessings on Mohamed.

'The Prophet, upon him be peace and blessings, said that two units of prayer are better than everything in the world and what is within it. Imagine going shopping on Boxing Day or Black Friday and the sales are such that you come home with great purchases. Will you be happy? God is offering you a great bargain with these two units of morning prayer, for with these you receive more than everything in this world. Let your imaginations, intellects and thoughts roam as far as possible and you will still not comprehend what God gives in response to your dawn prayers.

'From the moment you awake for prayers, in your heart and in your mind you are in the presence of God and prayers. You are filled with openness, hope and connection to God. You are far from every problem and close to God.

'The Prophet of God said, "Satan ties three knots on the back of your head while you are asleep. On every knot he puts the saying: 'The night is long, stay asleep.' When you wake up and remember God, one knot is undone. When you perform ablution, the second knot is undone. When you pray, the third knot is undone and you will wake up energetic with a good heart; otherwise, you will wake up lazy with a mischievous heart."

'May God grant us the ability to praise and worship God. There is no force or power other than the authority of God. Pray upon and remember your Prophet.'

The crowd recites prayers again, and the imam sits down, only to stand up again to deliver a shorter version of the sermon in Arabic-accented English, in which 'prayers' are '*brayers*' and his speech is littered with Arabic phrases in a way that native speakers of English would surely find hard to follow.

And then he prays, raising his hands, with the congregation responding '*Amen*' after every sentence:

'O God, bring blessings to us, to all the Muslim men and women, the living and the dead.

'O God, help us reform our characters and abide by our faith.

'O God, reform us and reform the affairs of the Muslims.

'O God, help the Muslims in Syria, Iraq, Kashmir, Palestine and in every country of the Muslims.

'O God, honour us with the honour of Islam.

'O God, help those who help this religion.

'O God, humiliate those who humiliate Muslims.

'O God, give us goodness in this world and goodness in the next world, and save us from the fires of hell.'

Judging by his Quran recital, the imam seems to be from North Africa, most likely Morocco. Most Quran reciters elongate the first syllable of the phrase '*malik yawm iddin*', describing God as the 'owner' (*malik*) of the Day of Judgement, but this imam gives it a short '*ma*', making Him its 'king'. This so-called *Warsh* style of recital, his focus on piety and the heart, and his smiles and clear love for Mohamed, all indicate Sufi leanings from North Africa.

After the prayers have ended and people begin to mill about, the buzz of this mixed culture of Arabs, Africans, Scots, Turks and South Asians reaches a climax as conversations, hugs and laughter, and also the continued recital of the Quran by others, fill the room.

As I head towards the reception area to leave the mosque, I hear Scottish-accented English being spoken.

On the wall in the reception area I spot a poster for a 'Politics and Media Masterclass' that will focus on who regulates the media, how to challenge it and how legislation is made. It is sponsored by MEND (Muslim Engagement and Development), a controversial group.

Outside the mosque, women and men mingle in the car park. I wander towards the back of the mosque and discover a restaurant called Mosque Kitchen. I pass small groups of Nigerians, Egyptians, Syrians, Turks, Bengalis, Punjabis and Indians, all chatting. Their languages and laughter fill the air. Inside Mosque Kitchen there are lots of white Scots having lunch, evidently completely unperturbed by its association with the mosque. I see blonde women, a brunette with a male partner, women without hijab and a gay couple holding hands. A menu in the front window advertises different types of curry, naan breads and kebabs at low prices; I guess that this place is popular with university students.

I follow a narrow alley just beside the restaurant out to the square behind the mosque complex, not wishing to disturb anyone having their lunch. Immediately outside Mosque Kitchen on Nicolson Street there are all shades of Scots mingling, shopping, chatting, waiting at bus stops. Further down the road, a grand neoclassical building with a pillared entranceway is signposted as 'Surgeons' Hall Museums'. There are halal butchers and ethnic clothing shops alongside coffee shops and betting centres. Nicolson Street is truly indicative of mainstream culture, fully integrated, not a ghetto. Why cannot Bradford, Birmingham or Rochdale be more like this,

I wonder. Why are their mosques isolated in specific communities? What have the Scots done right that we in England have not?

I walk past the car park that the mosque shares with a Lidl store. The air is still thick with the different languages of the mosque congregants.

'*Izzayyak?*' says an Egyptian to a friend. 'How are you?'

'*Ki khobor?*' I hear from a Bengali youth greeting someone. 'What's new?'

'*Zaroori aap aye,*' says an Urdu-speaking woman, looking very serious. 'You come too, urgently.'

'*Teşekkür ederim,*' I hear at my elbow. 'Thank you very much.' A man has just ended a phone call. Turkish-speaking, fair-skinned and youthful, balding and bespectacled, he is lingering beside his Volkswagen Polo. I see a small, royal blue trinket hanging off his rear-view mirror, to ward off the evil eye. In Turkey, Greece, Cyprus, even Syria and parts of the Arab Middle East, this is a symbol commonly placed in houses, shops, kitchens and offices, and worn by women as pendants and necklaces, which diverts attention and gives protection against human curses. The man is wearing a lanyard from the University of Edinburgh.

I briefly wonder what David Hume would have thought of this mingling of superstition and science, university and mosque, Turkish and Scottish in his home city.

'*Merhaba,*' I say to the man in Turkish. 'Hi!' I extend my hand to him in greeting. 'I'm guessing you work at the university?' I then ask in English, smiling and pointing at his lanyard.

'Yes, brother, I'm a senior technician at the science lab,' he responds warmly, with a Scottish burr.

'I'm visiting from London,' I say. 'A really mixed mosque you have here. I'm researching for a book. May I ask you a couple of questions?'

'Yes, of course,' he says, leaning against his car, relaxed.

Turks, much like Arabs and Greeks, Italians and Russians, are a deeply politicised people and always willing to talk politics. Placing my bets on that assumption, I plunge in with sensitive questions from the outset.

'I came from England last night, I prayed at your mosque here today, and people seem free, happy – and what a mixed congregation! I see people from so many ethnicities side by side on your streets here, and the mosque located right in the middle of the university and business. Yet the moment I check my social media, there's a government-sponsored advert about Anas Sarwar leading an inquiry on Islamophobia in Scotland. And despite the peace, I notice that your mosque is being leafleted by activists from MEND and the unions to mobilise against the British media and government. Is there really a Muslim-hatred problem here in Scotland?'

He pushes up his glasses. 'That's a good observation,' he says. 'I didn't see the leaflets at the mosque, but I have noticed Anas and other politicians talking a lot about Islamophobia, Palestine, Kashmir, and pressing the English for another referendum on Scottish independence. But look, here in Edinburgh, the car park's full and we need more space. Out there, there are beggars. Where's the policy from Scottish politicians on local issues that impact our lives here?

'It's the politicians that cause our problems here,' he continues. 'Look what's happening with the SNP. We voted to stay with the UK, but they want another referendum. I'm from Turkish parents. We have a Kurdish problem there, and the terror is killing our people. There's hatred of Kurds everywhere at home, yet in England I don't see any hatred of Scots, only love and admiration, even for the crazy ones.

'Do you know where Sarwar's father is now?' he asks, after a pause.

'No,' I say. 'I think he'd be retired now. He was the first British Muslim member of parliament, right?'

'That's the problem. He was meant to be a British MP, not a Muslim MP. He should be British first and foremost. His behaviour is what gives people Islamophobia. He left the British parliament a decade ago, handed the seat to his son, and then went back to Pakistan to become governor of Punjab. How is that British? How is that patriotic? To prefer politics in Punjab over Scotland?

And Labour politicians are silent on this sort of stuff, for fear of racism. They use Islam for political power, and now his son is using Islamophobia as an opportunity for leadership. I've been here for twenty years, and I have never seen Islamophobia in this country. People are easy-going, and religion is seen as a private matter. It's different in Glasgow, where there are Pakistani Muslim gangs and drugs, and politicians using Islam, like the Sarwar family. You have to visit Glasgow to see it.'

I want to tell him that I am going to Glasgow soon. But before I can say that or ask other questions, he has more to tell me.

'Did you ever hear about the two men who drove cars into Glasgow airport about ten years ago?' he goes on. 'They intended it to be a suicide attack, and they were later linked to the London car bomb plot in 2007. The Muslims in Glasgow have a problem they need to sort out, not just blame on Islamophobia. My father's always telling me that his sisters and cousins couldn't wear hijab growing up in Turkey; that is Islamophobia.

'A Muslim lad from Bradford came and killed an Ahmadi a couple of years ago in Glasgow. A lot of Muslim groups and politicians didn't join the funeral and ceremonies afterwards because he was a different type of Muslim. In Turkey, we have the Shi'a Alevis. In Iran, they have the Bahais. We have to respect these different faith groups and give them their full rights, the same as we enjoy here.

'On the other hand, in Turkey we kill the PKK. Here, at least the separatist party, the SNP, is in the London and Edinburgh parliaments; that is real democracy.'

'Why do you think they want independence from England?' I ask.

'I have colleagues in the labs who support independence, and also some who don't, but the SNP people are always looking back to that idealised, "Braveheart" type of history, before the countries united. They want to repeal the Acts of Union, ultimately, and go back to those days.'

Our discussion moves on to Turkey and Iran, relations between the two countries both now and historically, and my many visits to Turkey. He asks me questions about the Istanbul mosques and shrines I have seen. We really bond. True to Turkish traditions of hospitality, in a Scottish form, he invites me to lunch, but I politely decline.

'You've given me a task. I have to go to Glasgow!'

GLASGOW

I have arrived in Shawlands, on the south side of Glasgow. Minard Road is long, with a range of council flats, terraced redbrick houses and some shops. A Suzuki garage and a school are prominently visible just down the road.

'Hutchesons' Grammar School' reads a large board on the fence outside. Another Hutcheson, an Ulster Scot, Francis (1694–1746), was one of the leading figures of the Scottish Enlightenment. He rejected the extremist dogma of Calvinism that sprang up under John Knox during the Reformation. Hutcheson not only refuted Thomas Hobbes' interpretation of society that 'all are at war with each other' unless an all-powerful government controls us, but also helped to promote the belief that human beings are inherently kind and loving and find joy in service. Hutcheson taught moral philosophy for years at the University of Glasgow and reformed the syllabus so profoundly that it gave rise to a generation of Enlightenment thinkers including, most famously, Adam Smith and David Hume.

Yet in the shadow of his namesakes' legacy, I'm standing on the spot of a religious murder. I haven't come for the sake of the school but to see the Kayden 2 newsagent's on the corner of Minard Road. Half of a bright red banner advertising the *Sun* newspaper is missing, while the shop's former name, Shah Newsagents, is still visible.

On 24 March 2016, Asad Shah, an Ahmadi Muslim, was stabbed to death in his shop by a Muslim man from Bradford who killed him in the name of defending the Prophet's honour. Shah's murderer, Tanveer Ahmed, was a member of a Barelwi group. As an Ahmadi, Shah would have believed that Mohamed was not the last prophet of God, in contradiction of orthodox Sunni thought. In the subcontinent, Ahmadis are persecuted and attacked for their beliefs and are not seen as true Muslims. For Dawat-e-Islami, the denial of Mohamed's prophecy being the 'last message' of Islam is seen as the ultimate insult to the Prophet. Indeed, Shah's family had relocated from Pakistan to Scotland in order to escape religious-based violence against them and their property back home.

Dawat-e-Islami is also the Barelwi movement to which Mumtaz Qadri, the killer of Punjab Governor Salman Taseer, belonged. Tanveer Ahmed, Shah's killer from Bradford, allegedly idolised Qadri, even corresponding with him before he received his death sentence.

Ahmed allegedly committed the Minard Road murder in response to hundreds of YouTube videos Shah had posted in which he promoted compassion and neighbourly love. In some of them he claimed to be a prophet himself. This offended the Barelwis and many other Sunni Muslims, for whom Mohamed was incontrovertibly God's final prophet. Pakistani Muslims are particularly sensitive on this point and hostile to the Ahmadi sect, founded by Mirza Ahmed (d. 1908) of India: another battle from the days of empire that lives on in our midst.

I cannot bring myself to enter a building in which a murder has taken place supposedly for the sake of Islam and its different interpretations between Bradford and Glasgow. How could such a thing happen in the nation that gave birth to the Enlightenment?

Next door to Kayden 2 is the Bridge Café. It's just after 5 p.m., and the lady has closed the shop's shutters, but the door is still open so I go in.

'Can I help you, love?' she says.

'Thank you for letting me in,' I reply. 'Have you been based here for long? More than a few years, say?'

'No, love. Just about three months.'

'Ah, not to worry. Thank you anyway,' I say, and leave.

I continue along the street, gazing at the houses and the passers-by whom Shah must have known and served as the local newsagent. A man wearing a backpack is walking towards me. He is white, in his late thirties.

'Excuse me,' I say, standing before him. 'Can I ask you something?'

'Anything, anytime,' he says. Such willingness to help and engage with a stranger is a special blessing at such moments.

'Have you lived here for more than five years?'

'Yes, much longer than that,' he says.

'Do you remember the newsagent who was killed in 2016?'

'Mr Shah? Aye, of course. Lovely man. Wouldn't hurt a fly.'

'Tell me more,' I say. 'I'm from London, and I want to understand what happened, and how locals remember him.'

'Mr Shah always asked after my wife and kids. Then something happened online, and a Muslim from England came and killed him. We had politicians and Muslims come to Shawlands, and the area was full of media afterwards. I remember hearing that some Muslims from the Oakshields area didn't come to pay respects, and a lot of people were upset.'

'Where's Oakshields?' I ask.

'Not far from here. There are more Muslims living there. Mr Shah wasn't involved with them, or anything like that. He was just a peaceful man.'

Before leaving Minard Road I decide I will enter Mr Shah's shop after all, to pay my own respects to the innocent soul who lost his life in an act of violence that claimed to be carried out in the name of Sufi Islam and love for the Prophet. For all the Barelwis' talk of love, this was raw caliphism in action. In so many towns and cities I have been seeing caliphism as a subculture reflected in clerics' sermons, bookstores and marriage rights, but here in Glasgow it actually claimed the life of another believer.

I push the door open at Kayden 2 and see a young man sitting behind the counter.

'Hi!' I say, and he stands up. He sports a goatee, is slightly overweight and is wearing a Manchester United top.

'I'm visiting from London, and I'd like to ask you if you own the shop – and what you know of the previous owner?'

'Mr Shah?' he asks knowingly.

'Yes.'

'I've only heard his name from the locals, especially the older people here: they knew him, and they liked him. I'm working here for my friends, they own the shop.'

'Do you know what actually happened?' I ask.

'I've heard from the neighbours that Mr Shah was a very nice man, but very religious, and a different type of religious. He said something online and another religious man from England came and killed him for it.

'I'm Kurdish, I am Muslim, but I don't support this,' he adds.

I thank the young man as I leave, and then he's answering his phone, smiling.

Something is weighing heavily on my mind. Visiting the site of a sectarian religious murder, when an organisation that champions such acts is still openly active in Britain, seems wrong. And there's that other fact, which I have heard before: that the mosque in Oakshields didn't join the vigil for Mr Shah, which had support from all creeds and shades of opinion, and heard pledges and pleas for religious coexistence.

I look up the Oakshields mosque and realise that it is, in fact, Glasgow Central Mosque. It's the same mosque that the Edinburgh University technician spoke about, and the same one that the *hafiz* in London claimed to have studied at.

As my taxi takes me from Minard Road to the mosque, I call a friend in London and ask him to recommend a pub in Glasgow where I can chat with some more locals.

'You've got two problems there,' he tells me. 'One, Russia and Scotland are playing tonight, so the pubs are going to be packed.'

'So what?' I say.

'So, second, you're what they call BOGOF in Glasgow.'

'Bog off?'

'Buy One, Get One Free,' he laughs. 'You're brown and English – two for the price of one! The racist football fans will have a bargain if they get you – stay away!'

As the car takes me down Niddrie Road I notice a sign for something called Madinat ul-Uloom, meaning 'city of knowledge'.

Underneath it says Dawat-e-Islami, the controversial Barelwi organisation.

The mosque is near the south bank of the River Clyde. It's a vast complex made up of several buildings, and much larger than the one I visited in Edinburgh. There are separate male and female entrances, but the car park isn't segregated, so there are children coming in late to madrasa, the evening class. The young girls are all in hijab, the boys wearing white Arab robes. The mosque is redbrick with glass protrusions and a geometrically angled glass-and-metal dome. A slender minaret that reminds me of a sewing needle stands beside it. A cluster of buildings on the other side of the car park make up City of Glasgow College.

Inside, a sign on the mosque wall tells me there is a library, so I instinctively go to examine the book collection, but an elderly man stops me.

'Excuse me, where are you going?' he asks.

'To the library,' I say.

'Sorry, the library is closed. You can go and pray in the hall if you wish,' he concedes, as he guides me towards the main hall.

'May I see the imam?' I ask.

'Yes, he's in the office just there.'

I knock on the door. There are two offices for two imams. One imam is sitting with three teenage boys, all wearing white robes and white skullcaps. This is already a different world from Edinburgh. The imam has a long beard and looks at me, unsure if he should greet me. He isn't certain that I am even Muslim and seems to detect some hostility in me. In truth, my mind is on Mr Shah, and the fact that this mosque didn't attend the vigil for him, and because Mr Shah was an Ahmadi Muslim. Seeing the imam with his chest puffed up, arrogant, makes me think of the Cardiff shaikh and his horrendous story.

'Sorry to intrude,' I say, and head for the hall. His attitude is off-putting.

I remove my shoes and place them on the rack.

The hall is enormous, at least twice the size of the one in Edinburgh. There are groups of children sitting on the floor, bobbing to and fro along with the recital of the Quran. The other imam is sitting with them, wearing the distinctive Dawat-e-Islami turban and white *thawb*. I get out my phone and take a photo of the interior of the mosque. I would dearly like to say a prayer, but cannot bring myself to pray at a mosque that condones sectarianism and murder.

On the wall is an advertisement for a lecture by Shaykh Ahmad Ali, to which 'brothers and sisters are welcome'. Shaykh Ali is a British scholar of the Deobandi movement, which, though separate from the Barelwis and Dawat-e-Islami, still agrees with the theology of not allowing people to insult the Prophet. Large sections of the Deobandi school of thought in Pakistan have also been known to support the Taliban.

Anas Sarwar's pursuit of Islamophobia now seems so misdirected. The new generation here needs his help quite literally to get off the floor and take their seats. But the politicians are somehow not connected to this reality.

'Excuse me, brother,' I hear from behind me.

I look round. He hasn't said '*salam*' because I'm not wearing the right clothes. Dressed as I am in a Barbour jacket, jeans and a shirt and carrying a tote bag, he clearly thinks I'm not pious enough or worthy of Islamic greetings.

'Please don't take photos in the mosque,' he says.

'Are you serious?' I ask.

'Yes, that's our rule. No photography allowed,' he says, in a Glaswegian accent. It feels strange to hear those warm tones coming from a man dressed like a stereotypical Taliban member.

'Why not?' I ask.

'It's a rule. No photos,' he affirms, looking slightly unsure.

'But why? We live in a free country,' I say. He seems genuinely puzzled. I can't help but wonder if he's not had this conversation before.

'It's a rule, you can't ask why.'

'Clearly, you're teaching the kids here, right?'

'Yes, I'm a teacher for the advanced class here. I have to go back to my students.'

'Hold on,' I say quickly. 'Before you go, can you tell me something – why did this mosque stay away from Asad Shah's vigil, after that Barelwi guy from Bradford came and killed him? It was because you also think those who insult the Prophet must be killed, right?'

'I can't comment. Please ask the committee.'

He turns around promptly and leaves me standing there.

As I put my shoes on again, in the area by the racks, a young man appears – muscular, short-haired, alert. He glances at me twice, and then the third time I extend my hand. Hawk-like looks such as his often have a story behind them.

'*Salam alaikum*,' I say. 'I'm Ed, from London. How are you doing?'

'*Alaikum as-salam*,' he says. 'Abdullah. I'm dropping my brother off to class here. What's the teacher been saying to you?'

'No photos allowed.'

'And what you did you say to him?'

'That we live in a free country.'

'Thank God we do,' he says with conviction. 'What do you do?' he asks me.

'I'm writing a book on Islam and Britain,' I say. 'What do you do?'

'Don't quote me,' he says, 'and don't tell anyone around here ...'

'Oh, believe me, I don't foresee coming back here in a rush! I mean this mosque, not Glasgow ...' I hastily correct myself.

'I understand,' he says, with a staccato laugh. Here is a man who has learned to control his laughter, I think.

'I work for the British Army,' he confesses, the moment we step out of the mosque together. 'I'm Major Abdullah Batal.'[2]

'God bless you,' I say. 'Thank you for your service to our country.'

'Aye, thank you,' he says, a mild smile breaking out.

'We recruit in Glasgow,' he says, 'but the lads never talk in the mosques about their role. The community around here can't accept it.'

He's now heading towards his car, and I'm leaving the mosque complex to get a taxi to the Dawat-e-Islami centre I saw earlier.

'How many Muslims are there in the British armed forces?' I ask.

'Probably about five hundred, but we need a lot more. My grandfather served in the Second World War, so it's in the family for me. But the guys around this mosque don't understand that. We protect their freedoms, and they hate us.'

'I'm thinking of going to Luton later,' I say. 'The EDL was born there after Muslim extremists spat on British soldiers returning from Iraq and called them murderers.'

'You should definitely go,' he says. 'The EDL and others will start to recruit again in the army if mosques like these don't get on board with modern Britain. I mean, what's wrong with taking a photo? Why can't kids here come to our recruitment fairs?'

'Have you tried?' I ask.

'I haven't, because I don't want them to know and talk about me in the community. The Ministry of Defence has really made an effort – we have Muslim officers who go on Hajj, and there are provisions made for prayer times and for fasting during Ramadan.'

The idea that Muslims are disloyal to the United Kingdom, as so many people see it, is simply erroneous, I reflect: millions fought for the Allies in the two world wars. There is no incompatibility between being a Muslim and serving in the army; indeed, the armed forces now have a dedicated imam to provide for Muslims' spiritual needs.

Back on Niddrie Road, I notice that the Dawat-e-Islami centre is next to a bookshop called Category Is Books that advertises itself as a 'fiercely independent queer bookshop'. There is a big poster in the window supporting trans rights, and as I enter the shop I see events advertised for the LGBT community. 'I belong', it says above the counter. The bookseller is busy talking to an electrician who's there to fix a problem. I wonder what Dawat-e-Islami think of their neighbours, and how they would react to the advertised events.

Back out on the pavement, there's an advert outside the Dawat-e-Islami madrasa for the group's television channel. Their Charity Commission number is proudly displayed on the building. I can just make out an old advertisement for shirts painted on the side, and assume that the building has recently been taken over.

I go into the mosque, and little girls in all-black burkas run from the room as they see me, a man, entering. A notice on the door prohibits entry while children are being taught, so I go to the office where an elderly man is sitting there reading the Quran; he tells me to go and see the imam in the hall.

Taking his advice, I step inside the main room. About sixty boys with bright green turbans on their heads are sitting on the floor with several bearded elders.

'*Salam alaikum*,' I say. 'May I speak to the imam?'

A bearded young man in the far corner, who looks to be in his thirties, beckons me over.

'If I wanted to send my daughters here to study here in the evenings, how much would the fees be?' I ask.

He replies in Urdu. 'There are no fees, but please ask your wife to come and speak to the ladies about it.' Again in Urdu, he tells another teacher to give me an application form.

A youth who is surely no older than twenty gets up from the floor. He's not wearing a turban but a skullcap.

We return to the office together.

'How old are your daughters?' he asks, opening a drawer.

'Very young,' I say. 'Only nine and twelve.'

Eventually he finds the right forms.

'Everyone charges fees at madrasas, so how come you don't?' I ask.

'We in Dawat-e-Islami think knowledge should be for God, not money. At all our institutions around the world we do not charge money.'

He names people in Pakistan who contribute to the cause. He also mentions the importance of '*dawat*' (another way of transliterating '*da'wa*'), or proselytising.

'Do they have to wear the hijab and burqa to study the Quran here?' I ask, as we leave the office.

He points to a CCTV screen that I hadn't noticed until now.

'Look,' he says, pointing at a room full of black-clad girls. 'This is our uniform.'

'But they are not yet *balighat*,' I say, using the scriptural term for post-pubescent women, those who have reached the age of maturity at which, in seventh-century Mecca, they were required to cover their bosoms.

Noticing my use of Arabic, he also responds in Arabic.

'But it's *satr-e-aurat*,' he says. The phrase, also used in Urdu, means 'covering the private parts'.

'Children covering their hair and faces as "private parts"? That isn't any part of the sharia!' I protest.

'It is,' he insists.

'Where? Give me one reference anywhere, including all the *fiqh* books and *hadith* from a thousand years, that says young girls – children – have to wear hijab.'

He thinks for a moment, and then quickly responds. 'My father owns the mosque,' he says. 'He's a scholar, and he sets the rules. I'm sure he has answers from sharia.'

Clericalism once again. The need to consult scholars.

'Impossible,' I say. 'Nothing exists to say little girls must cover up. Can't you see that we're sexualising children? And why are the boys sitting on the floor? You went to school here in Scotland, right?'

'Yes,' he says.

'Can't you see that the kids spend their days in school science labs with their teachers as equal human beings, and then they come to the mosque and sit on the floor wearing turbans to memorise a seventh-century book under the strict control of their elders. What kind of sense does that make?'

'Our *Agha* wore those clothes!' The Urdu word means 'master'. He's referring to the Prophet.

'Yes, but so did the pagans, Jews and Christians; it was just what the local Arabs wore in Mecca at the time. How is that Islamic? It's just part of an ancient culture.'

Again he refers me to his father, and asks me to come back on Monday.

'Before I go, can I ask you one last question, please? It's about Mr Asad Shah, who was murdered by a Dawat-e-Islami man from Bradford: does this centre support the killing of those who insult the Prophet, *qatl-e-gustakh-e-Rasul*?'

'Why are you asking such difficult questions?' he replies evasively.

'Because in a free country we have to accept that those who don't believe Mohamed was a prophet can legally mock him, and that some Ahmadis will claim to be prophets, too, as Mr Shah did. He was killed in this city by a member of your organisation. Can't you see that we all lose our freedoms, all of us, if we can't accept different viewpoints and criticism of our religion?'

'We cannot criticise our religion,' he says.

He insists once again that his father owns the mosque and can provide the answers. My mind goes back to the Dawat-e-Islami bookshop in Birmingham, and its owner from Pakistan who dodged my questions about Salman Taseer. The group believe their historical mandate is to oppose any insult to the Prophet, and they use *hadith* to support this claim. Pakistan's blasphemy laws also support this interpretation and are often used against Ahmadis as well as Christians, with sanctions ranging in severity from fines to the death penalty.

I take the application form and leave the centre to catch my train out of Glasgow.

I have saved London, my home city, as my final destination.

9

London

The UK's capital city is home to the largest Muslim population in the country – almost a million Muslims among its population of eight million – and elected Sadiq Khan, a Muslim mayor, in 2016. I wonder if my experience here, as I continue my research, will differ from the other towns and cities I have visited so far.

Mufti Jalal is the deputy imam at one of the largest mosques in London and teaches at an Islamic seminary in Luton. Only thirty years old, the mufti is held in high regard among his congregants and is widely known through his popular appearances on satellite TV channels on Sky, such as Islam Channel, British Muslim TV and others.[1]

We are sitting at a table in Giraffe, a 'world cuisine' restaurant in Spitalfields. Spanish tango music is playing. The waitress is Italian. Mufti Jalal is wearing a head cap and long *thawb*. I ask if he is comfortable.

'This is the beauty of this country,' he says. 'We can wear whatever we want. After I studied sharia in Turkey and Yemen, I used to wear normal Western clothes, like you. But at the mosque, the elderly community leaders want me to wear Arab clothing, and I'm willing to do so if it will help me change their minds on the real issues that are damaging the lives of so many people here in this great country.'

He orders a bowl of spicy curry soup; I order salmon teriyaki. The mufti is relaxed in this all-Western setting catering for city bankers and lawyers working near Liverpool Street. We spend three hours in conversation.

'What are the top issues in your inbox, Mufti Jalal?' I ask, as we discuss the various challenges of being both a Westerner and a Muslim.

'I can't be open with you unless I apologise again for calling you a government agent,' he says: sincere, warm and pious, genuinely upset by the feeling that he did me an injustice. I reassure him that my work has never aimed to support any government, but to secure the freedom and best features of our country. I feel that too many Muslims have taken an anti-state, anti-West approach as a way of defining themselves. He instinctively understands and agrees.

'Our sharia is the British constitution,' he says. 'The *Maqasid* of the sharia are best preserved in Britain. I came back here after Egypt, Turkey and Yemen with a deeper recognition of the historical freedoms of England, but too many Muslims don't understand that turning against this country is to turn against our own selves.

'At one point I studied under Haitham al-Haddad, who thinks we need to implement Islamic law against the "liberalism" of the West. I didn't agree with this, so I left, but his influence is on the rise.'

The *Maqasid*, or Higher Objectives, are aspects of the sharia that were enshrined in Islamic law by jurists as early as the eleventh century, particularly by Imam al-Juwaini (d. 1085) in his *Ghiyath al-Umam* (*The Salvage of the Nations*) and his students over the centuries. There are five aspects to the *Maqasid* as laid out by al-Juwaini: the preservation of family, life, faith, intellect and property; these are intended to form the basis on which the sharia is followed. The British legal system, with its fundamental values of individual liberty and freedom of expression, is a perfect working model of the main aspects of the sharia, applied to the context of modern life.

To watch the confident way in which the mufti speaks, and with such clarity, feels like a sudden breath of fresh air. We compare notes on mutual friends, and he shares my concerns about the rise of radicalism and intolerance among the Barelwis, particularly in Birmingham.

'They're like the mafia,' he says. 'Do you know what they did to Dr Musharraf? They tried to control him and then silence him. They say we must kill those who leave Islam or insult the Prophet Mohamed. But why? We can even insult God. The Quran itself reminds us about those who believed, then disbelieved, and then believed again. In other words, because they weren't killed for their lack of belief the door to believing again was kept open.'

This is an important point that I haven't heard others make before, using Quranic ideals to refute the caliphists and those who want to kill people like Salman Rushdie and other ex-Muslims or mockers of Mohamed.

'Why don't more Muslim clerics see the issue of apostasy this way?' I ask.

'A Deobandi friend of mine said recently that it's because they were never trained to ask questions, so they can't answer them. There's a lot of truth in that. Meanwhile the Deobandis are taking over our mosques, Salafis are taking over prayer rooms on university campuses and even the Sufis are producing mafia bosses. For the future of us Muslims, there's an urgent need for change.'

I didn't think I'd meet a Muslim scholar who would be so bold.

As we speak, his phone lights up with messages from a friend, and then a phone call. 'No, I can't come,' he tells the person on the other end. 'Let's watch the next episode together later.' He hangs up, and then smiles and tells me that he's watching a Turkish show called *Diriliş: Ertuğrul* about the warrior founder of the Ottoman Empire, who is central to Turkey's national origin story.

'We're always attacking Britain for its history of slavery and colonialism, but what about Turkey's own history of slavery, castrating men and making eunuchs of them, and their conquest of Arab lands and even European kingdoms in the Balkans? Why don't we speak about our own Muslim slavery and imperialism?' he asks.

'Because it doesn't suit our victimhood narrative?' I venture.

'Have you seen *Ertuğrul?*' he asks me.

'Only once – it was too slow-moving for me.'

'The cast is touring Britain, and there are halls packed with young Muslims welcoming the actors,' he says. 'It's as if we want to recreate that caliphate again, and don't recognise the new world we live in.'

I later look this up and he is right: *Ertuğrul's* cast has been to London and Birmingham, and Turkey's President Erdogan regularly has photos taken with them to identify with the glorious Turkish past. So caliphism is also active in the cultural sphere. It is surely only a matter of time before it finds political expression again. The defeat of ISIS on the battlefield is not the end of the caliphist dream.

'What are the most popular questions that people bring to you for fatwas?' I ask Mufti Jalal next. As a religiously trained mufti, he is authorised to issue fatwas, rulings on points of Islamic law, for believers seeking guidance. His response, as with the imams of Bradford, Blackburn or Manchester, will indicate the most pressing issues on local Muslims' minds, especially in the case of this most popular of imams.

'Are you sure you want to know?' he asks.

'It can't be worse than what imams have told me in the northern cities, can it?'

He doesn't look convinced.

* * *

It's Friday morning and thousands of people are heading towards Regent's Park Mosque. There are groups of Arab students, traffic wardens, cleaners, estate agents in their suits, bank clerks, teenage girls in skinny jeans. I pass some beggars, lined up along the outside wall of the mosque complex. Some of them are women, heads covered with hijabs, the men sitting on the ground. One is orating the call to prayer. Women and men flow into the mosque together naturally, freely.

There has been Islamic worship in this city for almost eighty years: Winston Churchill and his Cabinet approved the construction of a mosque in London as early as 1940, guaranteeing it a considerable sum of money and a central London location.

Lord Lloyd, one-time head of the British Council, referred to it in a private letter as 'the best piece of propaganda' Britain could have for its relations with the Muslim nations of the Middle East.[2] The mosque, now London Central Mosque, just off Baker Street, was opened in 1976.

I make my way into an open courtyard in which men are gathered for the weekly prayers. The exterior of the building is pale, broken up by gigantic windows of dark-tinted glass. The huge, sparkling copper dome and unadorned minaret are striking. Cars and taxis make their way to the underground car park. To my right, the greenery of Regent's Park is visible past an apartment block, and on my left are the mosque's library and administration offices. Groups of women branch off from the throng, heading towards the women's sections – there is one in the basement and one on a raised gallery on the first floor overlooking the main hall.

Seeing men and women talking and entering the mosque together reminds me of a *hadith* that is often ignored. Abdul Rahman, one of the Prophet's companions, reported that 'the companions used to perform ablutions together'. He was then asked, 'You mean men and women together?' 'Yes,' replied Abdul Rahman.[3]

As a child I won prizes for Quran recitation at this mosque and have fond memories of the place, but have avoided praying here for several years; my last experience here was troubling and traumatic.

In 2016, at the height of the ISIS atrocities in the Middle East, an Arab Muslim political leader met several Muslim influencers in this mosque. He had drafted a letter to the head of ISIS, Abu Bakr al-Baghdadi, and asked a hundred Muslims from around the world to sign it, including senior Muslim scholars and authors. I met this politician here in Regent's Park, at his request. He was sitting in the corner of the mosque trying to get signatories to condemn ISIS and stop young Arabs from joining the caliphate. Leading Muslim voices in Saudi Arabia, Jordan, Egypt and other influential Muslim nations had already signed his letter. He asked me to sign it when I approached him, and I readily agreed. Yet I noticed that he looked desolate.

'Are you OK?' I asked. 'Do you want to go for a coffee?'

He sighed and looked me deep in the eyes. I could tell he was wondering if he could trust me. I didn't blink under his searching gaze.

'I asked Shaikh [***] to condemn ISIS and sign this letter,' he said, then fell silent again.

'And I'm sure he agreed!' I spluttered, stupidly.

'No, Ed,' he said, raising his voice slightly, 'he refused.'

'What?! Why?' I asked.

'Keep this to yourself, but he demanded I remove the parts of my letter rejecting slavery before he signed it.'

'What?! I don't understand,' I say.

'ISIS has started slave markets, and is selling women for sex from the Yazidi and other communities. Shaikh [***] insists that slavery is acceptable in the Quran, and that Imam Shafi'i from the ninth century upheld it, so we cannot reject it.'

'Don't change your letter,' I insisted.

'Of course not,' said the man. 'But how can a white English convert shaikh like him support slavery and still teach at universities here? What is going on in your country?'

'Did others do the same?' I asked.

'Yes, but none of them were English converts and university professors; the others who questioned that part of the letter were Muslims from Mauritania and Nigeria, where opposing slavery is seen as a Western project.'

'Do you think there are Christians or Jews trying to bring back slavery, too, because it's in the Bible?'

'You tell me,' he said morosely.

I left the politician that day with a sinking heart. Despite the legacy of abolitionists like William Wilberforce, and the human progress embodied in the worldwide abolition of slavery, it seems there is still high-level support for slavery among some Muslims. It was only officially abolished in Saudi Arabia in 1962, and among Islamists, especially Salafis and those inspired by Maududi and Qutb, it still receives support.

That conversation echoes in my head as I enter the mosque today.

The marble floor gives way to royal blue carpet just beyond the shelves where worshippers place their shoes. The interior of the hall is largely unadorned, the windows so large on both sides that it seems as if the walls are made of glass. The front of the space is painted white, with a niche for the imam decorated with Arabic calligraphy. Although it is bright outside, the ornate chandelier hanging from the interior of the dome is emitting a warm glow, drawing the eye upwards to the dome's intricate calligraphy and geometric tiled designs. It is an impressive space, befitting the central mosque of Britain's capital city.

An imam wearing the Azhari red cap wrapped with a small turban ascends the *minbar*. His attire reminds me of the imam in Cardiff. His assistant, the muezzin who will give the call to prayer, asks that we all switch off our mobile phones and then gives the *adhaan*.

The hall is packed to the rafters. Most men are not wearing any form of head covering. Standing with my back against the wall at the back of the mosque, I have a full view of this peaceful gathering of so many nationalities and peoples. I see three Nigerian hats, two Afghan turbans, one white Sudanese turban. I see dozens of Yorkshire flat caps, and many baseball caps turned backwards. I see Adidas trainers, the word 'Brooklyn' on a jumper, two Moroccan hoods. A man in a cravat, then three more. There are several in ties, most likely Lebanese or other Arabs. Here the languages are varied, reflecting the diversity of this great city. Where the mosque's announcement boards forbid mosque gatherings without permission, they do so in Bengali, Arabic, English and Urdu.

In the summer, the side doors are opened and the breeze passes through the space. Today, the doors are closed but the sun streams into the hall.

The imam speaks in Arabic for the first fifteen minutes, and then he reads a translation in English for the second part of the sermon, his voice heavily accented:

'One of the reasons why the family works in Islam is that each member of the family knows his or her role. Each one of you is responsible, and each one of you will be responsible on the Day of Judgement.' He mentions the father's responsibilities and the mother's responsibilities.

'Dear honourable Muslims, we look at the Quran and the *Sunnah* of the Prophet Mohamed, and we find many basic principles about the family, how the structure of the family – the duty of the mother, the duty of the father and the duty of the children – is important, because you cannot expect your rights without fulfilling your duties. You have to fulfil your duties before you can have your rights.

'Even the relations between husband and wife are in the Quran. The woman has rights similar to her duties; it is not for one side – each side has rights and duties.

He moves on to the rights of parents, as described in the Quran. 'Dear brothers and sisters, parents have rights over children, and their right is to know their duties towards them, and these include providing for them, if they are able to do that. Showing kindness to them, showing compassion and respect, praying for them and supporting them financially. Their right is also to be patient and make *dua* [prayers of supplication] for them, as it says in the Quran.

'Also, Allah provided that we should be kind to our parents even if they are not Muslims. The need to treat them with respect and kindness doesn't change, as mentioned in Chapter 31, Verse 15. The rights of parents can be achieved by showing respect and doing good deeds, giving them help and supporting them; even if they have hurt you, you must be kind to your parents. Don't listen to your parents blindly, it doesn't mean that. You must listen to your parents in the good things …

'There are things where you cannot listen to them … but you must support them and say good words for them all the time. He goes on to remind his audience of the importance of showing gratitude, respect and kindness towards one's parents, even after their death.

'Dear brothers and sisters, on the other hand children also have rights. Parents have responsibilities for the upbringing of their children; this is in the Quran and many statements of the Prophet

Mohamed. You are to protect yourselves and your families, and this protection can be achieved by guiding them, educating them – not only a religious education but also worldly education. Look after your children; as parents this is your responsibility. Keep encouraging them and supporting them to get other education, a full education for the society in which they live.

'When the scholars ask how we protect our family, they mention that for protecting them, you show them what's right and wrong, the difference between right and wrong.

'Dear honourable Muslims, as I mentioned before, it is not only one person in the family, it is their duty, both, everyone has a duty and a role. As the Prophet said, they are responsible on the Day of Judgement for providing for the family, looking after them, protecting them and supporting them.

'Dear honourable Muslims, finally, hold yourself to account before you are held to account. Know that the angel of death has already passed us to take the souls of others, and he will come to us too.'

After the sermon there are the two units of prayers, during which a man in a Deliveroo jacket dashes out. Afterwards, more people rush out, presumably back to their workplaces, as many are wearing fluorescent jackets over their suits and ties.

The bookshop based at the mosque, Darussalam, is a branch of a Riyadh-based publishing house. Men and women browse freely together in the shop, and the shop manager at this busy time is a woman. There is a route through from entering the shop, looking at all its many items, to paying and then exiting, reminding me of gift shops in many of London's tourist attractions. There are shelves of beard oil, perfumes, black seed oil, *miswak* tooth-brushing sticks, abayas, headscarves and head coverings for men. The commercialisation of Islamic literalism is here in full view.

The vast book collection in the shop is full of titles that have been translated in Saudi Arabia but are increasingly being removed from bookshops in that country on account of their literalism. Yet here they are on sale in liberal Britain. There are books by Ibn

Taymiyyah, one called *The Political Shariyah: On Reforming the Ruler and the Ruled*. Yusuf al-Qaradawi, an affiliate of the Muslim Brotherhood who has spoken of homosexuality as a 'perversion', is visible – his book *The Lawful and the Prohibited in Islam* is also for sale in the bookshop. Works by the Saudi Salafi Muhammad bin Salih al-Uthaymeen, including a commentary on Ibn Taymiyyah, are also for sale, as is the standard Salafi textbook on *tawheed* by Muhammad ibn Abd al-Wahhab: *Kitab at-Tawheed* (*The Book of Monotheism*).

Outside the mosque, women and men find each other after the service, chatting and laughing. Children run around and teenagers mingle, glancing at their phones. There is a man distributing leaflets just outside the gates of the mosque. 'Conflict in Kashmir', reads one, outlining a series of talks:

Talk 1: India & Pakistan: Exposing the Myths.

Talk 2: Kashmir: The Dangerous US Plan.

Talk 3: Pakistan Army: Let the Lions Roar.

Talk 4: The Caliphate: The Ummah's Shield.

The event is to be held in Luton, the same town where members of a Muslim extremist group, al-Muhajiroun, spat on returning British soldiers. It was this ideology, and the actions of its adherents, that shaped Tommy Robinson's anti-Islam campaigning, and here they are still alive and active a decade later. The movement of which al-Muhajiroun is a satellite, Hizb ut-Tahrir, is responsible for these leaflets promoting the caliphate just outside the central mosque of Britain's biggest city, in one of its wealthiest areas.

I catch sight of my colleague Atlanta, who has also attended the prayer service. She is not a Muslim but was interested in experiencing prayers at Regent's Park. As we head back to the station, she tells me about an elderly Yemeni woman who sat next to her and began chatting with her in broken English about her faith. The woman, Khadijah, told Atlanta that Islam is for everyone, not just Arabs, and said she hoped Atlanta would feel the spirit of Allah during the prayers. Just before Atlanta left the prayer room, Khadijah had given her a leaflet in English called *The Fundamentals of Tawhid – Islamic Monotheism*, produced by Salafi Publications, the same group whose shop we visited in Birmingham. The leaflet is soliciting donations. The woman is carrying out her perceived duty of *da'wa*, or proselytising.

Not far from Oxford Circus there is a prominent Islamic bookshop. Several months ago I was here browsing through books about philosophy and Sufism when I could have sworn I overheard an Arabic conversation in the basement about a second marriage. A man was talking about a woman he liked, and was considering bringing friends and witnesses to get married in the bookshop. Did I hear him right? I was pretty sure the bookshop clerk replied that nobody else would know. I now want to confirm the services on offer.

A book in the window called *Gendered Morality* catches my eye as the two of us step inside. A white Irish convert is sitting behind the desk, with half-moon glasses and a stern demeanour that could easily have marked her out as a Catholic nun.

'Do you conduct marriage vows in here?' I ask.

'Yes,' she replies, 'we do.'

'Do you register the marriage?'

'No, it's an Islamic marriage. You'll have to go somewhere else to do that.'

'Do you ask any questions about people's pasts?' I'm trying to hint that I might already be married, and be contemplating entering into a second marriage. That's what the man I overheard on my previous visit had been discussing. 'What do I need?' I ask.

At this point she assumes Atlanta and I are getting married, as she points to us both and says, 'You need to bring your passports; any children from the marriage must be raised as Muslims; and you agree a *mahr*, a dowry, between you.'

Somewhat embarrassed at suddenly being suspected of attempting to marry my colleague, I thank her and we leave, but then realise that we haven't asked about witnesses, a crucial part of Islamic marriage ceremonies. We return and put the question.

'Do we need a witness?'

'Yes, two witnesses.'

'Can they be women?' I ask.

'No, you must bring two male witnesses. Muslim men.' She raises a dismissive finger and we leave the bookshop.

* * *

The following day, I get a Facebook friend request from someone named Humera. I also get a message on Facebook Messenger: 'Were you at Regent's Park Mosque yesterday? I think I saw you from the women's section!'

'Who is this?' I ask.

'You forgot me very quickly!! It is Humera! From Newham College!'

I suddenly remember who she is. We did our A levels together, and despite being only seventeen I had a massive crush on her. This recollection suddenly brings back memories. I used to write notes of admiration, dedication and appreciation to her, and she would always respond graciously with conversations. Now, more than two decades later, she is the one doing the writing.

'My husband and sons were in the mosque, too, but I thought I recognised you!'

'Why didn't you stop me in the courtyard area afterwards?' I ask. 'It would have been lovely to see you!'

'Yes, but the husband wouldn't like it. How are you, anyhow? I see you've been travelling and being productive!'

At college, Humera decided to wear the hijab. Her background was not in east London, and I was surprised that she conformed so quickly to what all the other Muslim girls were doing. Now, on Facebook, I see that all her photos are with other women in hijab and her husband or brother. Despite seeing these photos, I fail to understand her current moral compass, and so I press her further.

'Are you in Regent's Park often?' I ask. 'It's been so long; it'd be lovely to see you again!'

'Yes, I bet you've changed so much,' she says.

'Give me a couple of dates that work and we can meet before or after prayers,' I say.

She sends back emojis of outbursts of laughter.

'I can't see you on my own. I need a *mahram*.'

My heart sinks. The girl I used to know has married into the caliphist subculture where she has to refuse a meeting with an old college friend without a sharia-sanctioned male chaperone. For more than two decades she has only met with women, never with men on her own, except with her brother and husband present. Her son is a teenager now and will soon be able to act as her chaperone, too.

'Do you think God is that petty?' I ask her. 'That he cares about a man and a woman meeting? Does anything justify all this fear of sex?'

Writing this book, and seeing the control exercised over women across the country, has made me extremely sensitive to this underworld imposing its laws and lifestyles on women.

If Humera had wanted to meet me before, I don't think she will now.

* * *

Hannah, my younger daughter, comes home from school with a violin one day. A discussion about music at school naturally follows. Both of our daughters have related stories of things they've encountered at school that I thought had ended with my own generation of younger, less settled and more confused British Muslims.

'Halima won't join us,' said Hannah to her sister Camilla one year, discussing their school Christmas concert. Halima, at the age of seven, was wearing a hijab to school. Halima was to sit on her own in the school office and not join the other children at the concert.

The following year my daughters told me that another girl, aged eight, had joined several others in wearing the hijab. At school sports days I've seen girls as young as five wearing headscarves. The teachers don't challenge this sexualisation of children for fear of being accused of racism or Islamophobia.

Hannah is friends with Lina from Pakistan. Lina will return to Pakistan in a few years, but while in England she already wears a headscarf. I met Lina at a sports day and found her to be a pleasant, reserved child. But Lina, my daughters tell me, refuses to play with Puja, because Puja is Hindu and Lina says she's 'dirty'. Hannah has tried to make peace between the two girls, but they still won't play together.

At Christmas, some of the girls mime the words to the carols being sung at school, but don't actually take part in the carol singing. Others sit out swimming classes, as these are not acceptable. And in religious education classes, some of the older girls put their fingers in their ears rather than listen to explanations of other religions.

* * *

My wife's friend hears that I'm writing a book on Islam in Britain and wants to share her views on Islamic schools, so we invite her over for dinner. She brings along her daughters, Muna, who is twenty-four, and Zoya, who's twenty. After dinner we all sit in the study and look over volumes of Bukhari's *hadith* and Quran commentaries from the tenth and twelfth centuries, and talk about mutual friends. The topic turns to the girls' education.

Both Muna and Zoya were in the first cohort of the first women-only Muslim school and seminary in London. Looking at them, fully comfortable with making eye contact with me, and speaking in clear, strong voices, it's hard to imagine that they spent their formative years in a Deobandi Islamic school. Here they are in my study at home, completely comfortable in their tight jeans and tops, with free-flowing hair and perfect English, while their mother sits beside them wearing a hijab.

'So what happened?' I say, laughing, for they know what I am thinking.

They are both raring to answer, but their mother interjects: 'It was my mistake.' She looks at the floor and says, 'I'm sorry, again.'

She then looks at me and says, 'I've been apologising to my daughters for years now. I listened to Shaikh Hamza Yusuf from America, who said we should remove our children from state schools because the education system was godless.'

'I remember that,' I say, with empathy.

'I asked several Arab Muslim scholars here, and they all said don't send your children to Islamic schools, but I thought that an American Muslim convert knew better.'

'It wasn't all bad,' interrupts Muna. 'Both of us sat for the first few weeks of the *alima* course, the *Dars-e-Nizami*. We didn't want to continue, but stayed with the GCSE curriculum in an Islamic atmosphere at the school, and then left to do our A levels.'

She speaks well, enunciating her 't's, and it is hard to tell that she went to an Islamic school, where the focus would have been on Arabic and Urdu. She straightens her bra strap as she crosses her legs with the confidence and charisma of a liberated woman in her early twenties.

'But why not do the *alima* course and become female clerics?' I ask, playing devil's advocate, for I suspect I already know what her answer will be.

Zoya jumps in to say, 'I'm studying history now at Durham. I always knew the perspective of the teachers at the school was out of date and hypocritical.'

'What do you mean?' I ask.

'Small things happened there that said a lot. All the teachers were female, so there was gender separatism, but they had conversations on WhatsApp and Facebook with men, so how was that being religious? They said we couldn't wear make-up, but they wore perfume. They banned us from doing our eyebrows, but they did theirs. There were drugs at school and other girls had boyfriends …'

'That's why I think it's like any other school, and a money-making scheme,' jumps in the mother again. But she clearly has a deep respect for her daughters' views and allows them to complete their thoughts in a way that shows she perceives them as her equals.

The girls tell me it was online that they found Muslim clerics, in Canada, who helped them find ways to remain Muslim, believe in God and address their identity questions.

'The biggest challenge for Muslims is toxic masculinity,' says Muna. Maryam nods in agreement.

'The Prophet was very effeminate,' continues Muna. 'He had long hair, applied kohl to his eyes, used perfume, and we know him as "a mercy and compassion to the world", in the words of the Quran.'

Zoya smiles.

'No disrespect to you, but your gender is the dominant problem among clerics and communities; the patriarchy controlled everything in our school and the women teachers were just a front.'

Muna then says, 'We need new third places, away from mosques and schools, for Muslim youth.'

My own daughters leave us at this stage to go to bed, and we continue talking.

Muna and Zoya's commentary on the Muslim patriarchy continues to play on my mind. 'What do you mean by toxic masculinity?' I ask Muna.

'It's the expectation that we – women and men and non-binary others – must conform to the cognitive expectations of traditional masculinity,' she says. She explains every part of the LGBTQIA++ spectrum with a fluency that makes me look out of touch, despite my Birmingham encounter at the LGBT Centre.

'What did you study at university?' I ask.

'Law and history at SOAS,' she says. We exchange comments on our common alma mater, but her razor-sharp definition of the toxic masculinity within Islam stays with me.

'So give me an example of how toxic masculinity has an impact on Muslim women like you today. You seem free and intelligent and have a reason-based approach to religion.'

'Yes, but I couldn't have become like this if my mother and father hadn't let me.'

Are these 'woke' young women outliers? I wonder. Or are there many more like them among the younger generation of British Muslims who are dissenting from the patriarchy, the clerics, the community?

'You should meet our other sister,' Zoya adds. 'She's involved in organising the third space, giving young women a voice, helping them express their identity, removing the toxicity of masculine imposition on all our lives.'

The evening ends with tea and cake made by Fatima, with her immense hospitality. I'm pleased that my young daughters witnessed this particular conversation, rather than some of the others I have had in the course of writing this book.

The number of Islamic schools across the country is increasing, many of them state-funded. As secular inspectors, Ofsted cannot probe the content of religious curricula. There are also a large number of private religious schools that have been founded, according to a 2017 Ofsted report, in order to avoid teaching 'fundamental values of democracy, mutual tolerance and respect'.[4] Even Darul Uloom Bury, whose religious syllabus, the *Dars-e-Nizami* (taught alongside GCSEs), has received 'good' or 'outstanding' ratings in the past decade from Ofsted, has still been criticised by countless graduates for its failings.

* * *

Two weeks later, on a Sunday morning, I'm attending the wedding of a distant family member. The bride lives in Colchester. Her father is an accountant and her mother a teacher, and she studied engineering at university. At thirty, she had worried that she might not marry. When we arrive at the home she shares with her parents, we find that her younger sisters have adorned the drawing room with flowers and other decorations. Several guests are already sitting there. Snacks and non-alcoholic drinks are served. There is a special decorated chair, with a floral sign above it spelling out 'Roxana', the name of the bride.

'She'll sit here,' says the youngest sister of the bride.

'No,' says her father, recently returned from Hajj, now wearing a beard and carrying even stronger religious convictions than before. 'The men will see her. Let her sit in her own bedroom.'

An argument ensues, with the younger sister continuing to indicate where Roxana will sit.

The imam who will be conducting the wedding ceremony arrives.

'I think this place has been declared for Roxana so she should sit here,' I say.

'Yes,' say the women, and now the men don't want to be seen to be opposing them, knowing that the imam will be asked for his opinion and we will be forced to disagree. For the sake of peace, the father remains silent.

The bride appears, wearing a lavender dress and a hijab. She has bridesmaids with her in similar outfits. She sits down but makes no eye contact with anybody present. The imam recites Quranic verses and *hadith* on marriage, women and the family. He then asks the bride if she accepts the groom, for the dowry of £10,000, as her husband, to whom he will go shortly. She doesn't respond, and her mother prompts her to say '*qabul*', which means 'accepted' in Arabic. She sniffles, and then says it. It's a sad moment and there are tears. The imam prays for everybody; there's more crying. The bride's relationship with her family ends today, for in the evening she will be 'given away'. Emotions are running high as she leaves the decorated drawing room.

The imam is still in the room. I am to be a witness to the marriage along with two other men. The imam asks me to sign a piece of paper.

I take the pen. 'What happens next?' I say with a smile, trying to lift the mood.

'We will go to the Darul Ummah mosque in Tower Hamlets. The groom will be there, and he will sign, too.'

'And then?'

'You and the other witnesses will confirm that you have seen and heard the bride say "*qabul*", and then in the evening the meal will take place for both families and the marriage is complete.'

'And when do you or the couple register this marriage with the town hall? It's Sunday today, so it'll be closed. Does Darul Ummah have a legal registrar?'

The imam looks dumbfounded. The paper is taken away from me. The processes of the sharia courts are beyond questioning, it seems. The conversation in the room suddenly switches to the Premier League and when Manchester United will be playing. Tea and snacks are consumed as the two other witnesses quietly leave the room with the imam.

I have been left behind for asking too many questions. Yet the marriage is a sham. If the girl wants a divorce next week, she lacks the right to get it. The law of the land does not apply here. But surely a few community leaders can't just decide that a woman is married, trapping her without access to her legal rights?

I ask some of the others in the room about the groom. Who is he? What does he do? I was supposed to be meeting him at the mosque, but that is delayed now until the evening. One of the bridesmaids, when I turn to her, looks embarrassed. She gestures towards the door to the back garden. I follow her out. A few men sitting in the corner of the room glower at me for starting up a conversation with a woman. The norms of British society seem to be suspended here.

'What is going on here?' I ask her. 'Why does it all feel so weird?'

'You're only seeing the tip of the iceberg.'

'So what is it with the imam, and not supporting a legal marriage?'

'I don't think Rox has even thought about that. Her parents wanted the imam so that the marriage would be legitimate in God's eyes, and now that's been done. I think she thinks she's now married, so she's having a mental breakdown upstairs.'

'Yes, it's a huge step. So who is the bloke?'

The bridesmaid looks away. 'They met online, on a Muslim marriage site. They chatted, he gave her his religious credentials: he has a beard, he prays. He's a practising Muslim. And she's trying to be a better Muslim, so she thinks the marriage will help her.'

'And what does he do?' I ask.

'He's a waiter in a restaurant.'

'What?! She's an engineer, and he's a waiter?! But they're marrying for religion?'

'She likes him,' says the bridesmaid. And then someone else comes into the garden, and we're not allowed the privacy to continue our conversation.

A large community hall has been booked for the evening. Large numbers of women sit at the back of the hall, but I insist my wife and daughters sit with me. I saw similar strict gender segregation in Saudi Arabia, and refuse to allow that to influence my family. Slowly, other families arrive who also sit together. The women at the back now come and go to and from the front, speaking to friends. Several who had their faces covered when they arrived now lift their face veils as they realise the atmosphere is more relaxed, less religious, than they expected. Quiet music plays in the background until someone complains and it's turned off. Islamic *nasheeds*, unaccompanied chants, are played instead. People slowly mingle, children run around. All of the men, without exception, are dressed in Western clothes, and I can only see three wearing Islamic caps on their heads.

The bride, who is now considered a wife because some clerics have signed a piece of paper with no validity in a court of law, cries as she takes leave of her family. Her new husband waits with his family to take her home.

She is an educated woman from Colchester, marrying a man from a council estate in inner-city Tower Hamlets, being 'given away' to live with him because of an ancient custom that says a woman must live under the protection of a man. After almost every 'Islamic wedding' the bride goes to live at the groom's home. The patriarchy that my friend's daughters spoke of comes alive before my eyes.

On the drive home, my mind is full of questions that cannot be answered yet. I have just witnessed caliphism at work again: applying a separate law, a separate social code and a separate way of existence. Why can't this marriage be legally registered? Why must standards of piety from the bygone age of the caliphs define a British Muslim marriage? Why must a professional woman be placed under patriarchal male protection, as developed by the caliphs of the past and imposed by the caliphists of today?

* * *

Leaving Liverpool Street station after a meeting one afternoon, I pass the independent coffee shops, barbers, cafés and clothing shops along the outer edges of Spitalfields Market. At the end of the road is Hawksmoor's imposing neoclassical Christ Church, its immense triangular spire standing out bright against the grey sky. Just behind it lies Brick Lane, famous for its many Bangladeshi restaurants but slowly being taken over by art shops and vegan cafés. The street signs are in English and Bengali.

Mere steps away from the bustling tourist thoroughfare lie endless council flats, grey and uninspiring. Washing is hanging out to dry from windows. A few solitary trees stand amidst the concrete. Children are returning from school in their smart uniform blazers. In the distance, the Gherkin and the gleaming towers of the City stand at odds with my surroundings. A banner attached to a garden fence advertises an Islamic supplementary school offering Arabic language lessons. Photos of pupils show tiny girls in hijab, fully covered.

I emerge on to Greatorex Street, where shops begin to appear between the blocks of flats. Ali's Superstore. Majabi Grill. A shop offering money transfers and airline tickets. A sign for Whitechapel Citizens Advice Bureau, with Bengali lettering underneath. Salahuddin Hajj and Umrah travel agency. On the corner, facing on to Whitechapel Road, is a branch of the Qatari-owned Al Rayan Bank.

Across the road is the massive complex of the East London Mosque, also known as the London Muslim Centre, its façade of brown brick accented with darker red arches and a pale dome, twin minarets above its main entrance. All along Whitechapel Road in the vicinity of the mosque are countless travel agents, Islamic banks, bookshops and stores selling Islamic merchandise. The caliphist culture I saw in Dewsbury's Savile Town is present here, too, in this much bigger, more political part of London's East End. Does anybody care or even notice that all this is here?

I go into the first few shops I see. All are selling black seed oil, headscarves, caps, Qurans and religious textbooks. I spot works by Qutb and Maududi in every single store I step inside. Shops on the other side of the road are much the same. There must be several dozen of them in this one square mile of east London. Every restaurant or café sign I see refers to the Middle East or Islamic culture: Ottoman Grill, Al Hambra Café, Makkah Charcoal Grill. Where is the 'British' part of British Islam, British mosques?

The streets behind the mosque contain similar shops. Many of them offer traditional methods of healing, selling black seed oil. I pass a 'Cupping Clinic' advertising 'natural health for all'.

The practice of 'cupping', or *hijama*, is increasingly popular as a homeopathic practice to cure anything from headaches to hay fever. It seems to be enjoying a newfound popularity in the Muslim world due to the revival of references to a number of *hadiths* that suggest the Prophet Mohamed subscribed to the practice.[5] I saw similar services offered in Blackburn. An Islamic school, Ebrahim College, is based in a large office block nearby.[6]

Just across from the back entrance to some of the mosque's extensive buildings is the Qurtubah Institute, a complex offering various Arabic and Islamic lessons for children and adults. Further along is the mosque's Maryam Centre, a new nine-storey development that provides spaces for women to pray, a girls' school, and a women-only gym.

Beside it are a number of charitable organisations, one with a banner proclaiming: 'Believe in the Power of Zakat!' Just above the banner, etched into the stone frame of the door, an old inscription is visible, with the date 1899. Two Stars of David flank the engraved name of Fieldgate Street Great Synagogue.

Back on Whitechapel Road, I pass a charity shop run by Islamic Relief, the Birmingham-based organisation that has been banned by a number of governments including the UAE for links to the Muslim Brotherhood. In Whitechapel Market, every single stall without fail sells modest clothing, headscarves and caps, or is staffed by a visibly Muslim vendor.

Where are the Irish? The Jews? The Russians? The East End was once their home. What happened? The London borough of Tower Hamlets, which encompasses most of east London and Canary Wharf, has the highest proportion of Muslim residents in the UK, at 38 per cent, and more than 40 per cent were born outside the country.[7] Today, it seems perfectly possible for a Muslim man, woman or family to live in this area with absolutely no contact with the wider world, with modern Britain. From taxis to butchers, schools to gyms, banks to post offices, all are owned and run by Muslims.

* * *

In a small room in a house attached to a mosque in north London I meet Shaikh Magdy. He is Egyptian, a trained barrister and sharia scholar in his fifties. His beard needs touching up with the henna he uses to dye it a dark shade of orange. Shaikh Magdy is a rotund gentleman. As a cleric and judge within the sharia courts, he is the sort of man that thousands of young Muslim women will come to for advice when their marriages, of the sort I attended last week, hit difficulties.

Magdy is a well-known Muslim in Britain, and the cleric of choice for educated Muslim women because he speaks fluent English and has accreditation from Egypt's ancient university, Al-Azhar. He has a pedigree and has never been in the newspapers for any sort of negative activity, unlike some others in the British sharia courts. His plain office contains a filing cabinet, a desktop computer, a mobile phone and a photocopier; on the walls there are photos of the holy cities, Mecca and Medina. The room smells of floral air freshener. It is neither warm nor cold on this autumnal November day, yet I feel like keeping my coat on, as it's the sort of place where you don't want to stay too long. There is a strangely unwelcoming feeling in the room.

I sit down opposite Shaikh Magdy. He crosses his arms and leans forward.

'How can I help you?' he asks with a smile, half-moon glasses resting on his nose, a Muslim fez on his head, reminding me of all those twentieth-century French and Italian soldiers who wore fezzes during the wars.

'Shaikh Magdy, I've come to see you because you were a student of the great Zaki Badawi, who was a friend of the Prince of Wales. Shaikh Zaki, God rest his soul, understood Britain and Islam, and yet he was attacked by all of us back then as going too far in his liberalism. I've just been travelling across Britain, and sharia courts kept coming up in conversation. How do you feel about where Islam and Muslims are headed in Britain?'

He smiles and sits back in his chair.

'Where have you been?' he asks me. I name the cities, mosques, and some of the people I met.

'Have you met Haitham al-Haddad?' he asks me.

'No, but you're not the first person who's mentioned him to me. Why is he so important? *The Times* and the *Daily Telegraph* have run stories on the man. He's a nonentity, surely?'

Haitham al-Haddad is a Salafi cleric and former sharia court judge based in Britain. He founded the wide-reaching Muslim Research and Development Foundation (MRDF) and the popular website Islam21c, which offers advice to twenty-first-century Western Muslims on how to follow the classical traditions of Islam. Al-Haddad was expelled from the Islamic Sharia Council in 2015, and examples of his literalist theology are rife.

Although al-Haddad has condemned Islamist terrorist groups like ISIS (despite referring to the caliphate as an 'Islamic obligation'[8]), his extreme Salafism is nevertheless problematic in its branding of non-believers as bound for hell, and its literalist interpretations of the Quran and the *hadith*. A 2014 Channel 4 documentary found that al-Haddad had told students that husbands beating their wives 'should not be questioned', and *The Times* has compiled a cross-referenced summary of al-Haddad's views taken from publications and lectures given between 2007 and 2018. Included are his opinions on the 'correct' method of female genital mutilation; the age at which it is permitted for a girl to be married ('the younger the better'); the niqab as a Quranic requirement; the requirement that apostates should be killed; and homosexuality being evil.[9]

In a YouTube video posted by Islam21c, al-Haddad has stated that British Muslims need to come together to build more institutions for Islamic education and finance, as Islamic finance will 'end the financial crisis' and solve the West's 'problems' and liberalism.[10] In another, he says that all the afflictions people suffer come from God, and that Muslims will be rewarded, and have their sins removed, for suffering through pain and proving their willpower by not taking painkillers. He cites a *hadith* stating that some of the early Muslims wished for more difficulties in life because of the reward they would receive for surviving them.[11]

'Away from the media, away from mosques, he's raising the next generation of Muslims here as Salafis,' Shaikh Magdy tells me. 'I'd say almost seven out of every ten Muslim professionals I meet are neo-Salafis. He has a large network of students who are working around the clock to spread a version of literalist, Salafi Islam that is commenting on contemporary social and political issues. Look at the Islam21c website. The popular Eman TV channel. The MRDF control almost a hundred Islamic student societies in our universities. He's also famous for launching and winning libel claims, so we are all silent on challenging him.'

'But why is this a growing issue?' I ask.

'Because it's not in the mosques yet, but growing in the younger generation, the ones now in their twenties and thirties who will soon be taking over the mosques and British Muslim organisations. Then you'll come back to me and ask me what went wrong, so I'm telling you now where we are headed. I have young men in their teens coming to me to share the news that they've received full bursaries for six years of study in Saudi Arabia, to study Islam in Medina. Yes, the Saudi government may be moving away from extremism, but the universities in Medina and Mecca haven't changed their curricula, which remain fundamentally opposed to the modern world. Where are we headed? When we have more Wahhabi and Salafi imams coming back into Britain?'

'Surely we can oppose them?' I suggest hopefully.

'Look, the Muslim mindset is predisposed to obedience and seeking sacred blessings from clerics. That shift hasn't yet happened, but look at the MRDF website. You'll see Muslim women born and raised in this country who don't have an individual identity; they're just mothers – "Umm Khadijah" or "Umm Salama",[12] and there are no photos of them, or any female teachers. How do they accept it? They're British, how do the men not complain? Because Haitham and others have laid down the law in Salafi terms, and British Muslims are obedient to clerics.

'Then we have the problem,' he continues, 'with the media and politicians who want "authentic" Muslims. I am a liberal, modern Muslim scholar; I teach gender equality; my female students don't wear the hijab. They're lawyers, bankers and doctors, but they aren't seen as "Muslim enough". Centrist Muslims are losing ground in their own communities and their own country – the more savage, the more violent Muslims are, the more "authentic" in these people's eyes. This culture war of authenticity is killing the very ideas we uphold in the liberal and modern world. The big beards versus the clean-shaven imams. Who is authentic?'

I find him perceptive in his descriptions of the social meanings we have created in our narratives of Islam. He goes further:

'The vast majority of mosques and organisations in British Islam are a huge problem. There, I've said it. But what I want to know is, are we alone? What about gurdwaras? Temples? Synagogues? Do they allow women in management positions? I'm not talking about becoming religious leaders, I'm saying that my students, who also give money to mosques, cannot become chairs, managers or trustees. Why not?'

I promise myself that I will get to the bottom of this issue later.

After thanking Shaikh Magdy for his time, I leave his office.

* * *

Today I am walking through Leicester Square en route to Charing Cross Road. I have a couple of hours free and am on my way to browse antiquarian bookshops and Foyles. On the Square, I hear the loud sound of the Quran being recited. I can see the tops of two men's heads above the side of a makeshift stall where a loudspeaker has been set up. I've seen these men here in Leicester Square before. Thousands of people must pass this way every day, but I have never seen anyone heckle them.

There's a woman approaching them from the other direction, and I'm drawn to the books they have on display. The men are sitting on the ground having some lunch. They see the woman and me and stand up to shake my hand. Both men have long beards and are wearing Western clothes. I can tell they are Salafi-oriented because they cannot eat their chips and burgers standing up. There is a *hadith* followed by Salafis that says Mohamed sat down to eat, and so Muslims should not stand or walk as they eat and drink but try to perform *sunnah* by emulating Mohamed's eating habits.

They are also upholding traditions from the ninth century as they shake my hand but refuse to shake the hand of the Danish woman who now stands beside me. The men indicate that they would like to speak with me, but I point to the woman and say, 'I think she may have some questions for you.' They appear not to have heard this, so I go ahead with my point of contention.

'Do you think Britain is an Islamophobic country, when in the middle of its capital city you are broadcasting the Quran and nobody stops you?'

One of the two, a mixed-race man with a shaved upper lip but a long beard, responds with, 'Are you a Muslim?'

'What does that have to do with my question?'

'If you answer, I will explain how it is connected to understanding Islamophobia.'

'In the heart of London you are freely preaching Islam, yet some Muslims claim this country is inherently Islamophobic – can you explain how that is?'

He repeats his question. After all my travels, this clerical sophistry, and the paranoia of preachers, is now beginning to annoy me: I have seen these games of manipulation all too often. I can't engage with it any more. I feel my phone buzz in my pocket as I turn around and walk off.

It is August 2019, and a Saudi journalist friend of mine has sent me a text message saying: 'Happy New Year!'

Has her message been delayed by eight months, I think at first. I check my phone's reception and connectivity. All is well. I respond to her with question marks.

'Islamic New Year!' she responds.

'Good heavens, yes, of course!' I reply. 'Which year are we in?'

'1440,' she replies.

'Wow. Jewish people are in 5779, Christianity has reached 2019. We Muslims are still at the point before Columbus, Leonardo da Vinci, Galileo, the Reformation and the Enlightenment.'

She agrees, and confesses she's not thought about that before, with emojis of laughter. I find out later that she has published a piece on a Saudi news site about Islamic reform and the question of whether the Muslim mindset is still stuck in the fifteenth century.

Within days of that digital exchange I start getting Facebook promotions and adverts for Ashura events commemorating the seventh-century Battle of Karbala, which is remembered by Shi'a Muslims on the tenth day of Muharram, the first month in the Islamic calendar.

The major difference between Islam's two principal sects concerns the lineage of Islam's leaders after the death of the Prophet Mohamed.* For Sunnis, the caliphs – literally 'successors' – who followed Mohamed, starting with his father-in-law Abu Bakr, were legitimate. To the Shi'a, it is still a deeply felt injustice that Mohamed's son-in-law Ali, and Mohamed's grandsons Hasan and Hussein, were not granted the caliphate after Mohamed's death in 632. The name 'Shi'a' literally comes from 'Shi'at Ali', or supporters of Ali.

Shi'as are definitely in the minority within the Muslim population of the UK, but there are nevertheless an estimated 400,000 of them living here.

The Battle of Karbala in 680 marked the entrapment of Hussein and his followers in the Arabian desert by supporters of the existing caliphate, who opposed the claims of Ali's progeny to the succession. Hussein, giving himself up to his enemies to preserve the lives of his companions, was impaled by arrows and suffered dozens of knife wounds. His horse made its way back to his supporters with an empty saddle. While to Sunni Muslims Karbala is an unfortunate episode in history, for the Shi'a it is central to every aspect of their religious life; their clothes and worship ceremonies reflect their dedication to Ali and his slain son, Hussein. They mourn his death every Muharram.

* * *

* For the history of Shi'a Islam and its genesis, please see *The House of Islam: A Global History*, Bloomsbury, 2018).

It is now the ninth day of the new Islamic year and I am walking to a Shi'a mosque in London. It is just after 9.30 p.m. and the streets are dark. There are two men guarding the entrance to the building. Just in front of me a man and his son head into the mosque, and I walk up right behind them. I am not stopped. The man in front of me quickly removes his sandals and touches a pole with many pieces of coloured fabric attached to it. He feels the fabric with veneration, then brings his hand to his forehead and wipes his face. Stupidly, I point out to him that he's forgotten his sandals. I later learn that the pole with the pieces of fabric attached to it is called the *alam*, and it symbolises the war standard of Hussein. The man was showing reverence for it by removing his footwear, which is considered dirty in Muslim culture.

He has now finished his ritual and is looking at me suspiciously. It is clear to him that I am not a Shi'a, for I'm supposed to know about the *alam*. Young men in fluorescent jackets that say 'volunteer' are sitting to the side with notepads, registering the details of people entering and those giving money to the mosque. They're raising funds for the *jaloos*, a procession that will happen tomorrow, and for food for the attendees afterwards.

Sheepishly I walk past them, remove my shoes and sit down on the floor of the mosque. There are men sitting on chairs along the wall looking at me. Others are praying, resting their foreheads on flat stones sourced from the site of the historic battle, at Karbala in modern Iraq. I saw such practices in Syria, but I don't know how to pray as a Shi'a, so I don't try to fake it but simply sit back to observe. Almost all those present, some 500 men, are wearing black, mostly salwar kameez. They are in mourning for the deaths of Ali's sons at Karbala. A few are wearing chadors around their upper bodies, some of them green. I am fortunately not wearing bright clothes, as I don't want to draw further attention to myself. Not a single congregant is wearing any headgear. Most have trimmed beards, and there is no Sunni shaving of moustaches. Some have tattoos and many of the younger men have earrings.

Sunnis believe that Omar, the second caliph, commanded the believers to trim their beards once a year at the Hajj, so they grow their beards long each year. But since Shi'as don't recognise the first three caliphs (Abu Bakr, Omar and Othman) as legitimate, believing the succession to Mohamed should have followed his bloodline through Ali, they don't wear their beards long.

There are a lot of young boys in the room, too, some as young as four or five. They are all wearing black headbands that say '*Ya Hussein*' (O Hussein) in red.

There are photos on the walls of persecuted Shi'a communities in Pakistan, Saudi Arabia and other countries. Sunni mosques tend not to have photos inside the main area of the mosque.

'*Ya Sahib al-Zaman*' it says in Arabic on the walls. 'O Master of the Age'. I saw that same writing in the doorways and windows of several houses as I walked over. This is code for the Shi'a messiah, the Mahdi.

The establishment of a global caliphate is not only a militant Sunni aim, but also a mass anticipation among most Shi'as. Sunni extremists will be content simply to instate a caliph, but the Shi'a version insists that it will be the reappearing Imam Muhammad al-Mahdi, who was born in 869 as the twelfth imam, or caliph, descended from the Prophet's daughter Fatima and son-in-law Ali.

The concept of a messianic Mahdi does not appear in the Quran, and is based solely on *hadith* dating from the tenth century onwards, together with the Shi'a belief that the twelfth imam, Muhammad al-Mahdi, did not actually die but merely disappeared from the world and will return one day to rule global Islam in the name of Allah. The majority of Shi'as today are Twelver Shi'as who expect, indeed await and yearn for, their Mahdi's imminent return.

I feel inquiring eyes turning on me. A man at the front of the room is standing with a microphone behind a table with two pink roses, symbolising Fatima, also known as Zahra, or Fatima al-Zahra, the daughter of Mohamed and mother of Hussein. On either side of the speaker there is a stylised hand of Fatima, a symbol of goodwill and protection in the Shi'a Middle East. Below the hands, and above the flowers, are more colourful flags tied in knots. There is also something on the table wrapped in cloth.

'*Salawat!*' orders the speaker, and everyone around me breaks out in chants of '*Allahumma salli 'ala Muhammadin wa aali Muhammadin*'. 'O God, send blessings upon Mohamed and the family of Mohamed.' The elders sitting on chairs look at me, wondering if this stranger among them will recite the prayer. I have seen such phrases uttered in unison on Arabic television, when Hasan Nasrallah of Hezbollah or Iranian clerics speak, and therefore am able to recite the prayer in the same slow, elongated, militant tone.

I feel a hand on my back, and someone says, 'Please.' I look behind me. 'Please go to the front,' he says. Terrified that I am being summoned for some kind of impromptu court martial, I ask, 'Why?'

Then I see volunteers asking other people to move forward, too. They're anticipating hundreds more people and want to make space by crowding us into the front areas of the mosque. I shift forward, sliding on my hands and knees rather than walking.

Another speaker takes the microphone. He starts with Arabic prayers, and then recites some folk poetry in Punjabi. I catch intermittent words and phrases – 'son', 'mother', 'kill', 'skies cry' – as he raises his voice while affecting to cry. After twenty minutes another speaker takes the microphone and again recalls the killing of Hussein at the seventh-century Battle of Karbala, reading aloud from a book while simulating tears. Speaker after speaker raises his voice and then breaks down as if crying, yet none wipes away real tears. In the audience, though, I hear sniffing, see tissues dabbing tears away.

And then an anticipated speaker walks up to the front of the room. '*Salawat!*' he orders, and we all obey with the expected chants. As the speaker recalls Fatima, most beloved daughter of Mohamed ... the death of Hussein ... and Hasan not being there to aid his brother ... the elders start to beat their chests. They repeatedly draw their right hands to their upper chests, landing a thudding slap each time. Two of the children are slapping their own faces. I suck in my breath in shock. A man on my right looks at me with red-rimmed eyes full of tears.

More children on the other side of him are slapping their faces and heads as the speaker tells us in Urdu about the death at Karbala of Hussein's young baby, Ali al-Asghar, when Hussein held up the infant to his attackers, begging for their mercy towards an innocent. Ali al-Asghar was pierced with an arrow and killed on the spot.

It is now 11 p.m. Do the children not have school in the morning, I wonder.

The men continue to thump their chests and some begin to wail. The loudspeaker is turned up to full volume, and it is hard to understand the speaker as its echo and the inordinate wailing and thrashing fill the room. A father or guardian several rows in front of me strokes his toddler's back in approval as the boy whacks his own face. As the father's hand appears, I see he is wearing *aqeeq* rings, set with precious stones. Then I look around and see that almost everybody in the room is wearing them. Imam Ali, the father of Hussein, husband of Fatima and son-in-law of Mohamed, is reported to have said that wearing such rings brings strength and peace.

The speakers curse the Caliph Omar and invoke curses upon him. This is all about the caliphate: they believe Hussein to have been the rightful caliph, so they curse the other caliphs.

The overwhelming emotion in the hall at the still unhealed wound of Hussein's killing, in 680, is palpable. The strong sense of vengeance and anger at history stealing the caliphate from the bloodline of Mohamed is still raw, more than a millennium after the fact.

Why are children being permitted to self-harm? Why are their parents not protecting them? Why are the parents, too, beating themselves so mindlessly? Thirteen centuries after Hussein's death, can we not move on? This is London, not Karbala.

But this is not the time for asking questions. I stand up amid the commotion, bend down and pick my way slowly between the shoulders of men, in between cycles of heavier and lighter self-beating. I avoid eye contact and make a final dash for the door, but my shoes have been moved from where I left them and it takes me a while to find them. Out in the street, after 11 p.m. in this residential part of London, I can still hear groups of Shi'a men singing songs about Zainab, Hussein's sister, who bravely stood before the rival caliph, berating him for the murder of her brother.

Little do I know it now, but worse is yet to come. Police notices have been placed outside the mosque about a 'Major Event Tomorrow', at 11 a.m., warning that roads will be blocked. This is for the *jaloos*, the Shi'a mourning procession to mark the anniversary of the historic battle.

* * *

I arrive at 11.20 the following morning. There are volunteer security guards outside the mosque and guarding the streets.

'Where's the procession?' I ask. They don't speak English. Then I see a man rushing up the street in a yellow vest and I ask him. He points up the road and says, very briefly, 'Over there.'

I walk in the direction he indicates, passing a parked ambulance. Just beyond it there must be more than 2,000 women dressed from head to toe in black, singing and wailing, walking slowly down the road. Ahead of the women I see thousands of men and boys processing, so I walk up beside them.

As I do so, I see others joining from the front of the procession, not the back. At the front there are men carrying the *alam*, and many come to kiss it or reach out to touch it with their hands, kissing them and wiping their faces with the blessing. The procession turns into a side street.

I walk ahead to take a look at the participants. Local residents, pensioners, mothers and carers come to the window, and some are outside their houses watching. I note numbers 225 and 237 where people are looking on. I want to go back later and ask them how they feel, what they think of this. For now, though, I keep my eyes on what the procession is doing. More and more men are arriving all the time, as the women continue wailing.

I see a horse decorated with tassels and tinsel, with bloodstains on its hooves and back. Without thinking, I ask the teenager next to me why the horse is bleeding.

'No, it's paint. Imam Hussein's horse had his blood on it after he was killed.'

There's a white man in his twenties nearby wearing a top hat and coat tails. He seems to be the rider, but it looks like he has been asked to accompany the horse rather than ride it. He looks terribly confused and out of place as he follows along and tries to keep the horse moving.

Now there are male singers joining in, with microphones and very loud speakers. They have black flags with the words '*Ya Hussein*' spelled out in red Arabic script. The singers break into an ecstasy of mourning. Suddenly the men remove their shirts and stop to stretch their right hands up towards the sky, their faces also looking upwards, then bring their arms down fully in a heavy blow to their chests. They repeat this with their left hands, before settling into a rhythm of blows: right, left, right, left. They line up opposite each other and thump their chests in unison. The group feeling and sense of concord draws in others. There are boys no older than thirteen or fourteen doing exactly as they see their elders do.

I spot the ambulance at the back of the procession. Who will be the first to collapse? They'll need more than just one.

The punching reaches a climax and falls away. Then the singer begins again, and the thumping pace accelerates. The younger boys seem most eager. The neighbours look on aghast.

I move further ahead and find another group of shirtless young men loudly thumping their chests. Two of them have open wounds on their upper bodies. There is actually blood dripping down them, and they wipe it with their shirts, yelling with pain as they hit themselves again and again. The shopkeepers look on. I can't bear to see the gushing wounds, so I move ahead again.

I notice the procession has police protection: five officers, all male, are coordinating with the men in black at the front. Is all this legal, I want to ask. We cross an intersection where buses and motorbikes are being held back, but the police protection means the procession is immune from any criticism or intervention.

Perhaps the ambulance doesn't know about the bleeding men with open wounds, I think. Perhaps I can alert them. As I try to head back, two men stop me. 'Don't go back, please,' they say. 'Only forward. Women at the back.'

'But I want to ...' I can't finish my sentence. 'No men allowed in the back,' they interrupt. 'The back's reserved for women. Men must be at the front.'

I reluctantly comply and keep walking forward. Some white women and a group of Sikh men leave the local Co-op and walk past in disgust, refusing to make any eye contact. Police protection ensures that no abuse is shouted.

As the procession turns a corner and heads towards the mosque, the men at the front demand that the women come forward and enter the mosque first. A volunteer puts his hand on my shoulder and says, 'No men allowed to walk near women. Let them go inside the mosque.'

I stand near the mosque for half an hour, allowing the women to pass me.

Scores of women, all in black chadors and head covers, walk in with their heads lowered, avoiding eye contact. I can't stop myself from questioning all this.

'Why are women at the back?' I ask a man who's commanding the section of the procession where I'm now standing.

'*Nahj al-Balagha. Nahj al-Balagha.*' He says it twice. The commotion is such that nobody wonders why I am asking questions.

I make a mental note to look into *Nahj al-Balagha*, a collection of sermons and sayings by Imam Ali, later. I've been prevented from walking freely on the public streets of London by the imposition of gender segregation. I also want to go back and ask the shopkeepers at numbers 225 and 237 what they think of this.

The men resume the beating but somewhat more raggedly now as they make their way into the mosque. The male singers are on a high and full of energy. They recite and sing together in mournful tones:

Mazloom zamanay te, Shabbir jeha koi nahi,
sada rahega Hussein ka ghamm.

Unjust age in which there is none like Shabbir,[13]
the grief of Hussein will remain alive.

Their chests look red and swollen from the beating. The moment the women have finished shuffling past, I leave the men to their left-right beating and head off to assess reactions from the neighbours.

A woman is sitting outside a launderette, smoking.

'That procession you just saw pass by, what do you think?' I ask her.

She smiles. I realise she is not smoking a cigarette.

'It's all new to us. It's all new. I don't really have an opinion,' she says, and returns to smoking her joint.

At number 225 the man is still outside, a dog at his feet.

'That procession you saw go by, what did you think?' I ask.

'Very loud,' he says. 'What was all that chest-beating?'

'I think they're mourning,' I say.

'But the women at the back, that's not our culture. We don't put our women at the back like that.'

For this white man in his late sixties, the worry is not the violence he has seen but the treatment of the women.

At the last house, 237, I knock on the door. A lady in her early fifties comes out and smiles at me.

'What did you think about the march that went past earlier?' I inquire.

'They do it every year. But what is it? Hindu?'

'No, it's Muslim,' I say.

'Oh, really? They're Muslim here, too. I'll ask them,' she says, pointing at her neighbours' house with a warm smile. 'But I feel upset about the girls and women being thrown at the back and the men leading them. That really upset me.'

I don't ask any further questions. Again, the gender segregation seems to have resonated more than the self-violence. Perhaps the onlookers didn't see what was happening as closely as I did, where the heavy beating happened on the side streets.

I head to the first side street that the procession turned down and knock on the door of one of the houses. A black lady opens it.

'Good afternoon. What did you think of the march earlier today? The one that passed your home?'

'Are you from the council?' she asks.

'No, I'm a writer, and I'm trying to understand people's reactions to it.'

'I'll tell you how we react: we don't like the shouting, the fighting, and the women being covered in black at the back. But they have the police on their side. The council allows them. The government doesn't care. Nobody is on our side.'

The sincerity and pointedness of her remarks bring tears to my eyes. I can't help myself.

'It's not right,' she adds, as she sees my reaction. 'They're going to destroy our country.'

I thank her for speaking with me.

To get back to the Tube station, I need to walk past the mosque again. The women have all gone inside now, and the men are no longer on the street. The police escort and ambulance are gone, too. I notice for the first time that the mosque is covered in black cloth, and I count twelve black flags flying from its façade. As I come closer, I hear the clinking of metal, an unfamiliar sound, as if sword fights are going on within its walls. There are loud chants of '*Ya Hussein! Ya Hussein! Ya Hussein!*' as they commemorate the caliph who was not, the caliph who should have been, in the eyes of the Shi'a. The Mahdi who is to return is the caliph who should be.

The gates of the mosque are guarded, but I am drawn towards it, curious to know what is happening now. The guards don't stop me. They must have seen me in the march earlier, so I slip in.

Row upon row of men, with knives and blades attached to whips, are slashing their own backs, blood pouring down from their bodies on to the floor. There are old scars and open wounds on every back, and some men have knife wounds on their chests, too, like those of the two young men I saw in the streets earlier.

On YouTube later that evening I discover many, many videos of *matam* (chest-beating) taking place across the West and in the British cities of Newport, Blackburn, Manchester, Leicester and several parts of London. Following the social-media trail leads me to the practice of *matam* and *zanjir* (a chain with blades for self-flagellation) in Britain's cosmopolitan capital. This is something entirely new and previously unknown to me.

Once home, I look into the *Nahj al-Balagha* mentioned by the man in the procession. The book, whose title means 'The Peak of Eloquence', is a collection of sermons and sayings of Imam Ali compiled in the tenth century. It's found in every Shi'a home and after the Quran is the sect's most venerated text. One of its most famous passages, addressed to the new governor of Egypt, is widely appreciated as a perfect encapsulation of the ideal Islamic government.

A major break between Sunnis and Shi'as is over the role of women, especially relating to Ayesha, Mohamed's youngest wife. After Ali became the fourth caliph, in 656, she led an army 10,000-strong against him. Sunni Muslims laud Ayesha's strength, while Shi'as hate and curse her for leading an insurrection against the 'true' caliph, Ali. It became known as 'the Battle of the Camel', because Ayesha led her troops atop a camel as she encouraged them in a strong and moving speech to attack Ali. To this day the Shi'a have not forgotten this attack on their imam and rightful caliph by a woman. The *Nahj al-Balagha* records a sermon from Imam Ali after the battle that is still read in Shi'a communities around the world:

'O people! Women are deficient in faith, deficient in shares and deficient in intelligence. As regards the deficiency in their faith, it is their abstention from prayers and fasting during their menstrual period.

'As regards deficiency in their intelligence, it is because the evidence of two women is equal to that of one man. As for the deficiency of their shares, that is because of their share in inheritance being half that of men.

'So beware of the evils of women. Be on your guard even from those of them who are [reportedly] good. Do not obey them even in good things so that they may not attract you to evils.'

Since the book is firmly embedded in Shi'a communal thought, women being treated as inferior, forced to the back of communal processions and barred from leadership positions clearly has something to do with this instruction from Ali in Sermon 80 of the *Nahj al-Balagha*.

Ali's argument for female inferiority, made in the context of a seventh-century war, on the basis that they are not permitted to observe faith rituals or receive equal shares in inheritance, and his insistence on their inferior intelligence, are all taken, literally, from verses of the Quran. It is this continued entrapment in historical literalism that is so damaging to many Muslim women today.[14]

* * *

After travelling the length and breadth of Great Britain, meeting Muslims from every major denomination, it is clear to me that blind reliance on scripture and clerics is overwhelmingly strong within British Islam. Adherence to the seventh-century Quran, ninth-century *hadith* and tenth- and eleventh-century Islamic scholarship is deeply embedded.

We live in a world of reason and logic, science and data, evidence and progress. How can Muslims still believe ancient *hadith* on the healing powers of flies, the flatness of the earth and black seed oil and honey as remedies for every illness? Early Muslims embraced the rational culture of the Greeks. Ibn al-Haytham (d. 1040) was the first scientist to establish that we see by means of reflected light penetrating our eyes. Earlier thinkers believed that our eyes themselves emitted light. Al-Zahrawi (d. 1023) created surgical innovations that formed the basis of medieval European medicine for centuries. Ammar ibn Ali al-Mawsili (d. 1020) came up with the concept of a medical syringe. Jabir ibn Hayyan (d. 815) laid down the forerunner of the periodic table, dividing elements into metals and non-metals. Al-Khwarizmi (d. 850), from whose name the word 'algorithm' is derived, developed key concepts in algebra in the ninth century.

Arab Muslims named stars and galaxies and took further the ancient Greek spirit of innovation and questioning. The ancient Arabs traced their lineage to the Qahtan tribe and believed that the Yunan (the Greeks) were their cousins. Those ancient Arabs proudly learned from and emulated the classical Greek philosophers.

Motivated both by what I have seen, heard and felt during this journey and also by what I have not, I arrange to meet with Shaikh

Abd al-Qadir, a *hadith* specialist of high repute, widely respected in London as a spiritual and scholarly figure, and with hundreds of young Muslim scholars currently being trained under his guidance.

The shaikh is holding a Quran commentary session at a mosque in east London, and we have agreed to meet minutes away in a dessert café near Canary Wharf. It is an autumn evening and the lights of the tall buildings, the signs for Barclays, HSBC, Citibank, shine above us as we greet one another.

Shaikh Abd al-Qadir is in his fifties, with a greying beard, a long overcoat that doubles as a *thawb*, and a dark green turban on his head. He smiles at me with a shyness that feels natural and a humility that seems sincere. We shake hands and he embraces me. Next to our booth in the café, three teenage girls are having milkshakes and looking at images on Instagram. This doesn't seem to worry the shaikh. He smells of rose musk, and slowly the aroma of tea and musk fills our immediate surroundings as we order English Breakfast tea.

'I have five questions for you that I just have to ask,' I say. 'Across the country I've seen some worrying issues at play. But before I ask, please tell me what you would say are the top three concerns that your own students, and their families and members of Muslim communities in London, come to you to address, to resolve.'

He breathes heavily, clasps his hands together and tells me that the first issue is the widespread use of drugs among Muslim youth. Someone is supplying them in great quantities, and the habit is spreading in schools, colleges and universities and is sometimes even brought into mosques. Secondly, domestic violence is so widespread and so regular that he feels depressed by it.

'What's the worst case you have seen?' I ask. 'I have come across this in Blackburn, but also many other places.'

Again he sighs as he carefully chooses his words.

'A mother being beaten by her husband while her children stood outside the room, hearing their mother cry in pain. The children jumped off the balcony of their council home and fell to the ground. When the ambulance and police arrived, the father was still beating the mother and didn't even realise that the children had almost died. In another case, a husband starved his wife for days and left her with orders to eat her own discharge. Word of this level of barbarity by Muslims reaches us *ulama* [clerics], and we have to try to resolve their marriage problems.'

He then tells me about the third issue he faces, which is women coming to him seeking his intervention to get divorces from men who refuse to give them. Some cases have taken up to four years of wrangling, involving familial pressure, community shame and drawing in more distant relatives. Often, even when the husband is already married to a second wife, the first wife is still denied divorce. 'It's a terrible power game they play,' he says sadly.

My question has brought out the underlying theme behind his concerns, and I am reassured, though saddened, to find that my own anxieties aren't aberrations.

'Everywhere I went, Shaikh, women were being widely discriminated against by Muslim men and institutions. They were either banned from entering the mosques or, if they were allowed to enter, they had a secondary place as mere worshippers and had no say or involvement in the management committee. They couldn't initiate their own divorces the way men can, nor could they inherit as equals – and that lack of equality, justified by ancient, literalist interpretations of scripture, is completely at odds with the modern world.'

Shaikh al-Qadir blames these issues on ignorance. He also blames his fellow clerics. He cites Ibn Abbas, a cousin of the Prophet Mohamed, who warned of the jealousy and pettiness of knowledgeable Muslims. Shaikh al-Qadir tells me that many clerics today still distrust modernity – and issues relating to women are at the forefront of the equal rights debate in the modern world. Many men cannot fathom or accommodate any change in their worldview, and the clerics broadly support them in taking this stance.

'This is not Islam,' says the shaikh. 'This is ignorance. Let me give you two examples of our Islam, the faith of reason and justice. In sharia, we have what is called *ikhtiyar al-shart*, the choice of conditions, almost a pre-nuptial agreement between a couple that says the woman also has the right to divorce. Clerics don't talk about this because it upsets them, but we should make this legal and widespread so that our women are free to divorce, too.'

'By legal, you mean *nikah* marriages should be part of civil law?'

'Yes. Islam teaches us to obey the law of the land. We must not have these different laws and practices away from regular society. We are part of this country and should be part of it legally, too. Secondly, we forget that Imam Abu Hanifa, in the ninth century, argued that women can marry freely, without the consent of guardians. It follows that women should be able to divorce freely, too. Women have rights in this country – why must Muslim men take away from those legal rights?

'But there is something else. I can find legal and sharia arguments to strengthen the position of Muslim women, but more importantly our Prophet, in his last sermon on his deathbed, counselled us to love our women. What happened to that love? The Quran also commands love and mercy, *mawaddah*. Fine, most Muslim men tell us that love has left their marriages after a few years, but what of mercy? How can mercy leave you? God *is* mercy. In the Quran, God prescribes mercy upon himself – *kataba 'ala nafsihi al-rahmah* – where is that mercy among Muslims in this country today?'

I find it hard to continue with my other four questions, given the shaikh's broad defence of love, reason, mercy and justice in Islam. When these become the criteria of what is right and wrong, it is hard to persist with the specifics of what this *hadith* or that verse says. Shaikh al-Qadir is saying that, ultimately, we must modernise in our own context, and he is dismissing his own people, the *ulama*, as being part of the problem. But he invites me to continue.

'What other questions did you have in mind?'

I open my notebook and show him the *hadiths* that the students from Dewsbury, Bury and other Darul Ulooms had concerns about:

'It was narrated from the Prophet (peace and blessings of Allah be upon him) that women will form the majority of the people of hell.'

'It was narrated from 'Imran ibn Husain that the Prophet (peace and blessings of Allah be upon him) said: "I looked into Paradise and I saw that the majority of its people were the poor. And I looked into hell and I saw that the majority of its people are women.'[15]

'According to her testimony in the *Hadith*, Muhammad physically struck Aisha, his favourite wife, for leaving the house without his permission: "He struck me on the chest which caused me pain."'[16]

'A woman came to Muhammad and begged him to stop her husband from beating her. Her skin was bruised so badly that it was described as being greener than the green veil she was wearing. Muhammad did not admonish her husband but instead ordered her to return to him and submit to his sexual desires.'[17]

In Blackburn, Fadil had called this reliance on ancient *hadiths* 'the monster behind the wall'. What about those *hadiths* that argue for the beating of women, stoning gay people to death, women being 'deficient in intelligence', black people being symbols of the plague, the killing of Jews and the necessity of removing Christians and Jews from the Arabian Peninsula, where they had practised their respective faiths for centuries before Islam?

The shaikh listens to me patiently. He then quotes some *hadiths* himself: 'The Merciful has mercy on those who are merciful to others', and one I read on the madrasa wall in Dewsbury that says, 'The best of you is he who serves humanity', a call to humanism.[18]

The shaikh then says that Bukhari gets a lot of negative publicity because of some of the *hadiths* I mentioned, but what of the *hadith* in Bukhari about a prostitute, a sinful woman, who enters heaven because she gave water to a thirsty dog?

He tells me of the great Persian Sufi Bayazid Bastami, who attained sainthood by healing the wounds of a dog because of his belief in the Sufi principle of *khidmat al-Khalq*, serving all creation. The great Sufi Bahauddin Naqshband was famous for taking care of stray cats and dogs, he reminds me.

'We can never take a single *hadith* and form a judgement on its compiler,' he says. 'Many of them are of doubtful veracity, some are forgeries, others need to be placed in a much wider context with other *hadith*. Quranic verses take precedence, and ultimately human reason, justice, and the spirit of Islam's compassion should be referred to above all. If we take a *hadith* and then go to town with it, we are doing what the Salafis, Deobandis or other literalists do. We must always remember the text in its context, but also listen to reason, the Quran, and the teachings of our masters.'

'That brings me to my third question,' I say. 'You've mentioned the Sufis. In dealing with the Wahhabis, the Saudi government is starting to address extremism. With the Deobandis and the Taliban in India, the government and the Deoband are trying to uproot the extremism there. There are attempts being made in Tunisia and elsewhere to combat Islamist extremism. But with the Sufis, especially the Barelwis, this *gustakh-e-Rasul* business, and the *wajib-e-qatl*, duty to kill, that has resulted in the loss of life, still goes unchecked. I've met members of the Dawat-e-Islami in Glasgow and Birmingham and people across the country who are deeply concerned by this. What is your position on killing those who insult the Prophet?'

'We are living in Britain, in the West,' the shaikh says. 'This is not a caliphate. In classical Islam, yes, the caliph killed mockers for treason. But we also know from *hadith* that the Prophet, in his love and kindness, forgave poets who insulted him in his own day, even when he was head of state in Medina. So if the Prophet forgave his detractors, who are we to kill in his name? Now, the most important aspect in any society is security and peace and justice. This is not a time where we need a caliph, or different laws while waiting for a caliphate to emerge. In the West we have freedom to worship, to be Muslim – much more so than in many Muslim societies. Sadly, Sufism is witnessing extremism and cultish ways, too. Like you, I am worried and think we should oppose any attempts to bring the politics of Pakistan or the verdicts of past caliphates into our country. Ours is a new reality, and we should keep the peace in our country.'

This brings me to my fourth question. 'In praying for peace, in the mosques, I have only heard prayers for Muslims and the victory of Islam. But in a church or synagogue, there are prayers for the Queen. Why don't we pray for the monarch?' I ask. 'When I lived in Syria, the imams in mosques always prayed for President

Assad. In Saudi Arabia, the mosques and congregation shouted
"Amen" loudly for the King. In Egypt, the United Arab Emirates
and every Muslim country I have visited, Muslims pray for peace
and security, provided by the head of state. In the US, they have
American flags flying at mosques. But here in the UK we can't even
pray for our monarch.'

Again he is silent, and he gently smiles. 'There would be an
uproar, but that doesn't mean we shouldn't pray for Her Majesty.
Ibn Arabi and other Muslim masters taught us that we mustn't
divide the world into us and them, that we are all God's creation,
and given that Her Majesty is head of the realm, yes, we should and
could pray for her.'

I arrive at my last topic of conversation. 'My father came to
England in 1953,' I say. 'Mine came in '63,' he chimes in. We
talk about how they both walked around in three-piece suits, as
Englishmen, and were proud to be in England, despite the end of
empire. The shaikh tells me how, back then, in disagreements on
the factory floor the foreman always wanted a Muslim to testify
because he would be honest, and our religion was seen positively.

'Now that is my question,' I say. 'That perception is changing.
There is something at play across the country. If we'd said to our
fathers then that in 1989 we'd have books being burned by Muslims
here, and Salman Rushdie hounded with death threats, they'd
have dismissed us as crazy. Yet that happened. And if we'd said in
1989 that by 1996 hundreds of Muslims would join Hizb ut-Tahrir
and other fascist organisations calling for a caliphate, they'd have
thought us facetious – but then it happened. And if we'd said in 1996
that by 2005 there would be race riots in Bradford, Birmingham
and elsewhere, and Muslims from northern towns would kill fifty-
two people on the London Underground, our parents would have
dismissed us as fantasists, just imagining trouble. Even in 2005,
if we had said that within a decade some Muslims would leave
England to fight for ISIS, and the government would then proceed
to monitor forty-three thousand people for signs of radicalism and
extremism, would they have believed us? What about the Ariana
Grande concert bombing, the Westminster Bridge attacks, the

bombings at airports and the car crashes? They'd have said we were watching too many sci-fi movies.

'But thinking about it now, what will the year 2050 look like? I can see several British towns and cities becoming Muslim-majority by then. If things don't change, what is the future for this country?'

Shaikh al-Qadir remains silent for longer than usual. His answer, when it comes, is brief.

'My brother, I am living in a bubble where I meet only Muslims, and where most clerics don't believe the moon landings took place.

'You are right to be worried. I see two things missing: love and soul. There is no soul in the people and places you describe, and there is no love to give birth to loved souls. We need to love God, we need to give our souls to God's creation, everybody, in service, and we need to stop these divisions.'

My analytical mind falls silent. The shaikh exudes an inner calm, that Sufi radiance, that touches something within me.

The lights of Canary Wharf continue to flicker.

Conclusion

Between Past, Present and Future: Whither Britain?

OUR PRESENT

The rise of mosques across Britain is a symbol of a great idea: tolerance. The conversion by the government of Turkey of a historic cathedral, the majestic Hagia Sophia of ancient Constantinople, to a mosque in 2020 is the demonstration of several bad ideas: intolerance, conquest and Muslim supremacy. The visible increase of Islam in the West and the decline of Christianity in the Middle East, including even in Bethlehem, is not just about people, but ultimately about the ideas that we choose to shape us and our future.[1] That choice, or the lack of it, is creating havoc not only in far-flung countries but in our midst, too, here in Britain.

It is a fact that Islam will be more visible and vocal through Muslim presence in our lives – so what type of Islam do we want? Discussing this issue is not about being left or right wing, increasingly dated political categories that mean less and less, but about ideas that sustain the harmony of a nation and its future. As early as the seventh century, the prophet Mohamed not only invited Christians to meet him in his mosque in Medina, but asked them to pray there, too. And they did. When his friend, Omar, visited Jerusalem in the year 637, he invited the Jewish people to return to their city. They returned after 500 years of Roman banishment. Omar was asked to pray in the Church of the Holy Sepulchre, though he refused to do so for fear of Muslims in the future claiming the Church as a mosque. The open confidence of Mohamed, the respectful vision of Omar, I found wanting in most of the mosques I visited. Britain's future calls for careful attention.

As a country we face a number of highly destabilising threats in the coming decades, including climate change, technology and automation (with 20–30 per cent of jobs expected to disappear by 2030), as well as geopolitical and economic challenges relating to the rise of China (the first time that the West has had to deal with an equally strong non-Western power in 350 years), and potentially further large waves of migration from the Middle East and Africa. In this context, we desperately and urgently need to build a country that is genuinely resilient, intellectually dynamic and flexible enough to ride out these coming storms. At present, the brittleness of society makes us ill-prepared to deal with these economic, environmental and other challenges.

Something deeply precious is being broken in this country. We don't have the language or the locations in which to talk about this breakdown openly. 'If a lion could talk, we could not understand him,' wrote the philosopher Ludwig Wittgenstein. Across Britain, the communities I met on my travels are not talking with each other from the heart, for they do not have a common emotional language or shared set of ideas. Speaking functional English is not enough. There is often mutual suspicion and distance, not cohesion. The deep grammar of a shared love for this land and loyalty to its liberties, laws and languages is under significant strain. How to heal our people?

We are becoming separate tribes with different and opposing identities. Because we cannot talk openly about Christian or atheist worries about Islam, or Islam's current fears of liberalism, we are all creating a huge void. Who will fill it? For fear of giving offence, we often remain silent. But feeling offended, or fearing offence, is not an idea or an argument.

Gibran K. Gibran, the Lebanese-American poet, warned, 'Between what is said and not meant, and what is meant and not said, most of love is lost.' We are losing something we love, but cannot articulate it at will.

The woman in Dewsbury who wants to fly the Union Jack – but is forbidden from doing so by the local council – is attached to a symbol of her love. The imam in Manchester who condemns homosexuality is not alone in failing to love his neighbour. The men in Blackburn who are scared of entering 'Muslim areas' do not know their fellow citizens. The parents in Bradford who forbid their disabled children to take part in drama and theatre are physically in Britain but mentally living elsewhere. The bookshops in Birmingham selling the works of authors who teach that 'women should purge their minds of the misconception that they are superior or equal to men' are not in conversation with women in leadership positions in business or politics. The rise of caliphism in Cardiff, the deep dislike of Muslims in Belfast and the widespread inability of Muslim women to divorce in London and the rest of the country go unnoticed in today's Britain. This feeds separatism and sows the seeds of further conflict.

If some groups make their interactions all about identity, based on race and religion, and if the government and others institutionalise this, then many of the 85 per cent of people in Britain who are white British of Christian heritage will start also defining themselves along racial and religious lines. What will a reaction from them look like?

There is, however, good news too.

Despite charges that Muslims are becoming a 'nation within a nation',[2] during the Covid pandemic the doors of every mosque in the land were closed in line with government guidance. There was no craving to defy science and secular politicians.

The Muslim soldier in Glasgow, one of several thousand, and the food banks in Birmingham and elsewhere that serve Brits from all backgrounds, show a love and loyalty to the inhabitants of this land.

The hijab-wearing Muslim worker at the LGBT clinic in Birmingham, and the women who manage the mosque in Belfast, and the open atmosphere of the mosque kitchen in Edinburgh, are all pioneers of what we can become.

Many ordinary Muslims have found a way to succeed in British society through making everyday compromises with their religious beliefs: the corner shop and supermarket workers selling alcohol and pork; Muslims working in banks that charge interest; Muslims working in fashion, television, music, the British armed forces and dozens of other fields that would have traditionally been *haram*. Millions of people are already making integration work. There is a new Western Islam progressing here; it is just that the people who are quietly developing it are shouting less than the caliphists.

Anti-Islam commentators who seek to hold Britain and British Muslims to a single interpretation of a literalist Islam cannot comprehend the complexity of human life. We are not robots enacting ancient scripture. Islam is an evolving religion, and we should encourage that evolution to adapt to modern realities. Scripture commands Muslims to pray in the mosque at dawn; most mosques across the country are usually empty at that time. Britain's Central Mosque in London's Regent's Park does not open its doors for morning supplications.[3] Literalist scripture does not trump reality.

This shows that maintaining Britain's open society of free individual choices is possible. If some can integrate, almost all can integrate. But we should be rigorous about this expectation and not be complacent – the collapse in communication between our peoples is real. Racial, religious and other divides are in many places increasing. In parts of Glasgow, Blackburn, Bradford, Manchester, Rochdale, Dewsbury, Birmingham and east London, a Muslim can spend months with no contact whatsoever with mainstream 'white' Britain.[4] From banks to hospital staff to taxis to grocery stores to websites and dating apps, a parallel Muslim-only environment has emerged for those who want it.

A 2019 poll found that 66 per cent of people in Britain were concerned about the possible rise of extremism in Islam.[5] Their instincts were right. In 2020, the British secret services confirmed that they were monitoring 43,000 terror suspects, of whom 90 per cent were caliphists.[6] How many more do they not know about? But for a free society, monitoring 43,000 people is already far too many. The mounting friction between our liberty and security is the outcome of long decades of tolerating intolerance.

Let us return to first principles. The idea of a mosque being welcome in Britain is only possible because this country upholds Enlightenment ideas of tolerance and diversity. Secularism makes this possible. Upon approval from a local government authority, most mosques then become 'race temples' – closed spaces for a single ethnic group. Most also become male-only zones: women cannot be in leadership or management positions, or even pray inside. Today, 95 per cent of mosques have single-ethnicity, all-male managements.[7] The proliferation of mosques is also connected to the sectarian silos of Barelwi, Deobandi, Salafi, Islamist, Shi'a and other divides that cannot cede ground to differences. So what happened to tolerance and diversity?

On my train journeys across the country, and in quiet evenings at hotels and silent moments at the mosque, I have spent much time reflecting on why we are at a historical inflection point. If we get our reaction wrong, we will be depriving future generations of their heritage of a vibrant, diverse and free Britain.

The Italian political scientist Gaetano Mosca said that an organised minority can control the disorganised majority. Most Muslims in Britain are focused on their families, jobs, mortgages and holidays, and wish to live in peace like everybody else. But the organised minority who control most mosques, bookshops, charities, schools and community organisations, and who are often the most vocal presences online, are playing a tune that does not belong in modern, secular Britain. Can they be made to change?

In the recent history of Muslims, clerics and advocates of a literalist sharia have, at various times from Turkey to India to Arabia, prohibited the use of the printing press as a Western innovation, together with microphones, radios, televisions, cars, planes, cash (allowing only gold dinars), coffee, trousers, skirts, ties, watches, razors, spectacles, mortgages, learning English or attending Western schools and universities and even the use of modern medicine. Today, the forces of progress and modernisation have won. The clerics no longer forbid what they did in the last two centuries.

I see three distinct trends, too often insulated from scrutiny, that are taking root across Muslim communities in Britain. They stare me in the face all the more obviously because, when I travel to the Middle East, none of these three factors is anywhere near as strong, organised and protected from scrutiny.

Firstly, a growing *communalism* that defines itself primarily as Muslim, with a secondary identity based on ethnicity and sect, whether Islamist, Sufi or Salafist. What – to my mind – is a private, religious identity has become a public and increasingly political label. It is a form of religious and sometimes ethnic nationalism that seeks to unify Muslims under a single identity. In the 1960s, 1970s, 1980s and early 1990s, Muslims came under the wider umbrella of being 'Asian', but that category included Sikhs and Hindus. The rejection of that identity for religious reasons, and the militant assertion of being 'British Muslim', is a communalism that expects its members, real and imagined, to adhere to communal standards. Something called the 'Muslim Council of Britain' seeks to be the face of this community and act as an intermediary with government. All too often these communal standards are enforced on those who wish to dissent, through social and family pressure, and sometimes through intimidation and violence.

In the 2019 election, Jeremy Corbyn's Labour Party courted the vote of 'the Muslim community' because it was potentially five million-strong, and its 'community leaders' were seen as capable of controlling the election result in more than thirty constituencies. For many party strategists, the historical model of a secular state composed of individual British citizens who can lobby their parliamentary representatives on a range of causes is not politically advantageous. Despite these concessions to communalism, the imams I met in Bradford, who are political figures of power, are nevertheless still unhappy. This shows historical blindness. Muslim political communalism never ends well: Pakistan separating from India cut off hundreds of millions of Muslims from India's rich intellectual and cultural life; Lebanon's civil war weakened Sunnis politically; and Bosnia's conflict, the Sudanese government's religious nationalism that triggered that country's break-up and Nigeria's north–south divide are all warning signs for us.

Unless it is confronted now, white British people will respond to Muslim communalism by developing their own communalism, leading to increased far-right radicalism, which will in turn encourage many Muslims to become more insular and potentially more militant.

Secondly, a strange *clericalism* is gripping British Muslim minds. The 'mullah' in Iran or Pakistan, or 'hodja' in Turkey, was, after increased modernisation, an object of mass mockery. For it was they who tried to stop ordinary Muslims from embracing the modern world of art, technology, innovation and science. Today, the brightest minds in Egypt or Pakistan do not study at the madrasa seminaries. But in Britain, madrasa study is booming: this is mainly because communalism needs clericalism to provide the religious justification for why and how separate charities, television channels, schools, banks and so on should become more 'Islamic'.

Rather than using the titles 'mullah' or 'hodja' from the Indian subcontinent or Turkey, this male clericalism has gained respectability by adopting the Arabic term 'shaikh'. With that exotic word 'shaikh' and claims of power to access God, there has been a rise of cults in which financial and sexual abuse is increasing. Charisma has replaced deep thought and learning. The open minds of young people are being closed. In Birmingham and Cardiff we saw and heard the harm being done by the cults of the clerics.

The power of the clerics can be seen in their conducting unregistered marriages, parents being swayed to send their children to become clerics and the increasing thought control on all matters deemed to be blasphemous, particularly clerical decisions on what or who is *gustakh-e-rasul*. Salman Rushdie was the first victim of this, followed by the killings of Charlie Hebdo's staff more recently. And there may be others yet to come.

Thirdly, the spread of *caliphism* as a social and political aspiration, on the grounds that secular Britain is flawed and failing, is embedded in speeches, sermons, books, websites and charities. At its core, caliphism is anti-Western and seeks to subvert British culture, laws and institutions from within. Whereas in Egypt, Saudi Arabia or the United Arab Emirates there is open rejection of the need for a caliphate in the modern world of nation states, in Britain's Muslim communities social and political caliphism is flourishing. Sexism is a second-tier consequence of caliphism in its social application: women inherit less, cannot instigate divorce or take leadership positions in mosques, and must not question male leadership or interpretation of scripture. To accept otherwise is to be 'Westernised'. Hamas and the Muslim Brotherhood might seem remote in Gaza or Egypt, but caliphism, their core ideology, is spreading in our country.

These worrying trends are underpinned by a narrative of reinstating the long-gone glory of the Muslims, who will regain a caliphate only if they learn from the clerics how to be true Muslims. This growing mutual three-way reinforcement of caliphism, community and clerics – an idea, a people and a leadership – is set for collision with mainstream Britain unless this troika is dismantled. But how? And why?

OUR PAST

Consider this political reasoning:

> There can be no question of coercing any large areas in which one community has a majority to live against their will under a government in which another community has a majority – and the only alternative to coercion is partition.

On that logic the communalism of Muslims in India was upheld. Those were the words of Lord Mountbatten, the last viceroy of India, on 3 June 1947 as Britain prepared to abandon India as a land divided. That cry from history should alert us as to where we will be heading when local councils and large metropolises in the Midlands and the north come to want more autonomy as they increasingly diverge from mainstream Britain.

What will happen when Birmingham or Bradford have a Muslim majority and organised caliphists hold the balance of power? Does the city begin by banning alcohol sales, using council funds to remove statues offensive to monotheism, enforcing new school uniforms for girls that exclude short skirts, banning nightclubs and gay bars, or making Fridays a local holiday for communal prayers?

Caliphism and clericalism are sequestering an entire community away from meaningful contact with mainstream Britain. The cordon sanitaire around many minds will become solidified unless we change course.

Muslim parliamentarians who represent 'Muslim areas' for the Labour Party, who see themselves as elected to represent 'Muslim interests' and Muslims at large, are playing a dangerous and divisive game of communalism, with support from clerics mobilising mosques as mass voting blocs. In the fashionable name of 'devolved power' and 'localisation', the logic of Mountbatten may come to harm our country.

The Muslim population is growing exponentially, but integration is not. We dare not utter these truths, for the language – and the implications – scare us. But unless we do, we are merely storing up these problems for our children and grandchildren.

On my travels across Islamic communities in Britain, what I did *not* see troubled me. Where were the many books of the Mutazilite thinkers? They were a school of popular and powerful early Muslim philosophers in Arabia and Mesopotamia, who believed in the power of reason, placed the Quran in the specific context of seventh-century Arabia and argued against literal interpretations.

Where were the works of the novelists and poets who have cherished individualism and free inquiry throughout Muslim history? Where, for example, was Ibn Tufayl's book on finding God and meaning on a desert island, which preceded *Robinson Crusoe* by several centuries?

Where were al-Farabi, Avicenna or Averroes – all Muslim scholars and philosophers who upheld the Aristotelian empirical tradition and continued the study of Greek philosophy?

What happened to the poetry of Khayyam or Hafez or Ghaleb, who celebrated wine drinking and free love of the divine?

What of the Muslim reformers in Egypt, say Huda Sha'arawi, who removed her headscarf in the 1920s as a public gesture of freedom?

The absence of such positive, inspiring and diverse role models for British Muslims reflects the fact that clerics and caliphists are nurturing a particular type of Islam whose ideas, values and culture are set to conflict increasingly with wider society. For too long, politicians and others have uncritically praised the 'Muslim contribution' to British society and glossed over the challenges of integration. On the ground, reality is the opposite of what politicians say: there is growing separatism and increasing confrontation. Terrorism is the most ugly demonstration of this separatism.

But it is wrong to blame only Muslims for this failure. Into what are they supposed to integrate? A fuzzy 'integration' whose success is judged by Muslims speaking English, baking cakes and playing cricket will not work. Caliphists are only successful in winning followers for their imagined utopia of an 'Islamic State' because the majority community is unable to tell a more compelling story of why Muslims should have a stake in maintaining Britain as a pluralistic, tolerant, secular democracy. After all, Shamima Begum and others went to fight for the slave-owning, people-beheading caliphate of ISIS, but when their caliphate collapsed it was telling that they sought to be tried under impartial British justice rather than the sharia-infused laws of the Middle East.

What is Britain? The *Shipping Forecast*, while comforting for an island nation, does not tell us of the storms to come in the battle of ideas. Squeamishness over defining the special qualities of our home and hoping that migrants will learn its political culture by osmosis has not worked so far. And it certainly won't work now in the screaming, segmented and polarised age of social media.

We are not even sure what we call our country. George Orwell identified this acute difficulty: '... we call our islands by no less than six different names, England, Britain, Great Britain, the British Isles, the United Kingdom and, in very exalted moments, Albion.'[8] To that one may also add Northern Ireland, Wales and Scotland, all increasingly at odds with England, the Union and London. Scotland's unity with England is not as strong as it looks. The unionist side fought the 2014 independence referendum on the economy. It won (with 55 per cent of the vote) but not overwhelmingly, and the EU referendum two years later proved that short-term economic arguments don't necessarily prevail over longer-term cultural change.

There is an increasing probability that Scotland will depart the UK in the next decade, and that the English will have to create our own national identity. It has been difficult enough getting Muslims to integrate into a British identity (which is, by definition, multi-national), so think how hard it will be to integrate Muslims into a post-Scotland English identity that is much more tightly based on race and ethnic heritage. The departure of Scotland would drastically increase the proportion of people in the country who are Muslim – at a guess, from 6 to 12 per cent (on a par with France and Belgium) – which would deal a further large psychological blow to the English people and state. This would then strengthen the argument for Muslim separatism. Will we sit back and watch, or act now to change the future?

What is Britishness? To what should newcomers and their children adhere in order to belong and feel at home? The weather? Queuing, apologising a lot, roses and gardens, Marmite, eccentrics, digestive biscuits, fish and chips, tea, Wensleydale cheese and sponge cakes are all endearing, but not enough. And have I just confused Britishness with Englishness?

Perhaps the quiet confidence of this country over the centuries, not to mention its effective racial homogeneity, did not require the delineation of identity. T. S. Eliot, in his *Notes Towards the Definition of Culture*, wrote: 'Just as a doctrine only needs to be defined after the appearance of some heresy, so a word does not need to receive this attention until it has come to be misused.'

Today, the misuse of ideas of tolerance and identity demands that we respond with better ideas.

Ibn Khaldun, the fourteenth-century Muslim historian and sociologist, wrote extensively about civilisations and settled peoples being disturbed by those who cannot find a home or somewhere to belong. He identified the need for a bond of group feeling: a shared way of life. Something must bind newcomers and settled people to enable them to honour the land and its laws. Fail to do that, and conflict ensues. Ibn Khaldun was no abstract theorist: he was famed for his practical thinking. When the Mongol conqueror Tamerlane was on the outskirts of Damascus in 1401, he summoned Ibn Khaldun to converse for hours about what causes the rise and fall of civilisations.

President Ronald Reagan, Prime Minister Boris Johnson and Facebook's Mark Zuckerberg have all cited Ibn Khaldun, but none has tried to unpack his insight on the rise and fall of countries and civilisations based on the energy and synergy of group-feeling. In the modern world, the idea that comes closest to the force that Ibn Khaldun identified is patriotism.

The English philosopher Roger Scruton defined patriotism as a feeling 'based on respect and love for the form of life that we have. It seeks to include, not to exclude, and to combine in the face of external threat. A patriot respects the patriotism of others, including that of the enemy.' Patriotism, therefore, is inclusive and, by definition, focused on love of the land and its institutions – the monarchy, armed forces, rule of law, the NHS, free and fair markets – that protect a way of life that we have come to cherish.

The secular and democratic nation state, with laws applied within a defined jurisdiction, with a people that agrees to be bound by these laws, and governed by parties that can be bloodlessly removed from power, is the greatest invention for consensual government of citizens. Of the nations of the ancient world, the Babylonians, Assyrians, Persians, pagan Greeks, Romans and others are no longer with us. But why do the Jews alone survive? The secret, that Ibn Khaldunian spirit of patriotism, love of the land of Israel and upholding Jewish laws, has kept the light of hope and longing burning bright for two millennia in exile for the Jewish people. It is from ancient Israel that we learn what Ibn Khaldun meant by a patriotism that is bonded to love of nation and land. In the *Muqaddimah*, his 1377 introduction to a planned book of world history, Ibn Khaldun singled out the Israelites for escaping slavery in Pharaoh's Egypt and arriving in Jerusalem, surrounded by Canaan as their Promised Land, with its liberty and laws. That nation, their persecution, their prototype is something we emulate across the world today, as nation states become the primary force for global relations.

Patriotism requires pride and confidence in the memory of a nation's past, but also hope and optimism in a country's future. It is time to stop unreservedly apologising for Britain's past. This country has done nothing that China, Turkey, Russia and Austria have not done in multiple forms. I am a product of the British Empire. Millions of Brits have a love for India or Egypt because of their family ties to those lands, both as administrators and administered. My father left India to come to Britain in 1953 willingly, freely. My mother's ancestors left Arabia. Diversity in Britain today is a consequence of the millions who made that decision: they did not come here because they hated Britain, but because they loved this country and its freedoms and opportunities. To loathe British history is part of a process of self-hatred that leads to a complete collapse in self-confidence and national identity, and creates a vacuum that can be exploited. From this wider culture we create a subculture in which communalism, clericalism and caliphism fester.

Why is Britain singled out repeatedly and constantly, despite having abolished slavery and pioneered human equality around the world? If not for Britain and her allies we would today be living under a different world order, led by German Nazis. Ours is not a nationalism of blood and race.

I could live for decades in Turkey, China, Nigeria or Japan, but I would never be accepted as Turkish, Chinese, Nigerian or Japanese. In 'moderate Muslim' Malaysia, the law contains a 'sons of the soil' affirmative action policy, favouring native Malays over members of other ethnic groups, even if these arrived centuries ago. In Britain, by contrast, newcomers can become British. Here they can become lawmakers, cultural icons, corporate leaders and scientific innovators. Here, they can thrive.

How did Britain become this special place? It is by telling that story that we strengthen our patriotism, but also include Muslims and others in this love of land and lifestyle. The past was complicated. People did things differently; at the time society considered some things right that we now see as wrong. Good people sometimes did bad things, and bad people sometimes did good things. Britain's contribution to history has, on balance, been positive and beneficial. We must tell our national story unashamedly, for in it there are themes that can strengthen us all.

Winston Churchill readily admitted that Britain could not have won the Second World War without the sacrifices and services of the Indian army – an all-volunteer force, millions of whom were Muslims. They chose to fight the Nazis. Muslim countries and diplomats gave shelter to Jews fleeing Nazism. Noor Inayat Khan, an observant Muslim woman, found herself the sole surviving radio operator linking the French Resistance with Britain. She was executed in Dachau in 1944, aged thirty. The 2018 film *Enemy of the Reich* captures her story, as does the book *Spy Princess* by Shrabani Basu, but there were many more such Muslim women and men who fought along with Britain.

Over 2.5 million Muslims travelled to Europe to fight for the Allies during the First World War. To side with Britain, against the Ottoman caliphate, was a powerful testimony to the depth of Islamic-British relations. Muslims died in the trenches in France upholding a British promise to defend Belgium: our ancestors fought tyranny together. It was Britain that helped Saudi Arabia, Egypt, Jordan and others find freedom from Ottoman Turkish imperialism. Gratitude for Britain's alliance with those countries then is a reality to this day. But the bond is older still.

Queen Victoria was obsessed with Muslims to the point of learning Urdu and studying Muslim poets, the Quran and the Sufis, and she learned to write with the Arabic alphabet. Her friend and teacher Munshi Abdul Karim travelled with the royal household and lived with the Queen in the Isle of Wight. He was beside her at her deathbed. The spiritual bond between Victoria and her Muslim friend was so deep that her son, King Edward VII, raging with anger and jealousy, later burned all the letters and photos she sent to him. After her death, Abdul Karim and his wife were sent away from court.

The madrasas in this country that are focused on literalist sharia – not mysticism, poetry, philosophy, music or art – are not wholly the products of pure Islam. As Georgian Britain's forays into India increased, Warren Hastings, the first Governor-General, took it upon himself to create the first madrasa in Muslim India, aiming to rival the traditional teacher-to-student apprenticeships in the Sufi monasteries, or *khanqahs*. In 1781, Hastings founded Madrasa 'Aliyah in Calcutta. He sat on the board of governors, and the curriculum that he introduced in Calcutta was not dissimilar to that of the madrasas I visited for this book in Dewsbury or Bury or now mushrooming across Britain. To be free from Hastings' imperial finances and influences, but not his syllabus, the Deoband movement later mimicked the madrasa system after the 1857 uprising. Britain modernised, left India and reformed its own educational syllabi as school education became compulsory; but the madrasas did not. The British-Islam relationship runs deep.

Going back still further in history, it was Queen Elizabeth I who did more than anyone to cultivate this relationship. During the Reformation, which might be considered the first Brexit, England was isolated by Europe's Catholic monarchs and, in 1570, Elizabeth was excommunicated by Pope Pius V. The Protestant Queen refused to bow to European intimidation, so she found new and willing allies in the Muslim Ottomans, then a 270-year-old empire with territories in the Balkans, North Africa, Central Asia and the Middle East. She also forged alliances with Muslim empires in Morocco and Persia.

Sultan Murad III wrote to Queen Elizabeth, issuing a new law for his subjects, that if 'her agents and merchants shall come from the domain of Anletar [England] by sea with their barks and with their ships, let no one interfere'. This imperial edict, the rule of law, facilitated British trade in Ottoman ports.

Muslim protection of British ships and commercial envoys helped England thrive despite the boycott by European powers. The consolidation of Protestantism, free trade and free inquiry in England that led to the Enlightenment had something to do with the Ottoman–Elizabethan pact. By the end of her reign English traders, diplomats, adventurers and others lived in or travelled through places such as Istanbul, Damascus, Fallujah, Aleppo, Raqqa, Algiers, Baghdad and Tripoli. The Queen was said to like Moroccan sugar so much that her teeth became black with decay.

The merchants who left England to trade with Muslims, writes the historian Jerry Brotton, transformed Elizabethan homes.[9] The wealthy filled their houses with Turkish carpets, silk quilts and embroidered tapestries. The language of sixteenth-century England was filled with Arabic words: 'sugar' from *sukkar*, 'crimson' from *kirmiz*, 'tulip' from *tulband*. The English fascination with Islam and Muslims did not end with the Elizabethans. In 1650, a Greek-Turk named Pasqua Rosee opened the first coffeehouse in the City of London. It was Sufi Muslims from Yemen who spread the drinking of coffee within the Ottoman Empire, to help believers stay awake at night for worship of Allah. The Arabic *qahwah*, or *kehve* in Turkish, became 'coffee' in English. Samuel Pepys visited the coffeehouse in 1660 and wrote: 'the first time that ever I was there, and I found much pleasure in it.'

This deeply interwoven history runs even further back through Tudor times with Henry VIII's gifts to and from Muslim monarchs. In Hans Holbein's 1537 portrait we see King Henry's cloak has bands of arabesque knots, the curtain beside him has an interlacing Islamic pattern and he is standing on a Turkish Ushak rug.

And during the Crusades Islamic influences from Jerusalem shaped medieval England's church architecture and early banking system; the chivalric conduct of Richard the Lionheart and Saladin is still the stuff of legends and bedtime stories 800 years later.

But perhaps the crowning glory of this proud history goes to Anglo-Saxon England's King Offa of Mercia (reigned 757–796).

Offa was a Christian king and yet he minted gold coins that carried, in Arabic, the Islamic declaration of belief: there is no deity except the one God. He introduced gold dinars stamped with his name 'Offa Rex', but encircled this with Arabic. Now held at the British Museum, an example of this unique coin highlights the age-old connection between Britain and Islam.

In sum, Islam and Muslims are firmly part of the story of these islands. We should use these stories to give us the confidence to challenge caliphism and communalism without fear of being accused of Islamophobia or racism. Mosques enjoy freedom from taxation, and madrasas receive state funding. In return, it is right that we ask that the positive characteristics of what it means to be British are shared with young British children.

But on what basis must this national conversation proceed? What sort of Islam, and what ideas?

OUR FUTURE

Across the European continent, we see the rise of political parties that define themselves by their opposition to Islam and Muslim immigration. France, Germany, Holland, Austria and Poland have all witnessed presidential candidates coming second in elections (even winning in Poland) partly due to their hostility towards Muslim immigration. It is easily conceivable that another civil war in the Middle East, a famine in Africa, or continued lack of economic opportunities in Egypt, Algeria and elsewhere will increase the flow of refugees and migrants to Europe, and then across the Channel to Britain. But with or without such further immigration, the integration of Muslims into the rest of Britain needs to be rigorous.

Migrants merely speaking English cannot embed the causes for patriotism I outline above. A shared culture is also important. To fail in our duty to integrate the peoples of our country is to leave ourselves open to the only other possible scenarios: social separatism, communal domination, conflict of some form, partitions of towns, and ultimately mass deportations. If not India or Beirut or the

Balkans, take a look at the Belfast partition walls, justified in the name of 'peace lines'.

What are our red lines today? For what did our ancestors die? We are heirs to a great and ancient tradition. If all of us living on this land can share in our way of life, foster an inclusive patriotism, rejoice in the six defining traits that I explain below, then we have a better future.

These six qualities are also the outcomes of a Protestant Christian ethic that has moulded today's Brits. The God-shaped hole in our souls cannot be left empty. Nihilism and meaningless lives strengthen our enemies. The doctrines and dogmas of organised religions today must not stop us from living the essential Christian message of 'love each other as I have loved you'. These were the words of a rabbi from Nazareth in anticipation of his death, in excruciating pain, nailed to a Roman cross. Granted, there are objections to Christianity today, but as George Bernard Shaw said, 'if your face is not clean, wash it. Don't cut your head off.' Christianity is part of our head. By Christianity, I mean the spirit of the words carved at the tomb of the unknown soldier in Westminster Abbey: 'Thus are commemorated the many multitudes who during the Great War of 1914–1918 gave the most that man can give life itself, for God, for King and country, for loved ones at home, for the sacred cause of justice and freedom of the world.' Our forefathers died for God, country and freedom: will we protect their legacy?

Discard this inheritance and we alter the country for the worse. Celebrate these attributes and bolster them in our public life – in schools, courts and all other institutions – and the mosques will follow. Shy away, and very soon caliphists, communalists and clerics will sniff weakness. This seafaring nation of traders and shoppers, inventors and thinkers, poets and philosophers, mystics and martyrs has, over the centuries, blended cultures and civilisations. This fusion constitutes modern Britain and has fashioned the six main attributes of its people.

I. *Rule of Law*, based on reason and the long English common law tradition, to ensure justice is upheld. The French-speaking Norman King Henry II, on the English throne in the twelfth century, instituted the common law by drawing on Anglo-Saxon customs, but also the cultures of his native France and the Mediterranean. Ultimately, our laws are derived from the teachings and practices of Moses and Aristotle. But it was Jesus who sowed the seeds for our world: 'Render therefore unto Caesar the things that are Caesar's, and unto God the things that are God's.' That synergy of secularism keeps us free. For as long as we uphold the secular rule of law in all jurisdictions, then sharia and separatism are kept at bay. One law for all, and the law of the land is supreme.

From Moses to Aristotle to Jesus to Magna Carta in 1215 and to our own times, we have evolved and progressed to create a modern citizen who has recourse to the independent courts of law without fear or favour. The Founding Fathers of the United States were inspired by the Magna Carta to institute their own rule of law in 1776. Magna Carta was the first written charter of liberty in European history, written against the background of the Pope's wrath against King John; later popes similarly excommunicated King Henry VIII and Elizabeth I. Against the religious tyranny of Rome the rule of law was born in these islands. The rise of sharia courts in which to settle divorces or inheritance or custody matters in England is the thin end of the wedge. All marriages should be registered or annulled through British courts, not a separate legal mechanism. There is nothing in the English common law tradition that contradicts the spirit of Islam.[10]

II. *Individual liberty* is a gift from our forefathers, the rejection of oppression by any form of collectivism – government or any other organisation – that prevents the individual from exercising their God-given freedom or inalienable rights. Examples of that freedom include Moses breaking with Pharaoh, Jesus defying the Temple priests, and Mohamed rejecting his tribe. It was individual liberty that powered Socrates to condemn the politicians of Athens, Cicero to challenge Caesar and Hypatia to confront zealots in Alexandria. Pericles, in his famed oration, argued that Athenians did not 'exercise a jealous surveillance over each other; we do not feel called upon to be angry with our neighbour for doing what he likes'. The individual is free in her home.

It was in that spirit that in 1628 the English chief justice Sir Edward Coke coined the phrase 'a man's house is his castle'. Coke also quipped that 'Magna Carta is such a fellow that he will have no sovereign'. The law was thus the guarantor of the individual liberty of all subjects, even against the monarch and parliament. Again, it was in these isles that individual liberty was protected and exported to America with the Protestant pilgrims.[11] The second American president, John Adams, regarded Coke as 'the oracle of the law' that guaranteed liberty. English ideas of freedom shaped the world.

The free individual is the building block of the family, society and then the country. The rugged individual, the eccentric, the free thinker are celebrated in our culture from the days of childhood in stories such as *The Ugly Duckling* or *The Emperor's New Clothes*. Caliphism seeks to kill that spirit: communalism eradicates the free individual.

III. *Gender equality* is among our greatest characteristics. What the ancient Greeks, Romans and others could not imagine, we have achieved with female and male equality in the eyes of the law. Women could not vote or own property in classical Athens. In Rome, women could not hold political office. When the Romans conquered Britain, they met fierce resistance from Queen Boudica of Britannia. The Romans raped her daughters and confiscated private property. Boudica's wild revenge, wrote Tacitus, was to kill more than 70,000 people and pillage London. Unlike other peoples, Brits liked strong women. Boris Johnson sees Boudica as an early model for Queen Elizabeth I, Victoria and even Margaret Thatcher.[12]

In India, widows were burned alive on the funeral pyres of their husbands until British administrators stopped the practice. That women and men are equal in court is testament to Britain's progress. In the entire dynastic existence of the centuries-long Ottoman Empire there was not a single female caliph. Among India's Mughals or Persia's Safavids, not a single female empress ruled. It was no accident that Queen Elizabeth I ruled on her own terms, not as a wife but as a woman and against the powers of a pope and a Europe that condemned her for her gender and her Protestantism.

In Britain, from Julian of Norwich to Mary Wollstonecraft to the suffragettes to Margaret Thatcher, we have changed the world by leading on gender equality. Benazir Bhutto and Indira Gandhi, female prime ministers of Pakistan and India respectively, were products of Oxford University. How can we tolerate so many women in this country today being unable to divorce, inherit equally, take leadership roles in mosques or live in fear under a different set of 'community' laws?

IV. *Openness* in our gatherings, thinking, writing and speaking is a hallmark of British identity. For freedom of speech, thought and assembly millions have laid down their lives. John Locke and others were expelled from England in the 1680s and returned to ensure society was more open to Jews, Muslims and Protestants. Locke's 1689 *Letter Concerning Tolerance* is part of our heritage. It was from that spirit of openness, along with the rule of law, that Adam Smith advanced an economic model to create and share wealth across all sections of society, not only the mercantilist elite. Creating open markets with Smithian economics was and is another example of the British trait of fairness and freedom in the marketplace.

It is no coincidence that Britain was the home of choice for some of the greatest German-speaking writers on freedom and openness. Leo Strauss, Sir Isaiah Berlin and Sir Karl Popper all found shelter in Britain's open society. Popper's masterful book *The Open Society and Its Enemies* praises the individualism and rule of law culture that characterise Britain as a nation state.[13]

In today's Britain, 89 per cent of people say they would be happy for their child to marry someone from another ethnic group.[14] The vast majority, 93 per cent, disagree with the statement that 'to be truly British you have to be White'. Such is our openness.

V. *Uniqueness* is an important British attribute to understand and celebrate. For too long we have been pretending that Britain is the same as every other nation; we are not. No, we are particular and different. British uniqueness is cause for both humility and patriotism. We are inheritors of a great legacy and trustees of a culture for future generations. I learned this the hard way.

Between 2010 and 2015, I was a senior fellow for Middle Eastern Studies at the US Council on Foreign Relations, a powerful think-tank nexus of politics, policy research, media and government advisory work. In 2011, the Arab Spring uprisings led us to believe that, at long last, democracy had arrived in the region. I travelled frequently to Egypt, Tunisia, Bahrain, Turkey and Syria. Many of my American colleagues were doubly enthused: every revolt seemed like 1776 to them, and every monarch or president was King George III. How wrong we were. In the smog of Molotov cocktails in Bahrain, tear gas in Tahrir Square in Egypt and fumes at the American Embassy's school in Tunisia I learned that Edmund Burke was right to warn against the French Revolution in 1789. 'Rage and frenzy will pull down more in half an hour than prudence, deliberation and foresight can build up in a hundred years,' Burke cautioned.[15]

My attempts to help Tunisia and Egypt failed. Many of the revolutionaries were not reasonable, did not understand the idea of the rule of law and did not believe in gender equality or intellectual openness. The culture in this country and those others shaped by Britain (the US, Canada, Australia) is not like that of China, Russia, Nigeria or others. Our mosques and Muslims will only understand and appreciate this if we conserve and acclaim this uniqueness. If we shy away, the flawed idea of 'sameness', and saying that we are no worse than China, will lead to a void that will be filled by those proclaiming caliphism.

VI. *Racial parity* is an important characteristic of the British people. Britain has come a long way since the 1950s, when racism was overt. Harold Pinter's *The Caretaker* captured a Britain stuck in suspicion, with backing for Enoch Powell from dockworkers, and mail from supporters – thankfully a bygone world. No, we are not perfect, and the dark cloud of anti-Semitism that lingers on social media, and the absence of black Brits on the boards of directors of Britain's businesses and among its top diplomats, tell us we still have work to do.

Yet we are a mongrel nation. Britain is a world leader in treating racial difference with the same relaxed attitude as when meeting someone who has, say, pink hair or a visible tattoo. We are not fixated on racial purity. We do not have a racist political party in parliament, in the way that many European countries do. Any person of colour who doubts me should go to France or Germany claiming to be European and smell the whiff of racism in the air. Calais has a mass camp because refugees in France from Africa and Asia via Spain and Italy do not want to stay in Europe: Britain is a better destination, despite the risks of taking lorries and boats to reach Dover. Humans don't behave like that to reach a racist country.

Brits know that the Queen's family roots are German. Prince Philip was Greek. Prime Minister Boris Johnson has Turkish ancestry. He is proud of reminding us that his Turkish great-grandfather memorised the entire Quran. Brits of Indian and Jewish heritage hold some of the greatest offices of state.

This is modern Britain, its identity based on ideas that have shaped us over centuries.* These characteristics structure the rights and responsibilities that make us all equal citizens.

If we lose any of this inheritance, we lose ourselves. Free societies can be self-destructive unless we are vigilant. For as long as we fly the flag with confidence in our national character, our Muslim and other fellow citizens will join the British mainstream with pride and a sense of belonging. The fault is not with immigrants and Muslims. The onus is on us stubbornly to uphold our way of life. We must not tolerate intolerance. For nothing less than the future of our country depends on it.

* R.I.G.O.U.R for short: **R**ule of Law, **I**ndividual liberty, **G**ender equality, **O**penness, **U**niqueness and **R**acial parity.

Glossary

abayah	A loose cloak worn on top of other garments
adhaan	Arabic call to prayer
'alim	A scholar – but in today's parlance, a cleric
Allahu Akbar	Lit God is Great, a prayer
bid'ah	An innovation in religious practice
dua	To ask God for something
dunyah	The earthly world
fitna	temptation or discord
Gustakh-e-Rasul	Someone ill-mannered against the Prophet Mohamed in speech or conduct
hadith	Sayings attributed to the Prophet Mohamed
hafiz	Someone who has memorised the Quran
hijama	Cupping therapy
izzat	Family or personal honour, usually linked to women and their behaviour dishonouring male izzat
jamaat	Group
khutbah	Sermon
madrasa	A school in Arabic, but a 'religious school' in non-Arabic speaking Muslim communities
mahram	A chaperone or person one is forbidden to marry, such as a brother or a father
maqasid	Higher aims of sharia, such as saving life

matam	Chest-beating by Shi'a Muslims in mourning for the Prophet Mohamed's family
mihrab	A semi-circular niche in which the minbar is normally situated
minbar	A seat from which an imam is expected to deliver his sermon
miswak	A twig used to rub the teeth clean
qari	A reciter of the Quran
qasida	An ode or poem
qawwali	Spiritual, passionate music and songs of the Sufis of the Indian subcontinent
raka'as	A unit of prayer
ruqya	Muslim exorcism
sajda	Prostration
talaq	Divorce
thawb	A long, loose shirt from the neck to the ankles
tilawat	Quran recitation
wajib-e-qatl	Mandatory to kill, particularly a Gustakh-e-Rasul or other blasphemer
wudhu	Ablution
zanjir	A chain with blades for self-flagellation for Shia Muslims
zawiya	A monastery for Sufis, but not upholding monastic practices – usually for spiritual retreats and then returning to daily life

Notes

INTRODUCTION

1 William Henry Quilliam (1856–1932) who changed his name to Abdullah Quilliam and later Henri Marcel Leon or Haroun Mustapha Leon. The Ottoman Caliph, Abdul Hamid II, granted Quilliam the title of 'Shaikh of Islam' for the British Isles.
2 See the demographic study of the non-partisan Pew Research Center's report, Europe's Growing Muslim Population (November 2017)
3 https://www.bbc.co.uk/news/uk-politics-eu-referendum-36501227

CHAPTER I
DEWSBURY

1 The movement was founded in Delhi by Muhammad Ilyas Kandhlawi, a cleric from the anti-British, ultra-conservative and traditional Deobandi movement founded in 1866 soon after the Indian Uprising of 1857. From these movements, the Taliban and others have emerged in our times.
2 The precise number of mosques in Britain is unknown due to there being no government requirement for registration, and to the lack of any comprehensive database of mosques. Many houses and offices, university campuses and community centres serve as mosques and facilitate daily prayers and Friday gatherings. These take the number of mosques to more than 3,000. Fifty years ago there were fewer than fifty mosques in Britain.
3 By India, I mean greater India, thus including Pakistan and Bangladesh.
4 In most mosques an imam earns less than £25,000.

5 *Sahih al-Bukhari*, Book 59:126.
6 *Intermingling of the Sexes*, Idara, New Delhi, 2013, p. 7.
7 Ibid., p. 8.
8 Ibid., p. 12, citing Shaykh Mustafa as-Siba'ee.
9 Ibid., p. 13.
10 al-Kawthari, Muhammad Ibn Adam, *Islamic Guide to Sexual Relations*, Huma Press, London, 2008, p. 1.
11 Ibid., p. 70.
12 M. Azmi, *Guidance for a Muslim Wife*, Idara, New Delhi, 2013, p. 2.

CHAPTER 2

MANCHESTER

1 Listed in Quduri, citing *al-Bukhari*.
2 Mustafa, meaning 'the Chosen One', is a name given to the Prophet Mohamed.
3 The centre receives local and central government funding and is also supported by the Turkish company Onder. Community rumours abound as to which foreign government helped purchase the centre.

CHAPTER 3

BLACKBURN

1 *The Casey Review: A review into opportunity and integration*, 2016, p. 44.
2 https://www.newstatesman.com/politics/uk/2018/07/blackburn-town-stopped-working
3 https://www.bbc.co.uk/news/uk-england-41930457
4 Rural Education And Development.
5 https://www.kalamullah.com/Books/Mukhtasar%20al-Quduri.pdf Abu Dawud.
6 Ibid., Al-Tirmidhi in chapter on Suckling on the authority of Ibn Mas'ud.
7 Ibid., 2.4.7.
8 Quoted in Bassam Tibi, *Islam's Predicament with Modernity: Religious Reform and Cultural Change*, Routledge, London, 2009, p. 226.
9 *Bahishti Zewar*, p. 12. http://www.islamicbulletin.org/free_downloads/women/bahishti_1_2_3.pdf
10 Ibid., p. 14.
11 Ibid,. p. 27.

12 Ibid., p. 26.

13 http://shiloh-project.group.shef.ac.uk/interview-with-saima-afzal-founder-of-sas-rights/

14 https://www.bbc.co.uk/news/uk-england-lancashire-51561654

15 In Preston, Kidderminster, Bradford, Bolton, London, Dewsbury and Dundee. https://islamicportal.co.uk/obituary-shaykh-yusuf-motala/

16 Cardiff University academic Sophie Gilliat-Ray has written on the barriers thrown up by Deobandi institutions in Britain to external investigation. See, for example, 'Closed Worlds: (Not) Accessing Deobandi *dar ul-uloom* in Britain', *Fieldwork in Religion*, vol. 1, no. 1 (2005), pp. 7–33.

17 Sophie Gilliat-Ray, 'Educating the *Ulama*: Centres of Islamic Religious Training in Britain', *Islam and Christian-Muslim Relations*, vol. 17, no. 1 (2006), pp. 65–6.

18 Quoted in Hamid Mahmood, 'The Dars-e-Niẓāmī and the Transnational Traditionalist Madāris in Britain', Queen Mary University London thesis (2012), Appendix 1, p. 85.

19 Noted by Hamid Mahmood; http://www.cambridgemuslimcollege.ac.uk/wp-content/uploads/CMC-Prospectus-2016-WEB-Feb-231.pdf

20 *Sahih al-Bukhari*, 8.73.68: Narrated Abdullah bin Zam'a: The Prophet forbade laughing at a person who passes wind, and said, 'How does anyone of you beat his wife as he beats the stallion camel and then he may embrace [sleep with] her?' And Hisham said, 'As he beats his slave.' And 7.62.132: Narrated Abdullah bin Zam'a: The Prophet said, 'None of you should flog his wife as he flogs a slave and then have sexual intercourse with her in the last part of the day.'

21 *Sunan Abu Dawud*, Book 38, *Hadith* 4447: Narrated Abdullah ibn Abbas: The Prophet said: 'If you find anyone doing as Lot's people did, kill the one who does it, and the one to whom it is done.'

22 *Sahih al-Bukhari*, 1.45.2415: Narrated Jabir: A man manumitted a slave and he had no other property than that, so the Prophet cancelled the manumission (and sold the slave for him). Nu'aim ibn Al-Nahham bought the slave from him.

23 *Sahih al-Bukhari*, 65.4350: Narrated Buraida: The Prophet sent Ali to Khalid to bring the Khumus (a fifth of the war levy) and I hated Ali, and Ali had taken a bath (after a sexual act with a slave-girl from the Khumus).

24 *Sahih al-Bukhari*, 6.304: Narrated Abu Sa'id Al-Khudri: Once Allah's
Apostle went out to the Musalla [to offer the prayer] of Eid al-Adha
or al-Fitr prayer. Then he passed by the women and said, 'O women!
Give alms, as I have seen that the majority of the dwellers of Hell-fire
were you [women].' They asked, 'Why is it so, O Allah's Apostle?' He
replied, 'You curse frequently and are ungrateful to your husbands.
I have not seen anyone more deficient in intelligence and religion
than you. A cautious sensible man could be led astray by some
of you.' The women asked, 'O Allah's Apostle! What is deficient
in our intelligence and religion?' He said, 'Is not the evidence of
two women equal to the witness of one man?' They replied in the
affirmative. He said, 'This is the deficiency in her intelligence. Isn't it
true that a woman can neither pray nor fast during her menses?' The
women replied in the affirmative. He said, 'This is the deficiency in
her religion.'

25 *Sahih al-Bukhari*, 9.87.161: Narrated Abdullah: The Prophet said,
'I saw [in a dream] a black woman with unkempt hair going out
of Medina and settling at Mahai'a, i.e. Al-Juhfa. I interpreted that
as a symbol of epidemic of Medina being transferred to that place
[Al-Juhfa].'

26 *Sahih al-Bukhari*, 437: Narrated Abu Huraira: Allah's Messenger said,
'May Allah's curse be on the Jews for they built the places of worship
at the graves of their prophets.'

27 *Sahih Muslim*, 1767: Narrated Umar ibn al-Khattab that he heard the
Messenger of Allah say: 'I will expel the Jews and Christians from the
Arabian Peninsula and will not leave any but Muslims.'

28 *Sahih al-Bukhari*, 4.52.176: Narrated Abdullah ibn Umar: Allah's
Messenger said, 'You [Muslims] will fight with the Jews until some of
them will hide behind stones. The stones will [betray them] saying,
"O Abdullah [slave of Allah]! There is a Jew hiding behind me; so kill
him."'

29 *Sahih Muslim*, 1731: It has been reported from Sulaiman ibn Buraida
through his father that when the Messenger of Allah appointed
anyone as leader of an army or detachment he would especially
exhort him to fear Allah and to be good to the Muslims who were
with him. He would say: 'Fight in the name of Allah and in the

way of Allah. Fight against those who disbelieve in Allah. Make a holy war; do not embezzle the spoils; do not break your pledge; and do not mutilate [the dead] bodies; do not kill the children. When you meet your enemies who are polytheists, invite them to three courses of action. If they respond to any one of these, you also accept it and withhold yourself from doing them any harm. Invite them to [accept] Islam; if they respond to you, accept it from them and desist from fighting against them. Then invite them to migrate from their lands to the land of the Muhajireen and inform them that, if they do so, they shall have all the privileges and obligations of the Muhajireen. If they refuse to migrate, tell them that they will have the status of Bedouin Muslims and will be subjected to the Commands of Allah like other Muslims, but they will not get any share from the spoils of war or *fai'* except when they actually fight with the Muslims [against the disbelievers]. If they refuse to accept Islam, demand from them the *jizya*. If they agree to pay, accept it from them and hold off your hands. If they refuse to pay the tax, seek Allah's help and fight them.

30 *Sunan Abu Dawud*, 2142: Narrated Umar ibn al-Khattab: The Prophet said: 'A man will not be asked as to why he beat his wife.'

CHAPTER 4
BRADFORD

1 'When Cousins Marry' documentary, Only Human Channel. https://www.facebook.com/748719995296565/posts/134735138210008 7?sfns=mo

2 The Bradford Council website says that only 50–100 refugees a year (or 0.1 per cent of its population) will be brought into the city from 2015. A *Telegraph and Argus* article found that, while Bradford had the highest rate of acceptance of Syrian refugees in the Yorkshire/ Humber region, it was still only 188 individuals in the 2014–16 period.

3 I mentioned this meeting and conversation to William Shawcross, author, journalist and head of the Charity Commission, and he added a fourth way: Muslims eventually form a majority in many of Britain's towns and cities. Demographic projections suggest this will happen in the coming decades, as noted in the Introduction.

CHAPTER 5
BIRMINGHAM

1 *5Pillars* Facebook video, 'Activist Shakeel Afsar's message of encouragement', posted 2 August 2019 at 03:30; accessed 7 August 2019. https://www.facebook.com/490858150969676/posts/22792037 25468434?s=690045284&v=e&sfns=mo.

2 'What is No Outsiders?', Paul Salahuddin Armstrong, 3 May 2019, *The Association of British Muslims*, http://aobm.org/what-is-no-outsiders/

3 The Ummah Welfare Trust is a client of the Qatari-owned Al Rayan Bank, which provides services to numerous Islamist groups such as the Islamic Forum of Europe.

4 https://www.thetimes.co.uk/article/8b0d84b6-105d-11ea-aa63-2a87a83b86bb

5 'Polygamy (Polygyny): Would it better to be one of a few wives instead of being on your own? (Islam 5.5)', Abu Khadeejah Abdul-Wahid, 20 January 2019. https://www.abukhadeejah.com/polygamy-in-islam-better-than-being-alone/, accessed 7 August 2019.

6 'Divorce, Three Talāqs In One Sitting, Taking One's Wife Back, Waiting Period and Remarriage (Islam 5.3)', Abu Khadeejah Abdul-Wahid, 10 September 2018. https://www.abukhadeejah.com/divorce-talaq-iddah-remarriage-khula/, accessed 7 August 2019.

7 'Child Custody in Islam after a Divorce or Separation (Part 1): Shaikh Sālih Al-Fawzān', Abu Khadeejah Abdul-Wahid, 22 March 2018. https://www.abukhadeejah.com/child-custody-in-islam-after-a-divorce-or-separation-part-1-shaikh-salih-al-fawzan/, accessed 7 August 2019.

8 'The LGBTQ Movement: Homosexuality and Islam: Understanding Muslim Attitudes To Homosexuality (Islam 5.7)', Abu Khadeejah Abdul-Wahid, 30 January 2019. https://www.abukhadeejah.com/lgbtq-homosexuality-gay-muslims-and-islam/, accessed 7 August 2019.

9 https://twitter.com/fawadchaudhry/status/1066052445552472065

10 https://www.dailymotion.com/video/x4e50as

11 *The Reality of Sufism in Light of the Qur'aan & Sunnah*, Shaykh Muhammad ibn Rabee' ibn Haadee al-Madkhalee, translated by Aboo Talhah Daawood ibn Ronald Burbank, Birmingham, Al-Hidaayah Publishing, 2nd edn, 1999, p. 37.

12 Ibid., p. 24.

13 Shaykh Ehsan Elahi Zaheer, *The Reality of Bareilawi'ism: Their Beliefs and Practices*, The Orthodox Press, 2011, p. 8.

14 Ibid., p. 37.

15 Ibid., p. 112.

16 Ibid., p. 183.

17 *The Evils of Music: The Devil's Voice & Instrument. [Taken from 'Delivering the Afflicted from the Plots of ash-Shaytan by Imam Abu Abdillah Muhammad bin Abi Bakr bin Ayyub bin Qayyim al-Jawziyyah (691–751 AH)]*, translated by Qasim Mutiva, Hikmah Publications, 2011, p. 49.

18 Ibid., p. 65.

19 Ibid., p. 66.

20 Ibid., p. 72.

CHAPTER 7

BELFAST

1 A. Herman, *How Scots Invented the Modern World*, Crown Publishers, New York, 2001, p. 14.

2 One of the Prophet Mohamed's companions.

CHAPTER 8

EDINBURGH AND GLASGOW

1 Author's translation of the Arabic and substantive sermon.

2 Name changed to protect his identity.

CHAPTER 9

LONDON

1 Ofcom ruled that Islam Channel broke the broadcasting code for advocating marital rape, violence against women and describing women who wore perfume outside of the home as 'prostitutes'. (https://www.theguardian.com/media/2010/nov/08/islam-channel-ofcom" Guardian, 8 November 2010). In 2018 and 2019, Ofcom again ruled that the broadcaster failed to comply with rules (https://www.ofcom.org.uk/about-ofcom/latest/bulletins/content-sanctions-adjudications/decision-islam-channel-limited). See Quilliam Foundation's report *Re-Programming British Muslims: A Study of the*

Islam Channel (2010) for further information. Between 2013 and 2015, Jeremy Corbyn made numerous appearances on the channel, and was the keynote speaker at one of its Gala dinners in 2019 (https://order-order.com/2019/12/03/corbyn-2019-keynote-speaker-islam-channel-censured-antisemitism-advocating-marital-rape/)

2 Warren Dockter, *Churchill and the Islamic world: Orientalism, Empire and Diplomacy in the Middle East*, I. B. Tauris, London, 2015, p. 231.

3 See Muwatta' al-Imam Malik, 24.1 and Musnad Ahmad ibn Hanbal, 103.2.

4 Ofsted Annual Report 2017.

5 E.g. *Sahih al-Bukhari*, 10.136: 'If there is any good in your medical treatments, it is in the knife of the cupper, drinking honey, or cauterisation with fire, as appropriate to the cause of the illness, but I would not like to be cauterised.'

6 My book *The Islamist* (Penguin Books, 2007) devotes several chapters to caliphist activity that occurred in this area in the 1990s. Today the impact of caliphism is even more pronounced than it was then.

7 https://www.towerhamlets.gov.uk/Documents/Borough_statistics/Research-briefings/Population_2_BP2018.pdf

8 *Mainstreaming Islamism: Islamist Institutions and Civil Society Organisations*, Quilliam Press, Cambridge, 2019, p. 7.

9 'Haitham al-Haddad: Adulterous Western women are begging to be stoned to death', *The Times*, 8 October 2018.

10 'Sh. Haitham: Islam is bound to flourish, but what do we need to do?', 15 December 2018. https://www.youtube.com/watch?v=aYUYIikopHY

11 'Why I didn't take painkillers – Sh Haitham', 1 May 2019. https://www.youtube.com/watch?v=rUPm2BPja5Q

12 Meaning Mother of Khadijah or Mother of Salama.

13 Another name for Hussein.

14 Unequal gender rights have affected non-Muslim women, too. In Egypt, for example, which follows a sharia-based interpretation of inheritance laws, a Christian woman named Huda Nasrallah was only granted half the inheritance her brothers were after their father's death. After a lengthy legal battle she was granted equal inheritance. https://www.bbc.com/news/world-middle-east-50544239

15 *Sahih al-Bukhari*, 3241; *Sahih Muslim*, 2737.

16 *Sahih Muslim*, 4.2127.

17 *Sahih al-Bukhari*, 72. 715.

18 The great humanists Sir Thomas More (d. 1535) and Desiderius Erasmus (d. 1536) were not atheists. Too many Muslims today confuse the concept of giving precedence to the human mind as a dismissal of scripture. More and Erasmus were both observant Christians. Human reason need not necessarily contradict revelation. For example, Averroes and Thomas Aquinas, in Islam and Christianity respectively, advanced this important thesis, which was a precursor to the Enlightenment.

CONCLUSION

1 In 1950, Bethlehem and the surrounding villages were 86 per cent Christian. By 2016, the Christian population had dropped to 12 per cent, according to the mayor. (Source: *National Catholic Reporter*, December 2016.)

2 Trevor Phillips, *Daily Telegraph*, 11 April 2016.

3 At the time of writing in September 2020, the mosque only offered four of the other daily prayers in congregation and remained closed for *fajr*.

4 To see only whiteness or blackness is to reduce ourselves only to skin colour. Martin Luther King was right to call for us to judge each other by the content of our character, not the colour of our skin.

5 YouGov, February 2019.

6 *The Times*, 12 April 2020.

7 Abdal Hakim Murad, *Travelling Home: Essays on Islam in Europe*, Quilliam Press, Cambridge, 2020, p. 49.

8 George Orwell, *England Your England*, 1941, Penguin Books, London, 2017.

9 See Brotton's *Orient Isle: Elizabethan England and the Islamic World*, Penguin Books, London, 2016.

10 Ed Husain, *The House of Islam: A Global History*, Bloomsbury, London, 2018.

11 Larry Siedentop, *Inventing the Individual: The Origins of Western Liberalism*, Allen Lane, London, 2014. The Jewish author sees the roots of modern liberty in Protestant Christianity.

12 Boris Johnson, *Johnson's Life of London*, Harper Press, London, 2011.

13 Not to be confused with George Soros. Soros saw the Nazis in his homeland and found all nationalism repugnant; Karl Popper saw

the Nazis and knew the antidote to all totalitarianism was individual liberty.

14 Ipsos MORI's June 2020 poll 'Attitudes to Race and Inequality in Great Britain'.

15 See Jesse Norman's brilliant *Edmund Burke: Philosopher, Politician, Prophet*, William Collins, London, 2013, or Burke's prophetic *Reflections on the Revolution in France* (1790).

Appendix

Sermons Attended and Locations

Acknowledgements

Writing this book has been difficult. The encounters and conversations forced much soul-searching and mental agony. But family, friends and kind colleagues helped keep the book alive across the towns and cities, pages and chapters.

My particular thanks to:

Mum, who prayed *always* for safety and sanity.

My wife Faye, and daughters Camilla and Hannah, for their love and courage to keep going back again and again, and for their unfailing checking-in phone calls every evening. Being a father to daughters is among the greatest honours for a man: the ability to see the world not only for the next generation, but for women of the future. I measure progress in the book by whether the world is a better place for women, Camilla and Hannah, or not.

Nathan Feldman, my brother. He knows why. Through his love, kindness and patience, God shines. Only Nathan knew every nook and cranny of Britain and had been there before me. As always, with head and heart, connecting the dots, he is strategically ahead of most. Your Davidic Majesty.

Dr David Green and Meg Allen at Civitas: Institute for the Study of Civil Society, for a space in Westminster for thinking, convening, conversing, comparing. David's deep patriotism, a rare selfless loyalty, and Meg's long-range concerns and support are the sort of traits that make the English-speaking people concurrently live in the present and shape the future.

HM Shura for love, laughter, loyalty and light, even when we disagree. Especially when we disagree.

Tony Blair, David Cameron, Daniel Hannan, Tom Tugendhat, Dean Godson, Jessica Douglas-Home, Nick Timothy, David Goodhart and John Woodcock for conversations directly about the book and indirectly about its contents on the state of Britain's communities, towns and cities provoked me to think boldly and probe anew.

Friends (you know who you are) in the United States, United Arab Emirates, Bahrain, Israel, Saudi Arabia and Egypt have been a constant source of spiritual sustenance and fidelity. Thank you.

Atlanta Neudorf, then at Civitas, an outstanding researcher, discerned my unconscious switch from colourful notepads to black. Atlanta's persevering and deciphering my scribbles in the margins made this book take shape.

Heba Yousry for always reading the manuscript, answering questions and being shocked, but also asking insightful philosophical questions as is her wont, daughter of Socrates. If there was one person more impatient than me, it was Heba. That shared impatience spurred the writing over the line.

William Neal for always thinking ahead, evaluating an idea by testing against reality. Will's intelligence and instincts for reading of people and places are always the deep foundations for his wise counsel.

Peter Welby for his vast grasp of historical and theological facts, reading between the lines and helping unpack assumptions, but also assessing their consequences.

Sam Woodcock for astute judgement and long walks in Canary Wharf and Pall Mall worrying about the future, but finding solutions too.

Will, Peter and Sam combined are the youngest and best brains trust any writer can seek when struggling between ideas and reality. They 'get it'.

Isabella Woods and James Brandon read chapters and provided critical feedback and made the text better each time. Thank you.

Susan Smyth helped me to compare observations from the UK with other countries. Her intellectual clarity and real-life reflections helped me think.

James Pullen at the Wylie Agency for brainstorming, patience, unstinting support and guidance from conception to delivery. James is never AWOL: always there, always thoughtful, always offering a new perspective.

Michael Fishwick, my prudent editor and mentor at Bloomsbury, cut out the fat in my writing and clarified my thinking, while helping to avert landmines. If not for Michael's wisdom, this book would have been lost between Covid and my initial folly to make this about France and Germany, too.

Lilidh Kendrick has enthusiastically and thoughtfully now helped to steer two of my books at Bloomsbury. Her feedback on chapters was uplifting, especially Edinburgh!

Sarah Ruddick has been incredibly patient and professional with the final stages of editing and rereading over months at Bloomsbury. Thank you.

The musicians who provided theme tunes for writing about land, country and peoples: Beck Goldsmith for 'I Vow to Thee My Country', Elissa for 'Mawtini' and the Israeli choir for 'Hatikvah'.

Finally, to all the kind people – some of whom I was privileged to meet in the course of my travels – who make this nation special from Land's End to John o'Groats. Thank you.

Index

A Note on the Author

Ed Husain is a British writer and political advisor who has worked with leaders and governments across the world. He is an adjunct professor at Georgetown University in Washington DC and has held senior fellowships at think tanks in London and New York, including at the Council on Foreign Relations (CFR). Ed is the author of *The Islamist* (2007) and *The House of Islam: A Global History* (2018). His writing has been shortlisted for the George Orwell Prize. A regular contributor to the *Spectator* magazine, he has appeared on the BBC and CNN and has written for the *Telegraph, The Times*, the *New York Times*, the *Guardian* and other publications.

A Note on the Type

The text of this book is set in Adobe Garamond. It is one of several versions of Garamond based on the designs of Claude Garamond. It is thought that Garamond based his font on Bembo, cut in 1495 by Francesco Griffo in collaboration with the Italian printer Aldus Manutius. Garamond types were first used in books printed in Paris around 1532. Many of the present-day versions of this type are based on the *Typi Academiae* of Jean Jannon cut in Sedan in 1615.

Claude Garamond was born in Paris in 1480. He learned how to cut type from his father and by the age of fifteen he was able to fashion steel punches the size of a pica with great precision. At the age of sixty he was commissioned by King Francis I to design a Greek alphabet, and for this he was given the honourable title of royal type founder. He died in 1561.